Challenging the Monolingual Mindset

MULTILINGUAL MATTERS

Series Editor: John Edwards (*St Francis Xavier University, Canada*)

Multilingual Matters series publishes books on bilingualism, bilingual education, immersion education, second language learning, language policy and multiculturalism. The editor is particularly interested in 'macro'-level studies of language policies, language maintenance, language shift, language revival and language planning. Books in the series discuss the relationship between language in a broad sense and larger cultural issues, particularly identity-related ones.

Full details of all the books in this series and of all our other publications can be found on http://www.multilingual-matters.com, or by writing to Multilingual Matters, St Nicholas House, 31–34 High Street, Bristol BS1 2AW, UK.

MULTILINGUAL MATTERS: 156

Challenging the Monolingual Mindset

Edited by
John Hajek and Yvette Slaughter

MULTILINGUAL MATTERS
Bristol • Buffalo • Toronto

Library of Congress Cataloging in Publication Data
Challenging the Monolingual Mindset/Edited by John Hajek and Yvette Slaughter.
Multilingual Matters: 156
Includes bibliographical references and index.
1. Language and languages—Variation. 2. Languages in contact. 3. Intercultural communication. 4. Multilingual education. I. Hajek, John, editor. II. Slaughter, Yvette, editor.
P120.V37C43 2014
306.44'6–dc23 2014019601

British Library Cataloguing in Publication Data
A catalogue entry for this book is available from the British Library.

ISBN-13: 978-1-78309-251-2 (hbk)
ISBN-13: 978-1-78309-250-5 (pbk)

Multilingual Matters
UK: St Nicholas House, 31–34 High Street, Bristol BS1 2AW, UK.
USA: UTP, 2250 Military Road, Tonawanda, NY 14150, USA.
Canada: UTP, 5201 Dufferin Street, North York, Ontario M3H 5T8, Canada.

Website: www.multilingual-matters.com
Twitter: Multi_Ling_Mat
Facebook: https://www.facebook.com/multilingualmatters
Blog: www.channelviewpublications.wordpress.com

Copyright © 2015 John Hajek, Yvette Slaughter and the authors of individual chapters.

All rights reserved. No part of this work may be reproduced in any form or by any means without permission in writing from the publisher.

In the manufacturing process of our books, and to further support our policy, preference is given to printers that have FSC and PEFC Chain of Custody certification. The FSC and/or PEFC logos will appear on those books where full certification has been granted to the printer concerned.

Typeset by Techset Composition India(P) Ltd., Bangalore and Chennai, India.

Contents

Contributors	vii
Acknowledgments	xiii
Introduction *Yvette Slaughter and John Hajek*	1

Part 1: Language Use and Policy in the International Context

1. English in Scandinavia: Monster or Mate? Sweden as a Case Study   17
   Catrin Norrby

2. Language in Singapore: From Multilingualism to English Plus   33
   Francesco Cavallaro and Ng Bee Chin

3. English as an International Language: A Multilingual and
   Pluricentric Perspective   49
   Farzad Sharifian

4. German or Swiss? Address and Other Routinised Formulas in
   German-speaking Switzerland   63
   Doris Schüpbach

5. Meet and Greet: Nominal Address and Introductions in
   Intercultural Communication at International Conferences   78
   *Heinz Kretzenbacher, Michael Clyne, John Hajek, Catrin Norrby and
   Jane Warren*

**Part 2: Immigrant Languages in Australia: Understanding
and Advancing Multilingualism**

6. L1 and L2 Chinese, German and Spanish Speakers in Action:
   Stancetaking in Intergenerational and Intercultural Encounters   97
   Marisa Cordella and Hui Huang

7 Linguistic Diversity and Early Language Maintenance Efforts in a
    Recent Migrant Community in Australia: Sudanese
    Languages, their Speakers and the Challenge of Engagement   113
    Simon Musgrave and John Hajek

8 Language Maintenance and Sociolinguistic Continuity among
    Two Groups of First-generation Speakers: Macedonians
    from Aegean Macedonia and the Republic of Macedonia   131
    Jim Hlavac

9 The Role of Professional Advice in Shaping Language Choice
    in Migrant-background Families with Deaf Children   149
    Louisa Willoughby

Part 3: Language Policy and Education as Tools for Change in Australia

10 Losing Bilingualism While Promoting Second Language
    Acquisition in Australian Language Policy   165
    Howard Nicholas

11 Mainstreaming of Italian in Australian Schools: The Paradox
    of Success?   182
    Yvette Slaughter and John Hajek

12 Understanding the Role of Professional Development and
    Influences on Teacher Practice: An Australian Case Study
    of Community Languages Teachers   199
    Margaret Gearon

13 'A Somewhat Disconcerting Truth': The Perils of Monolingualism as
    Seen Through the Early Years of the RAAF School of Languages   213
    Colin Nettelbeck

14 'Die Erfüllung eines Traums': Challenging the Monolingual
    Mindset Through the Establishment of an Early
    Immersion Language Programme   227
    Averil Grieve

Index   241

Contributors

Francesco Cavallaro is an Associate Professor in the Division of Linguistics and Multilingual Studies at Nanyang Technological University, Singapore. He has worked at various universities in Australia and he now lives and works in Singapore. His research interests are in sociolinguistics and the social aspects of bilingualism, especially of minority groups in multilingual contexts. He has published on language maintenance and shift, the demographics of the Italian community in Australia, language attitudes in Singapore and on the use of technology in the classroom. He is the author of the book *Transgenerational Language Shift: From Sicilian and Italian to Australian English*, published in 2010 by the Italian Australian Institute, La Trobe University, Melbourne.

Ng Bee Chin is an Associate Professor in the Division of Linguistics and Multilingual Studies at Nanyang Technological University. She works mainly in the area of bilingualism and multilingualism with a focus on the impact of language contact on individuals and the communities they live in. Her research approach is to explore both the cognitive and social aspects of language acquisition and use. Her current research focus is on the relationship between language and identity and language and emotion in multilinguals. Her research is interdisciplinary in nature and she also works in the area of language as a source of intangible heritage with collaborators in art and design studies. She is the co-author of *Bilingualism: An Advanced Resource Book* (Routledge, 2007).

Michael Clyne was Emeritus Professor of Linguistics at Monash University and Professorial Fellow in Linguistics at the University of Melbourne. He produced over 300 publications in a number of areas of applied linguistics and linguistics, including sociolinguistics, bilingualism, language contact and intercultural communication. He was awarded the Australian Cross of Honour, the German Cross of Merit, and an honorary doctorate of the University of Munich, and was elected to the Royal Netherlands Academy of Arts and Science. Professor Clyne passed away in October 2010.

Marisa Cordella is an Associate Professor in Spanish Linguistics at the University of Queensland. She has published extensively, conducted research and supervised postgraduate students in the areas of medical communication, intercultural communication, interactional sociolinguistics, critical discourse analysis, pragmatics, teaching methodologies and translation studies. She has conducted joint research projects with the Faculty of Medicine at Monash University and the Pontificia Universidad Católica de Chile, and is currently completing a cross-disciplinary ARC linkage project that connects upper secondary students learning Chinese, German or Spanish with older native speakers. The project focuses on the synergies between students' language development and older native speakers' health and wellbeing.

Margaret Gearon is Adjunct Senior Lecturer in the Faculty of Education at Monash University, Melbourne. Her research interests include: the classroom oral discourse of second language teachers; curriculum renewal and programme evaluation of languages other than English courses; designing and implementing content and language integrated learning approaches; and the development of teacher education models for teachers of second/foreign languages in universities and community languages schools. She has published widely in these areas in French and English.

Averil Grieve's research interests are bilingualism and bilingual education, language acquisition, sociolinguistics and identity. She completed a Masters degree in cross-cultural communication at the University of Sydney and a PhD in applied linguistics at the University of Melbourne. Her PhD focused on the relationships between acquiring features of adolescent language, length of stay and host family integration among a cohort of German exchange students to Australia. From 2004 to 2006 she was a board member of the Deutsche School Melbourne (DSM) and she continues to support local bilingualism by presenting at DSM open days and Raising Children in More than One Language seminars offered in Melbourne through the Research Unit for Multilingualism and Cross-cultural Communication (RUMACCC) at the University of Melbourne.

John Hajek is Professor of Italian and Director of the Research Unit for Multilingualism and Cross-Cultural Communication (RUMACCC) in the School of Languages and Linguistics at the University of Melbourne. He is also founding president of the Languages and Cultures Network for Australian Universities (LCNAU). Trained originally in Italian, French and Romance linguistics, he completed his studies in Italy and Great Britain before returning to Melbourne. He has extensive experience in teaching language (Italian and Tetum) and linguistics (Italian, Romance and general) and has published extensively across a wide area, including sociolinguistics, phonetics, phonology and linguistic typology, with a special interest in Italian, the languages of Australia and of the wider Asia-Pacific region. He recently co-edited *Uniformity and Diversity in Language Policy: Global Perspectives* (2011, with Catrin Norrby) for Multilingual Matters.

Jim Hlavac is a Lecturer in Translation and Interpreting Studies in the School of Languages, Literatures, Cultures and Linguistics at Monash University, Melbourne. He is an accredited professional interpreter and translator for Croatian and German. He has published widely in the field of translation and interpreting studies and also in the related disciplines of multilingualism, contact linguistics, intercultural communication, pragmatics and language maintenance/shift. He has published studies on language contact among speakers of the following languages in Australia: Arabic, Assyrian, Bosnian, Chaldean, Chinese, Croatian, Macedonian and Serbian. He is completing a book featuring cross-generational analysis of language use among Macedonian-Australians.

Hui Huang is a Lecturer in the School of Languages, Literatures, Cultures and Linguistics at Monash University, Melbourne. She has researched and published in the area of second language acquisition, language pedagogy, teaching Chinese as a second language and utilising ICT in teaching second languages. Her recent publications cover the topics of the effect of intergenerational encounters on second language learning and identity reconstruction, the educational uses of 3D MUVE environments, the animation and learning of Chinese characters, and cross-cultural communication.

Heinz Leo Kretzenbacher has been a member of the German Studies programme at the University of Melbourne for almost 20 years. Before that, he worked at the University of Munich and the Academy of Science and Technology in Berlin. His main research interests are sociolinguistics, language for specific purposes and academic communication, and German as a second or foreign language.

Simon Musgrave is a Lecturer in the School of Languages, Literatures, Cultures and Linguistics at Monash University, Melbourne. He was previously a post-doctoral fellow at Monash, and before that a post-doctoral researcher at the University of Leiden. His doctoral thesis examined aspects of the syntax of Indonesia and Austronesian languages, which continue to be among his research interests. These also include language endangerment, African languages in Australia, communication in medical encounters, and linguistics as part of the digital humanities.

Colin Nettelbeck is Emeritus Professor of French at the University of Melbourne, where he was formerly head of the School of Languages. He is a

Fellow of the Australian Academy of the Humanities and a lead team member of the Languages and Cultures Network for Australian Universities.

Howard Nicholas is Senior Lecturer in Language Education at La Trobe University in Melbourne. He has been involved in the development of approaches for the teaching of languages other than English in early childhood and primary school settings since the 1970s. He was a participant in a number of the conferences that contributed to the shaping of Australian language policy initiatives. His publications, research and professional development activities have focused on second language acquisition and bilingual education in varied settings. In addition to his work in Australia, he has worked and taught in Germany, the United States, Canada, China and Vietnam.

Catrin Norrby is Professor of Scandinavian Languages at Stockholm University, and Principal Fellow in the School of Languages and Linguistics at the University of Melbourne. She has published monographs and edited books, textbooks and articles in the areas of sociolinguistics, discourse analysis and second language acquisition, both in English and in Swedish. She is co-author of *Language and Human Relations: Styles of Address in Contemporary Language* (2009, with Michael Clyne and Jane Warren) and co-editor of *Uniformity and Diversity in Language Policy: Global Perspectives* (2011, with John Hajek).

Doris Schüpbach is Honorary Research Fellow in the School of Languages and Linguistics at the University of Melbourne. Her main research interest is in sociolinguistics, focusing on societal and individual multilingualism and their interaction, languages in contact, and qualitative research methods.

Farzad Sharifian is Professor and Director of the Language and Society Centre at Monash University, Melbourne. He is the author of *Cultural Conceptualisations and Language* (John Benjamins, 2011) and the founding editor of the *International Journal of Language and Culture*. He is also the founder of the academic programme of English as an International Language at Monash University. In 2008 he guest-edited (with Michael Clyne) a special issue of the *Australian Review of Applied Linguistics* on 'English as an International Language: Challenges and Possibilities'.

Yvette Slaughter is a Research Fellow in the Research Unit for Multilingualism and Cross-Cultural Communication (RUMACCC) in the School of Languages and Linguistics and a consultant in the Melbourne Graduate School of Education at the University of Melbourne. She completed her studies on Asian languages in Australia in 2008. Her research interests include language policy, language education (policy and implementation), bilingual education and sociolinguistics. She has worked and published on languages education at primary, secondary and tertiary levels in Australia. Her recent publications include 'Bringing Asia to the home front: The Australian experience of Asian Language Education through national policy', in C. Norrby and J. Hajek (eds) *Uniformity and Diversity in Language Policy: Global Perspectives*.

Jane Warren is Honorary Fellow in the School of Languages and Linguistics at the University of Melbourne. She has published at the juncture of sociolinguistics and cultural studies. She is co-author of *Language, Citizenship and Identity in Quebec* (2007, with Leigh Oakes) and *Language and Human Relations: Styles of Address in Contemporary Language* (2009, with Michael Clyne and Catrin Norrby).

Louisa Willoughby is a Lecturer in Linguistics at Monash University, Melbourne. Her main research interest is in issues affecting speakers of minority languages, particularly in education and health settings. She is also interested in language maintenance and shift more broadly, language and identity and Deaf studies.

Acknowledgments

This volume is dedicated to the memory of Professor Michael Clyne, linguist, sociolinguist and language activist. As noted in the Introduction, each of the editors and authors worked closely with Michael in some capacity in Melbourne, Australia.

A number of the contributions to the volume are based on papers given at a colloquium held on 23 February 2012 at the University of Melbourne. The colloquium, 'Challenging the Monolingual Mindset', celebrated the 10th anniversary of the founding of the Research Unit for Multilingualism and Cross-Cultural Communication (RUMACCC) by Michael, and remembered his passing on 29 October 2010. The Michael Clyne lecture delivered as part of the event was presented by Catrin Norrby who returned from Stockholm for it. It has since been rewritten by Catrin as a chapter in this book.

We wish to acknowledge the School of Languages and Linguistics at the University of Melbourne for its support of the colloquium, as well as that of Irene Donohoue-Clyne and Johanna Clyne.

Special thanks must go to Jane Warren and Doris Schüpbach, who are both contributors to the volume but who also provided significant help with the preparation of the volume. Jane provided invaluable editing assistance, while Doris compiled the comprehensive index.

Finally, we wish thank each of the contributors. It has been a pleasure to work with such understanding and amenable colleagues, dispersed around the globe, who so kindly agreed to share their expertise across a range of languages and language-related issues.

Introduction

Yvette Slaughter and John Hajek

Challenging the Monolingual Mindset

> The greatest impediment to recognising, valuing and utilising our language potential is a persistent monolingual mindset. Such a mindset sees everything in terms of monolingualism being the norm, even though there are more bi- and multilinguals in the world than monolinguals. (Clyne, 2005: xi)

Professor Michael Clyne was a passionate academic who dedicated his life to the pursuit of linguistic knowledge, and to its application for the wider benefit of society. Sadly, Michael passed away in October 2010, but he left behind a wonderful legacy. Michael's breadth of research was remarkable. Over his long career, Michael pioneered or played a critical role in the development of many fields within linguistics and applied linguistics in the Australian and international contexts, including sociolinguistics, bilingualism and multilingualism, contact linguistics and pluricentricity, inter- and intracultural communication, pragmatics, second language learning, language policy, linguistic demography and German, Dutch and English (including Australian English) linguistics.

The diversity of Michael's academic interests stems from his childhood experiences as a second-generation German-English speaking Australian (see, for example, Hajek, 2012; Nettelbeck, 2011; Sharifian & Sussex, 2010) and subsequently through his doctoral work on German-English language contact in the migrant context in Australia. The German language was, among Michael's very broad range of interests, a lifelong passion for him (see, for example, Clyne, 1967, 1985, 1995) for which he was awarded the Austrian Cross of Honour and the German Cross of Merit, as well as the Jacob and Wilhelm Grimm Prize for German Studies (1999) and the Humboldt Research Prize (2003). It was through Michael's early collection of oral histories from German speakers in Australia that he began to explore what he saw as missing elements of Australian history (Clyne, 1975, 1988).

> A few decades ago, I was in Lobethal (South Australia) tape-recording bilinguals whose ancestors had arrived there in 1841. One of the leading questions I would ask was: 'How has this place changed since you were a child?' 'Oh', said the elderly man in the museum in fluent German, 'it really has changed. The New Australians have come from England and they make such a noise on their motorbikes'. It brought home to me the fact that in some parts of Australia, the Germans were the old Australians and the English were the new Australians. Multilingualism was a fact of life in Australia long before the post-second World War immigration scheme. (Clyne, 2005: 1)

Michael documented the great linguistic and cultural diversity in Australia from the mid-19th century, a diversity that had largely been forgotten but which extended into Australia's political life, education system, newspapers and across the public landscape in the towns and cities of the burgeoning nation. He identified the development of forced monolingualism, imposed following Australia's Federation in 1901, which led to the closure of dozens of bilingual schools and newspapers and the stigmatisation of bilingualism, particularly the use of German during the war years (Clyne, 1975, 1991a). This experience of the 'monolingual mindset' (e.g. Clyne, 2004, 2005, 2008; Ellis *et al.*, 2010) has echoed for centuries across the globe (see Christ, 1997, who was also the first to introduce the phrase 'monolingual mindset' as a translation of *'monolingualer Habitus'*, coined by Gogolin, 1993, that Michael came to adopt). The monolingual mindset is a fundamental issue which continues to preoccupy academics and language advocates worldwide (e.g. Ellis, 2008; Reagan & Osborn, 2002, and many others) and one which Michael was keen to address. He was always a fervent advocate for the linguistic rights of multilinguals and pursued an unwavering agenda to educate the broader community about the benefits of multilingualism that accrue to individuals and to their communities. He worked for decades with ethnic communities, schools, parents, educators and governments and made the case, through research and advocacy, for the linguistic rights of migrants. He highlighted the importance of language maintenance for their communities in Australia and elsewhere, of language education programmes in schools for *all* students, and of the benefits the knowledge and use of more than one language provides for social cohesion and intercultural understanding, as well as for individuals, regardless of linguistic background.

Our Purpose

Academically, Michael had not only a prolific output, but also an enduring impact on his students, co-researchers and colleagues, many of who have prospered in their academic careers due to Michael's patience, passion, collaboration and 'willingness to listen to any point of view which was put forward with sincerity' (Sharifian & Sussex, 2010: 373). The purpose of this volume is to highlight the breadth of Michael's influence over a range of fields by bringing together research by 18 of his former colleagues – many of whom were his students at some point – who collaborated with him and were inspired by his intellect, sense of duty and understanding of languages.

The original impetus for this volume was a special half-day symposium entitled 'Challenging the Monolingual Mindset' held in memory of Michael Clyne on 23 February 2012 at the University of Melbourne. Almost all the contributors to this volume were present at the Symposium – as presenters or as part of the audience. Despite the title of the event, organisers specifically placed no restrictions on the content or approach of the papers presented, in order to highlight the diversity of the research conducted by Michael's colleagues and the many different academic contexts they now operate in. This freedom of approach and framing is continued in this volume – indeed the editors were explicit with contributors that this should be the case – in reflection of Michael's own wide-ranging approach. As a result, while some chapters explicitly reference the monolingual mindset and its impact, others do not. The concept was a very useful one for Michael, but his explicit treatment of it was only one part of his diverse research output, something we also wished to be reflected here (see also below). Bringing language issues to the attention of a wider audience is in itself a useful, even if implicit, challenge to the monolingual mindset.

The contributions in this volume focus on linguistic situations around the world, including specific case studies across three continents: Australia, Europe (Sweden and Switzerland) and Asia (Singapore), as well as analysis and discussion of the use of languages within and across a range of contexts, including post-migration settlement, policy, education, language contact and intercultural communication. Languages referred to and/or discussed include Arabic, Auslan, Boyanese, Cantonese, Danish, Dinka, English and varieties of English, German, Hokkien, Italian, Macedonian, Malay, Malayalam, Mandarin, Otuho, Spanish, Swedish, Swiss German and Tamil, among others. It is not surprising that a particular geographical focus of this volume is Australia – this is where Michael spent most of his life, conducted most of his research, supervised students, collaborated most with fellow researchers and worked hardest to promote multilingualism. Australia was also, for a time, a leader in language policy and the promotion of multilingualism and multiculturalism, although Michael came in later years to be disappointed by retrograde movement on these fronts (Sharifian & Sussex, 2010). Nine contributions to the volume look at a wide range of issues in the Australian context, past and present, providing a useful overview of the complexities of understanding and fostering bilingualism and multilingualism in a major English-dominant context – a context that finds parallels well beyond the English-speaking world (see, for example, Ellis *et al.*, 2010; Park 2008). At the same time, in recognition of Michael's lifelong dedication to German, three chapters in the volume have a specific focus on that language – in Australia and Switzerland.

The chapters in this volume sustain important threads found through Michael's work (see Sharifian & Sussex, 2010: 373–374). His research was wide-ranging, data-rich and 'focused on differentiated and overlapping human communities and languages in use' (Sharifian & Sussex, 2010: 373). He was interested in how languages are used, how languages interact and how people use languages to interact. Part 1 of this volume, *Language Use and Policy in the International Context*, looks at how languages are used and managed, through such themes as the impact of language policy, the rise of English as a global language, and the pragmatics of address in intracultural and intercultural communication. An important theme that emerges in the first few chapters is the potential expansion and contraction of linguistic repertoires, at both a societal and individual level, which can occur through the incorporation of foreign, global or post-colonial languages such as English, and the ensuing changes and challenges that arise. The role of English as a preferred first and second language can touch upon national sensitivities in many countries around the world, particularly when its use broadens across domains and it is increasingly integrated into the language use of younger generations. In highly multilingual post-colonial contexts, its increasing dominance can accelerate a reduction in linguistic diversity, as political, educational and economic pressures suppress the intergenerational transmission of many languages. However, it is also important not to position non-native speakers of English as passive users of the language, but to develop an understanding of how they use the language, and why, in order to improve intercultural communication.

In Chapter 1 Catrin Norrby investigates the interplay between English and the languages of Scandinavia, with a particular focus on Sweden. Travellers to Scandinavia are often struck by the generalised high level of English proficiency in the region. According to the language survey of the Special Eurobarometer 243 (EC, 2006), the overwhelming majority of respondents in Denmark, Finland and Sweden speak at least one language in addition to their mother tongue. English holds a privileged position: 89% of Swedish respondents claim to speak English and 97% believe that English will be useful for their personal development and career. Focusing on Sweden as a case study for Scandinavia, the chapter discusses how English predominance has come to be the norm. It considers recent trends in attitudes towards English as seen in official Swedish language planning in language policy and reality in Swedish universities, as well as in its use and attitudes towards it among the general public – including its visibility in the streetscape. The analysis suggests that while there is a significant tension between contrasting trends of accepting and controlling the role of English in Swedish society today, an increasing English-Swedish bilingualism in Sweden is in the end inevitable and not to be feared.

Chapter 2 focuses on the complexities of language use in a highly multilingual, multi-ethnic and multicultural society. Francesco Cavallaro and Ng Bee Chin examine the changing role of languages in Singapore, detailing the ongoing manipulation and contraction of the average Singaporean's linguistic repertoire. With active language planning policies in force since before its independence as a nation in 1965, the linguistic situation in Singapore has undergone dramatic changes in the past 60 years. By drawing on previous studies, as well as census and survey data, Cavallaro and Ng show a rapid shift in the languages used by Singaporeans to English – as a result of post-colonial policy – as both supra-ethnic *lingua franca* but also increasingly as the preferred language of the home. Their research also shows that Chinese vernaculars have largely disappeared as the preferred home language, with Mandarin becoming – at least for the moment – the de facto mother tongue of the Chinese community. Although a shift to English as preferred language of the home has occurred at different rates for the three main ethnic groups (Singapore Chinese, Malays and Indians), there is no doubt that English is making inroads everywhere, especially among the young – a trend which will undoubtedly continue to strengthen. Ongoing tensions also exist in relation to whether Singapore Colloquial English (Singlish or SCE) exists or should exist as a separate variety from Standard Singapore English (SSE). Cavallaro and Ng also discuss the challenges facing Singapore, with the need to integrate new residents from different cultural and linguistic backgrounds, to harness the resources of post-independence Singaporeans to meet the needs of the nation's blueprint for success, and to manage the increasing language gap between many of Singapore's elderly and the rising English-dominant youth, for whom there may be no common language.

In Chapter 3 Farzad Sharifian takes a different perspective on the role of the English language in multilingual contexts, exploring the basic assumptions of the paradigm of English as an international language from a multilingual and pluricentric perspective. Rather than viewing the globalisation of English as having had a diminishing effect on other languages, he argues that the globalisation of English can be linked to an increase in multilingualism. Furthermore, the global diversification of English has increased the pluricentricity of the language at all levels, from the sound system to the deeper layers of cultural conceptualisations. The chapter discusses the implications of these observations for the field of English language teaching. It argues that teaching English as an international language should also be directed to native speakers of English and should aim at developing improved meta-cultural competence. This can be achieved, in part, through exposure to the culturally determined conceptual variation that increasingly characterises the language in the contemporary world.

We then move to the area of address in intracultural and intercultural contexts. In Chapter 4 Doris Schüpbach investigates the practices of linguistic politeness, such as how people address and greet each other, in

German-speaking Switzerland. Contrastive studies of address practices in German tend to concentrate on Germany and Austria. This chapter reviews the available research and examines current practices and perceptions of address and linguistic politeness in German-speaking Switzerland in contrast to those seen as representative of Germany. This is done by analysing first-hand accounts of Germans living in Switzerland and advice given to Germans moving to Switzerland in the last decade when migration from Germany to Switzerland increased considerably. Pronominal address is the focus, with some consideration given to nominal address and other formulaic routines, in particular greetings and leave-taking formulas. Findings include divergences between German and Swiss politeness patterns, the widespread use of names in conjunction with greetings (but hardly any titles), and extensive exchanges of formulaic routines, particularly when taking leave. This lends support to Manno's (2005) claim that, in the case of Switzerland, the sociocultural context overrides shared language in influencing politeness practices. It also highlights the phenomenon that speakers of what is supposedly the same language who are socialised in different sociocultural contexts may be less prepared than might be expected for communicative problems when interacting with one another ostensibly in the same language.

Chapter 5 reports on the use of nominal address and introductions in intercultural communication at international conferences. Heinz Kretzenbacher, Michael Clyne†, John Hajek, Catrin Norrby and Jane Warren document and analyse how academics report on address and introduction practices as they occur in this specific context – both in English and in their first languages. They frame their research within a model of address developed for *intracultural* purposes by Clyne et al. (2009) and show how the basic principles of that model can be useful in understanding address behaviour in *intercultural* communication. Their findings illustrate a number of important points, e.g. self-introductions are the least distancing and formal, while age is an important factor in influencing reported behaviour. Perhaps not surprisingly, their results also point to substantial cultural variation in the perception and expectations of address norms and usage, as well as a level of uncertainty about how to introduce and address others in an intercultural context. The (in)appropriate use of nominal address is frequently brought up by respondents – as a source of both irritation and satisfaction. The results also highlight the potential – among non-native speakers of English – for English-language routines and patterns to be influenced by differing cultural norms operating in other languages and cultures.

In Part 2 of this volume, *Immigrant Languages in Australia: Understanding and Advancing Multilingualism*, the focus moves to the experience of migrants and their languages in the Australian context – a major focus of Michael's research and of his advocacy work. Researchers in Australia, with Michael in the lead, have been fortunate to have access to national census data collected every five years (since 1961, although there was considerable variation in data availability until 1981). Combined with extensive fieldwork, they have compiled a detailed and nuanced understanding of the complexities and challenges of language maintenance and transmission and intercultural communication (e.g. Clyne, 1991a, 1991b, 2003; Clyne & Kipp, 1997, 2006; Kipp *et al.*, 1995; but see Rubino, 2010 for an overview). Although the postwar migration scheme in Australia resulted in hundreds of thousands of Europeans coming to Australia, the focus of Australia's migration policies has changed considerably over the decades, moving from predominantly unskilled workers and refugees from Europe, to a new humanitarian focus on Asia with the arrival of Vietnamese refugees in boats in the 1970s, to the acceptance of a much wider and more diverse intake from around the globe in more recent decades. Large numbers of migrants continue to arrive in Australia each year – across a range of categories, including skilled and sponsored workers, refugees, family reunions, international students and working youth. As a consequence, migrants to Australia bring with them a new multiplicity of languages and cultures, motivations and attitudes, and pre-migration experiences, all of which impact on language use and identity re/formation (Clyne & Kipp, 2006). These different experiences are illustrated – among others in this section – for the more established Macedonian community (Chapter 8) and for the recent wave of migration from Sudan (Chapter 7).

The increasing and rapidly changing social and linguistic complexity of migration in Australia, and of Australia as a result, is shared with many other countries. This global phenomenon marked by the intensification of scope, type (e.g. skilled workers, students, refugees) and volume of migration has recently come to be described as 'superdiversity' (Vertovec, 2007, 2010) to distinguish it from earlier patterns of global movement (see also Blommaert, 2010; Blommaert & Rampton, 2011). It is important, as Vertovec (2007: 1025) argues, to avoid using the notion of ethnicity and country of origin to create a 'one-dimensional appreciation of contemporary diversity'. Vertovec's (2007: 1024) articulation of 'superdiversity' foregrounds the 'dynamic interplay of variables among an increased number of new, small and scattered, multiple-origin, transnationally connected socio-economically differentiated and legally stratified immigrants'. The need to reframe the migrant experience has been apparent over decades in Australia, not only as the migration experience has changed, but as the needs of migrants have diversified (as detailed by Clyne & Kipp, 2006, for instance, for the very different Filipino, Macedonian and Somali communities). Examples treated in this volume include: (a) the challenge of the inherent linguistic diversity of Australia's recently established Sudanese community (see Chapter 7); and (b) the impact of deafness on language development and transmission in migrant communities (see Chapter 9).

However, the notion of reinterpreting diversity should not be simply left to the newer migrant experience. It was one of Michael's passions that the cultural and linguistic experiences of older Australian migrants should not just be ignored but should also be used as a resource for younger Australian language learners. This led to the large-scale research project *Connecting Younger L2 Learners and Older Bilinguals: Intergenerational, Intercultural Encounters and Second Language Development*. Marisa Cordella and Hui Huang's research presented in Chapter 6 is part of this broader study which aims to promote intergenerational and intercultural communication as a way of enhancing second language development, as well as documenting the social and cultural benefits of such encounters for both migrants and students. Their study focuses specifically on investigating which stances were adopted when older migrants conversed in their native tongues – Chinese, German and Spanish – with young language students. The emphasis is on how people situate themselves and others in discourse through stance projections and attributions. Results of the study show that the migrants positioned themselves very strongly as language instructors, and also took the stance of sociocultural guides and ethical-moral advisers. The students sometimes corrected the English language of their migrant partners (language instructor stance) and contributed to discussions about social and cultural issues (stance of sociocultural guide), but did not take on the stance of an ethical-moral adviser.

The next three chapters focus on language maintenance in non-mainstream communities (migrant and deaf) in Australia. In Chapter 7 Simon Musgrave and John Hajek document the experiences of one of Australia's newer migrant groups, the Sudanese. There has been a rapid increase in the settlement of migrants originating from Sudan in recent years. Sudan is a country with great linguistic diversity, especially in the south (now the Republic of South Sudan), whence most have come. This extreme diversity in the mother country is reflected as superdiversity in the Australian context: there are at least 40 Sudanese languages spoken in the city of Melbourne alone, where this study is located. Language maintenance is therefore a complex issue for this community. This is true for languages with larger and smaller speaker populations but it is as yet barely understood by linguists and the relevant authorities in Australia. This chapter provides an overview of educational maintenance efforts, and the issues they involve, across the Australian Sudanese community, reporting specifically on three languages, Arabic, Dinka and Otuho. It also highlights the important role that linguists and others could play in assisting newer migrant groups from Africa, such as the Sudanese, with language maintenance efforts.

In Chapter 8 Jim Hlavac investigates language maintenance and sociolinguistic continuity among two groups of first-generation speakers of Macedonian – from (a) Aegean Macedonia in Greece and (b) the Republic of Macedonia. The chapter focuses on an immigrant group in Australia which records a high level of continued use of their first language (L1), in this case Macedonian. Data on pre-migration language acquisition and language use within the family, immediate environment and schooling have been collated from two groups of 50 Macedonian speakers. The differences in the sociopolitical environment and language planning features of the informants' countries of origin are a feature that could potentially result in post-migration patterns of language use that differ between the two groups. However, analysis of informants' reported language use across the domains of home/family, friendship/social contacts and the workplace, transactional and neighbourhood domains shows few major differences. Post-migration replication of Macedonian-language communicative networks is a characteristic that supports both groups' maintenance of their L1. Despite its 'minor' status, Macedonian continues to record robust levels of maintenance and can even claim some 'marketplace' value as a code employed with some non-Macedonians.

While services for migrant communities and the maintenance of their languages have improved dramatically in Australia over the last 50 years, in Chapter 9 Louisa Willoughby presents an overview of the somewhat fractured support and advice available to migrant families with deaf children. For most migrant background families living in Australia, the decision to maintain their community or heritage language with their children or shift to English is a personal matter. However, if a child has a disability such as deafness that affects their ability to use spoken language, parents are likely to receive advice about communication from a wide variety of professionals. A key issue in these situations is what role, if any, the professionals see the heritage language playing in family communication and how parents respond to this advice. This chapter explores these issues through a case study of seven Melbourne families from non-English-speaking migrant backgrounds with deaf children. Providers are found to behave differently in regard to the monolingual mindset, with those advocating an auditory-verbal approach in general taking the strongest view against first language maintenance and in favour of speaking English only. This research shows that in cases where families went along with the advice outright, problematic outcomes have occurred for the families and the children concerned.

While Michael was passionate about the languages of all communities in Australia and elsewhere, he also made it a priority to improve the status and quality of the learning of languages in the education system. He also saw language policy and language education as inextricably linked keys to developing Australia's language potential and spent many years advocating language policies and language education from the federal to the family level. Indeed, supported by the work of academics and activists such as Michael, Australia was seen to lead efforts in language policy development in the late 20th century (see also above). Language policy is, however, complicated by many variables including political will, issues of identity, and national cohesion, among others. While language policy and language education are undoubtedly important in supporting multilingualism and challenging the monolingual mindset, their consequences can also be unintended and surprising. Part 3 of this volume, *Language Policy and Education as Tools for Change in Australia*, illustrates the development and impact of language policies and education-related initiatives in various contexts.

In Chapter 10 Howard Nicholas explores the notion of bilingualism in the context of Australian language policy and its development, particularly within the most active time frame for language policy development. History tells us that Australian language policy was intended to promote bilingualism, but policy pronouncements have undercut attempts to foster bilingualism for all. This chapter examines how stakeholders have participated in a process of marginalising bilingualism in a grand but flawed endeavour. A selection of Australian language policy documents and statements, dating from the 1970s, is analysed to show how despite the intentions and starting points of many key stakeholders, the resulting documents and programmes have firstly, marginalised minority language development; secondly, disconnected English as a second language from an overall view of bilingualism; and thirdly, as a consequence, prioritised the development of elite bilingualism through second language programmes for (presumed) English-speaking monolinguals.

In Chapter 11, Yvette Slaughter and John Hajek examine the unintended outcome of the mainstreaming of migrant languages in schools by focusing on the path of Italian in the Australian education system. Although Australia is an English-dominant country, hundreds of languages are spoken in communities across the nation. The challenge for the Australian education system has been to cultivate the linguistic competence that already exists within Australian society, as well as fostering second language acquisition among all students (Lo Bianco & Slaughter, 2009). Australia's Italian community has been particularly successful in achieving the widespread introduction of the Italian language as a subject within the nation's primary and secondary education system. This chapter highlights some of the intricacies and effects of the relationship between language communities, maintenance and transmission, and the mainstreaming of languages in the school system. It points to a concomitant decline in the maintenance and development of bilingualism among Italian background speakers, and the disappointing performance of Italian in the upper years of secondary education. These trends, and the reasons for them, need to be carefully considered and addressed in order for Italian, and other community languages, to properly thrive through the entire school cycle in Australia. They clearly illustrate the need for ongoing advocacy and oversight for both the transmission of Italian as a second language in schools and as a community language.

In Chapter 12, Margaret Gearon, a language teacher educator, details the challenges for community languages teachers in the Australian context in developing their teaching practices. Learning to become a second language teacher through formal training and qualification is considered essential for teaching language in mainstream schools. This is, however, not the case for teachers in Australia's large network of community (heritage) language schools on which many migrant communities are dependent for the formal teaching of their languages. These teachers, with varying competence in their first language and English, are able but not obliged to undertake a 30-hour course focused on the teaching of languages and cultures. This training is to ensure that they have a basic understanding of second and bilingual teaching and learning principles and practices, and of the official languages curriculum framework of the state of Victoria. This chapter explores the views of teachers undertaking the basic methodology course, examining their views on language teaching and learning in their schools, and the extent to which the course in question influences these.

In Chapter 13, Colin Nettelbeck takes us on a surprising journey into language planning and education by Australia's military services. Nettelbeck argues that those in the Australian education system who have joined the struggle against the culture of monolingualism have for over half a century had a largely invisible ally: the Royal Australian Air Force (RAAF) – since 1993 the Australian Defence Force (ADF) – School of Languages. The School began during the Second World War to teach Japanese, and was suspended in 1948, but after its re-establishment in 1950, it quite rapidly grew into a dynamic and innovative institution providing instruction in more languages than most Australian universities. This study, based on the very few existing published accounts and on extensive archival material, offers an historical account of the early years of the School, giving special emphasis to the seminal role of its then commander, Toby Garrick. It argues that a fuller understanding of the policies and practices of language learning at the 'front line' of Australia's interactions with the outside world will be of benefit to all who seek to transform the 'monolingual mindset,' not least because the School's story demonstrates quite starkly how pervasive and deeply entrenched that mindset has always been.

The volume ends with a chapter dedicated to German in the Australian context. Although second language programmes have become widely established in Australian schools, few students have the opportunity to study in a bilingual environment. While a small number of bilingual schools are operated by government education systems around Australia, there are considerable difficulties involved in establishing bilingual schools outside this context. In Chapter 14, Averil Grieve reports on the successful development of an English/German bilingual primary school in Australia, the Deutsche Schule, and provides an in-depth discussion of the complexities involved in: (a) undertaking such an endeavour due to a continued resistance to total immersion language acquisition in Australia; and (b) establishing bilingual models that cater for a wide range of language abilities and interests. The case study explores such issues as adaption of early immersion models, school governance, curriculum development and how differences in language abilities can be used as a resource in bilingual classrooms. It also discusses the complexity of issues that need to be taken into account when establishing a new bilingual programme. These include the interests of potential parents and pupils, legal implications, governmental registration hurdles, funding and the monolingual mindset. As such, it provides a useful and informative model for similar initiatives everywhere. The Deutsche Schule, as the title and the author make clear, was truly the fulfilment of a dream for Michael.

Through a broad focus on everyday use of language, languages in contact, migrant languages, language policy development and application, language in education, and the use of English in different contexts, this volume will give readers a greater understanding of the opportunities and tensions that can develop in managing and understanding multilingualism and communication within and across communities and societies. We hope that this volume will be useful in making clear how ongoing research across a broad range of topics, just as Michael Clyne did, can benefit both multilinguals and monolinguals in understanding and fostering the linguistic potential of our communities – in Australia and around the world.

References

Blommaert, J. (2010) *The Sociolinguistics of Globalization*. Cambridge: Cambridge University Press.
Blommaert, J. and Rampton, B. (2011) Language and superdiversity. *Diversities* 13 (2), 1–21.
Christ, H. (1997) Language attitudes and educational policy. In R. Wodak and D. Corson (eds) *Encyclopedia of Language and Education, Volume 1: Language Policy and Political Issues in Education* (pp. 1–11). Dordrecht: Kluwer Academic Publishers.
Clyne, M. (1967) *Transference and Triggering*. The Hague: Nijhoff.
Clyne, M. (1975) Aspects of cultural diversity in Australia. In J. Campbell (ed.) *Papers Presented at the 2nd Oral History Conference* (pp. 2–6). Bundoora: La Trobe University.
Clyne, M. (1985) *Language and Society in the German-speaking Countries*. Cambridge and New York: Cambridge University Press.
Clyne, M. (1988) Bilingual education – what we can learn from the past? *Australian Journal of Education* 32, 95–114.
Clyne, M. (1991a) *Community Languages: The Australian Experience*. Cambridge: Cambridge University Press.
Clyne, M. (1991b) Patterns of inter-cultural communication in Melbourne factories. *Language and Language Education* 1 (1), 5–30.
Clyne, M. (1995) *The German Language in a Changing Europe*. Cambridge: Cambridge University Press.
Clyne, M. (2003) *Dynamics of Language Contact*. Cambridge: Cambridge University Press.
Clyne, M. (2004) Trapped in a monolingual mindset. *Prime Focus* 37, 40–42.
Clyne, M. (2005) *Australia's Language Potential*. Sydney: University of New South Wales Press.
Clyne, M. (2008) The monolingual mindset as an impediment to the development of plurilingual potential. *Sociolinguistic Studies* 2 (3), 347–366.
Clyne, M. and Kipp, S. (1997) Trends and changes in home language use and shift in Australia. *Journal of Multilingual and Multicultural Development* 18, 451–473.
Clyne, M. and Kipp, S. (2006) *Tiles in a Multilingual Mosaic: Macedonian, Filipino and Somali in Melbourne*. Canberra: Pacific Linguistics.

Clyne, M., Norrby, C. and Warren, J. (2009) *Language and Human Relations: Styles of Address in Contemporary Language*. Cambridge: Cambridge University Press.

EC (2006) *Europeans and their Languages*. Special Eurobarometer 243. Brussels: European Commission. See www.ec.europa.eu/public_opinion/archives/ebs/ebs_243_en.pdf.

Ellis, E. (2008) Defining and investigating monolingualism. *Sociolinguistic Studies* 2, 311–330.

Ellis, E., Gogolin, I. and Clyne, M. (2010) The Janus face of monolingualism: A comparison of German and Australian language education policies. *Current Issues in Language Planning* 11 (4), 439–460.

Gogolin, I. (1993) *Der monolinguale Habitus der multilingualen Schule*. Münster: Waxmann.

Hajek, J. (2012) Homage to Michael Clyne: Linguist, colleague and advocate. In R. Muhr (ed.) *Non-dominant Varieties of Pluricentric Languages. Getting the Picture. In Memory of Michael Clyne* (pp. 11–22). Vienna: Peter Lang.

Kipp, S., Clyne, M. and Pauwels, A. (1995) *Immigration and Australia's Language Resources*. Canberra: AGPS.

Lo Bianco, J. and Slaughter, Y. (2009) *Second Languages and Australian Schooling*. Melbourne: Australian Council for Educational Research.

Manno, G. (2005) Politeness in Switzerland: Between respect and acceptance. In L. Hickey and M. Stewart (eds) *Politeness in Europe* (pp. 100–115). Clevedon: Multilingual Matters.

Nettelbeck, C. (2011) Michael Clyne (1939–2010). In E. Webby (ed.) *The Australian Academy of the Humanities Proceedings 2010* (Vol. 35) (pp. 98–103). Canberra: Australian Academy of the Humanities.

Park, J.S-Y. (2008) Two processes of reproducing monolingualism in South Korea. *Sociolinguistic Studies* 2, 311–330.

Reagan, T.G. and Osborn, T.A. (2002) *The Foreign Language Educator in Society: Toward a Critical Pedagogy*. Mahwah: Lawrence Erlbaum.

Rubino, A. (2010) Multilingualism in Australia: Reflections on current and future research trends. *Australian Review of Applied Linguistics* 33 (2), 17.1–17.21.

Sharifian, F. and Sussex, R. (2010) Michael George Clyne (1939–2010): Scholar and champion of languages. *Current Issues in Language Planning* 11 (4), 371–377.

Vertovec, S. (2007) Super-diversity and its implications. *Ethnic and Racial Studies* 30 (6), 1024–1054.

Vertovec, S. (2010) Towards post-multiculturalism? Changing communities, contexts and conditions of diversity. *International Social Science Journal* 199, 83–95.

Part 1

Language Use and Policy in the International Context

1 English in Scandinavia: Monster or Mate? Sweden as a Case Study

Catrin Norrby

Introduction

When Swedish Crown Princess Victoria and Prince Daniel recently became parents, the prince explained his feelings at a press conference, hours after their daughter was born, with the following words (cited from *Svenska Dagbladet*, 23 February 2012):

> *Mina känslor är lite* all over the place. *När jag gick från rummet så låg den lilla prinsessan på sin moders bröst och såg ut att ha det väldigt mysigt*
>
> [My feelings are a bit *all over the place*. When I left the room the little princess was lying on her mother's breast and seemed to be very cosy]

The use of English catchphrases and idioms in an otherwise Swedish language frame is not unusual and it is no exaggeration to say that English plays a significant role in contemporary Scandinavia. The following areas of use at least can be distinguished: (1) English taught as a school subject; (2) English used as a lingua franca; (3) English in certain domains; (4) English as an act of identity; and (5) English in the linguistic landscape.

The term 'Scandinavia' is used in this chapter as shorthand for Denmark, Norway and Sweden (where Scandinavian languages are spoken) as well as for Finland (which is part of the Scandinavian peninsula together with Sweden and Norway). English is taught as a mandatory subject in schools throughout Scandinavia, usually from Grade 3 or 4, meaning that school leavers normally have 9–10 years of English teaching. In recent years there has been an increase of CLIL (content and language integrated learning), where content subjects are taught in English (see, for example, Washburn, 1997). The availability of English instruction throughout the education system is a prerequisite for the generally high level of proficiency in English among Scandinavians (see below).

English is used as a lingua franca by Scandinavians for communication not only in international contexts but also nationally, as well as for inter-Scandinavian communication. Danish, Norwegian and Swedish are often taken as examples of mutually intelligible languages, enabling speakers to use their native language in communication with their neighbours, sometimes referred to as semicommunication (Haugen, 1972). Recent studies, however, indicate that mutual intelligibility might be diminishing, as adolescents generally understand English better, and also display poorer understanding of the neighbour languages compared to their parents (Delsing & Lundin Åkesson, 2005). Turning to the national level, English is also used for communication within many domains, in particular in research and higher education, business and large companies, as well as in popular culture and advertising. In this chapter, the focus is on the domains of research and higher education.

In Scandinavia, code-switching between a national language and English is a phenomenon which has been particularly observed in young people's discourse. For example, Sharp (2001) found on average one code-switch to English per minute among Swedish youths. Most of these code-switches were unintegrated English language material in an otherwise Swedish frame, and were often made up of phrases from films, songs, advertising, and so on. Sharp (2001: 117) refers to these switches as 'the quoting game', where the speakers flag the shift to English by a change of voice quality or laughter. In other words, these code-switches can be interpreted as an act of identity where the speaker appeals to shared knowledge of global trends and in-group commonalities (see also Preisler, 2003 for similar results in a Danish context).

English in the linguistic landscape refers to the documentation of visible signs of English language use in a society, e.g. linguistic objects such as signs in the streets, in shops and service institutions. An important underpinning of linguistic landscaping is the understanding that public spaces are symbolically constructed by linguistic means (Ben-Rafael *et al.*, 2010). In this chapter, we explore the extent of English presence in a large shopping mall in downtown Stockholm.

The points above are not discrete but overlapping categories. For example, use of English as a lingua franca clearly overlaps with its use in certain domains, and English as an act of identity encompasses not only spontaneous use in interaction: its use in the linguistic landscape can also often be interpreted as promoting a certain identity. Furthermore, the various points refer to practices at different levels in society. Some can best be described as forces from above (e.g. English in the education system, and in the domains of business or research) whereas others pertain to forces from below, at the grass-roots level (e.g. in private interactions, use in certain subcultures and music scenes). It has been argued that this combination of movements from both above and below accounts for the strong position English enjoys in Scandinavia (Preisler, 2003).

English Language Skills and Attitudes to English Among Scandinavians

In this section, the general level of English skills and attitudes to English among the Scandinavian population are outlined and compared to those of other Europeans.

Skills and attitudes among high-school students

In a study of English skills and attitudes among Grade 9 students in eight European countries – *The Assessment of Pupils' Skills in English in Eight European Countries* (Bonnet, 2002) – student results from Denmark, Finland, Norway, Sweden, Germany, the Netherlands, France and Spain were compared. The results were based on a random sample of 1500 students from each nation (with the exception of Germany where the sample was much smaller and therefore not included in the overview below). The test was the same for all countries, but with instructions in the national languages. It was part of a survey of foreign language skills carried out on behalf of the European network of policy makers for the evaluation of education systems. Four skills areas were tested through multiple-choice and gap-fills: listening and reading comprehension, language correctness and written production. Students were also asked to evaluate the level of difficulty of the test and to assess their own English skills. In addition to the test and self-evaluations, both students and their teachers were asked about their use of and attitudes to English.

The results for each skills area can be divided into three tiers, where the Scandinavian (including Finnish) students tend to appear to the left, with higher skills, whereas the southern Europeans appear to the right, with lower skills. Norway and Sweden appear in the top tier for all four skills, and for reading and correctness we also find Finland among the top performers, as outlined in Table 1.1.

The strong results for the Scandinavian students can no doubt be linked, in part, to their positive attitudes towards English. The highest scores in this regard were recorded for the Swedish students, where 96% claimed to like English in general, followed by Denmark (90.2%), Finland (89.6%) and Norway (88.8%), compared with an overall average of 79.9% for the seven countries. As many as 98% of the Swedish students said it was important to know English, again followed by the other Scandinavians: Denmark (96%), Finland (92.7%) and Norway (91.6%).

Table 1.1 English skills among Grade 9 students in seven European countries

Results	Top tier	Middle tier	Bottom tier
Overall	Norway, Sweden (69)	Finland, Netherlands, Denmark (64–61)	Spain (46), France (38)
Listening comprehension	Sweden, Norway (>70)	Denmark, Netherlands, Finland (65–60)	Spain, France (<40)
Language correctness	Finland, Norway, Netherlands, Sweden (68–64)	Spain, Denmark (59–54)	France (48)
Reading comprehension	Sweden, Norway, Finland (86–80)	Denmark, Netherlands (78–77)	Spain (64), France (57)
Written production	Norway, Sweden (<60)	Finland, Denmark, Netherlands (<50)	Spain (<30), France (<20)

Note: Figures in brackets indicate correct answers in percentages.

The positive attitudes among the Swedish high-school students support earlier research results, which have shown that Swedes in general are very well disposed towards English (Oakes, 2001; Wingstedt, 1998), and this observation is particularly true of younger generations. For example, in his comparative study on language and national identity in France and Sweden, Oakes (2001) found that young Swedes reported much more positive attitudes towards English than their French counterparts. They even rated English as more adapted to modern society and as more beautiful than Swedish. Such attitudes also work in tandem with perceived skills and Oakes suggests that being good at English is indeed part of a Swedish national identity. Frequent code-switches to English, particularly among the young, can also be linked to positive perceptions of English where the use of English can be a means of constructing an identity as a member of an urban, global community. Similar findings have also been reported for Denmark, with abundant use of English being a characteristic feature of youth language (Preisler, 2003).

A recent study on the use of and attitudes towards American and British English accents among Norwegian adolescent learners (Rindal, 2010) indicates a high level of English proficiency in that the students managed to exploit the two English varieties for their own purposes of self-presentation. It was found that most students preferred British English pronunciation for more formal and school-oriented interactions, whereas American English was favoured in informal contexts and peer-group interactions. Rindal (2010: 255) argues that 'learners create social meaning through stylistic practice by choosing from the English linguistic resources available' and that the findings 'give strong indications that the learners make use of L2 in their construction of identity'.

Skills and attitudes among Scandinavians in general: The Eurobarometer

Results from the Eurobarometer survey of language skills of Europeans (EC, 2006) show that the overwhelming majority of Scandinavian respondents speak at least one other language in addition to their first language (see Table 1.2).

The results for the Scandinavian members of the EU are, as can be seen from Table 1.2, significantly above the EU average, based on the 25 member states at the time of polling (results for the UK, which displayed the lowest command of other languages, have also been included for comparison). As many as 90% of Swedish respondents report they know one foreign language well enough to have a conversation in that language.

Setting aside first language speakers of English, the language that most respondents say they are able to have a conversation in is, not unexpectedly, English (see Table 1.3). It is also worth noting that the dominance of English is particularly pronounced in Sweden. There, the tendency to invest in one language is stronger than in the other Scandinavian countries, where many more also say they can have a conversation in at least two languages in addition to their first language (see Table 1.2).

Overall, respondents from all 25 EU countries are very positive towards knowledge of foreign languages. Most positive are the Swedes, where 99% agree with the statement *'Do you think knowing other languages than your mother tongue is, or could be, very useful ... for you personally?'*, with 97% of respondents saying English is the most useful language. These results are almost identical to the Swedish Grade 9 students' positive evaluation of the usefulness of knowing English (98%).

So far the overview points to the widespread knowledge of English in Scandinavia where English language proficiency is regarded as something positive, in particular for international contacts and cross-cultural

Table 1.2 Which languages do you speak well enough to be able to have a conversation excluding your mother tongue? (percentage of respondents)

Country	One language	Two languages	Three languages	None
EU (25)	56	28	11	44
Sweden	90	48	17	10
Denmark	88	66	30	12
Finland	69	47	23	31
UK	38	18	6	62

Source: Special Eurobarometer 243 (EC, 2006).

Table 1.3 The most widely known languages (percentage of respondents)

Country	Language 1		Language 2		Language 3	
EU (25)	English	38	French	14	German	14
Sweden	English	89	German	30	French	11
Denmark	English	86	German	58	French	12
Finland	English	63	Swedish	41	German	18
UK	French	38	German	9	Spanish	8

Source: Special Eurobarometer 243 (EC, 2006).

communication. Being good at English, as noted above, even seems to be a marker of national identity, at least for young Swedes (Oakes, 2001). These are factors that all promote the use and increased spread of English. As outlined in the next section, debate about the role of English in Scandinavian countries has mainly concerned the rapid spread of English in certain domains, where concerns have been raised that the high level of proficiency might prove to be a threat to the long-term survival of the national languages.

English in the Domains of Higher Education and Research in Sweden

The following section examines the role of English in the domains of higher education and research, and explores the link between the actual linguistic situation and language policy and planning, using Sweden as an example.

Transnational student movements in an increasingly global education market have led to significant increases in the number of international students enrolled at Swedish universities. In 10 years the number of international students tripled to 36,600 (2008/2009 academic year), which means that one in four newly enrolled students was an international student. No doubt this development is linked to the high number of courses and programmes offered in English: 18% of all courses, 36% of all Masters-level courses, 25% of all programmes and 65% of all Masters-level programmes were offered in English (Cabau, 2011; Salö, 2010). In other words, the higher the level, the more likely that instruction takes place in English. In 2007 Sweden was in fourth position in Europe with regard to the number of programmes offered in English (123), after the Netherlands (774), Germany (415) and Finland (235) (Wächter & Maiworm, 2008). However, by 2008 the number of programmes offered in English in Sweden had increased exponentially to 530 (Cabau, 2011). These figures lend support to the argument that the globalisation of higher education has led to increased linguistic uniformity across Europe, as more and more countries offer courses taught in English to attract international students (Graddol, 2006: 77).

The large number of courses and programmes offered in English, however, does not necessarily mean that English is always used. On the one hand, Swedish is often used, to some extent, in subjects that are advertised in the university handbook as being offered in English. Söderlundh (2010) investigated the use of Swedish in university courses offered in English with a large proportion of international students. She studied language choice both in the classroom and in more socially oriented contexts during breaks. Her results show that Swedish-speaking students often use Swedish among themselves in group work and when addressing the teacher. Also, if no non-Swedish speakers are present in the classroom, interaction usually shifts to Swedish. On the other hand, subjects advertised as being offered in Swedish are not 'islands of Swedish', as the required reading is often partly in English.

As the language of research dissertations, English has increased its share significantly and is now completely dominant. For example, in 1920 about 15% of all doctoral theses were written in English, in 1960 its share had increased to 70%, and in 2008 87% were written in English. During the same period, the use of Swedish for doctoral theses steadily decreased from 50% in 1920 to 12% today. However, it is worth noting that the use of English is very unevenly distributed between disciplines, with 94% of theses in natural sciences written in English compared to only 38% for the humanities. The reason for the high overall figure is that the vast majority of all theses are written in natural sciences (for statistics, see Cabau, 2011; Salö, 2010).

The increased use of English in research can be seen as a means for smaller language communities to participate in international scientific communication, and in this role the use of English is not questioned per se. The significant increase of English in higher education is also clearly linked to student mobility and the language needs of international students. This, in turn, potentially leads to tension within the domestic market and its needs, which we now turn to.

Domain loss?

A dominant discourse over the past decade has been about the strong position of English in Sweden. In particular, the debate has concerned domain loss (e.g. Gunnarsson, 2001; Melander, 2001). For example, the English version of the website of the Swedish Language Council (Språkrådet, n.d.) states that 'English has started to compete with Swedish in a growing number of fields in Swedish society – in large, international companies, in the educational system and in the media industry'.

It has been argued that decreased use of Swedish in a particular domain is the first step towards a loss of that domain to English (e.g. Melander & Thelander, 2006). With decreasing use it will also be more difficult to make full use of Swedish in related domains, and domain-loss proponents argue that loss of one domain will, inevitably, spread to other domains.

Although few would argue seriously that Swedish is destined for extinction, many have interpreted the risk of domain loss as a warning sign – if no action is taken now, a diglossic situation will be reached where English is used in the public domain with Swedish limited to the private domain. Such a development would undermine democratic values, as those with limited English skills would not have full access to all domains in society (e.g. Josephson, 2004).

The debate on domain loss in favour of English thus provides an impetus for taking action through language policy and planning. The recent Swedish Language Act (Swedish Ministry of Culture, 2009) described below, which makes Swedish the 'principal language' of Sweden, could be interpreted against the background of fear of domain loss. However, some researchers challenge the domain loss theory. According to Boyd (2011), a certain domain does not have to be either English or Swedish, but both languages can be used side by side within it. Further, there is no firm evidence that loss of a language in a particular domain creates a domino effect, where other domains are necessarily affected (Boyd & Dahl, 2006).

(Re)actions 1: The Language Act

The Swedish Language Act came into effect in 2009, after over a decade of preparatory work, dating back to the *Draft Action Programme for the Promotion of the Swedish Language* (Språkrådet, 1998) commissioned by the Swedish Government and drawn up by the Swedish Language Council. (For further background on the Language Act see, for example, Boyd, 2011; Norrby, 2008.) The Language Act regulates the principles that were passed by Parliament in 2005, and specifies the 'position and usage of the Swedish language and other languages in Swedish society' and intends to 'protect the Swedish language and language diversity in Sweden, and the individual's access to language' (Language Act, Section 2). The Act states the following objectives for the position of Swedish in Sweden (Sections 4–6):

> Swedish is the principal language in Sweden
>
> As principal language, Swedish is the common language in society that everyone resident in Sweden is to have access to and that is to be usable in all areas of society
>
> The public sector has a particular responsibility for the use and development of Swedish.

Furthermore, the Act regulates language use in the public sector, stating that: 'the language of the courts, administrative authorities and other bodies that perform tasks in the public sector is Swedish' (Section 10). Finally, 'Swedish is the official language of Sweden in international contexts' (Section 13). In regard to the individual language user, the Act specifies that '[a]ll residents of Sweden are to be given the opportunity to learn, develop and use Swedish' (Section 14).

It could be argued that the Language Act simply states what is obvious to everybody who lives in Sweden, namely, that Swedish is spoken by the vast majority, either as a first or second language. However, making this explicit through legislation can be interpreted as a symbolic act to safeguard the position of Swedish as the common language at a time where there is a perceived threat from the outside. It is, however, interesting to note that there is no specific reference made in the Language Act to the use of English in Sweden, although it is no exaggeration to say that some of the impetus for the legislation is the increased role of English in some domains, such as in higher education (Cabau, 2011; Norrby, 2008).

(Re)action 2: University language policy

In recent years, an increasing number of universities in Scandinavia have begun to address the language situation in higher education, and several universities now have language policies in place. The first university in Sweden to implement such a policy was the University of Gothenburg, whose language policy (University of Gothenburg, n.d.) includes several provisions that are clearly consonant with the provisions of the Language Act. The decision to establish a language policy for the university was made by the University Board in 2006, and in 2010 the Vice-Chancellor made provisions for its implementation through the University's Action Plan for Language Issues 2010–2012 (University of Gothenburg, 2010). For example, the language policy of the university states that 'Swedish should be the main language of teaching in first cycle courses (Bachelor level) unless it is necessary to use another language, such as in foreign language courses', that 'dissertations in languages other than Swedish are to include extensive summaries in Swedish', and that 'all the scientific fields of the university should endeavour to use adequate terminology in Swedish' (University of Gothenburg, 2010: 6). Demanding Swedish summaries of theses, for example, is one way of safeguarding the continued use and development of appropriate terminology in Swedish – a direct response to the fear of domain loss.

While the policy aims at promoting the use of Swedish for the domestic market, however, the tone is quite different in relation to the international market, where the aim is to position the university as an attractive destination for students, researchers and teachers from outside Scandinavia by widespread use of English, both at undergraduate and postgraduate levels (University of Gothenburg, 2010: 8):

> The number of courses in which English is used as the language of teaching ... should, therefore, increase to encourage mobility and heighten the

quality of research and education according to the objectives of the Bologna Process.

Use of English at the undergraduate level – in set texts and in the classrooms – is not simply seen as a service to incoming international students, but as equally important for enhancing the English comprehension skills of local students and preparing them for higher levels of study, where English is used more extensively. At the postgraduate level (Masters and doctoral levels) and in research, the use of English should be even more prevalent in order to facilitate mobility – both in terms of increased numbers of incoming international students and researchers as well as outgoing Swedish students and researchers who wish to study abroad or engage with the international research community (see University of Gothenburg, 2010: 8).

There are clear tensions between the domestic and international policy statements, as seen in the quotations above, and the same language policy can have conflicting objectives as it tries to combine domestic demands for strengthening Swedish with the increasing internationalisation of higher education, and hence the use of English. Typically, the national language (Swedish) is promoted at the undergraduate level, in particular at lower levels, in courses aimed at the domestic market and Swedish students, whereas English is promoted at the postgraduate level, but also to some extent in advanced undergraduate-level courses, and in courses aimed at the international market more generally.

The successful implementation of the language policy and its call for increased use of English naturally depends on the cooperation of teaching staff, and here the policy simply states that '[a]ll teaching staff should be prepared to teach in English or at least teach bilingually with visual support in English' (University of Gothenburg, 2010: 9). What is implicit in such a statement is that all Swedish university teaching staff are indeed capable of switching to English, or teaching bilingually – an assumption that might not prove correct in reality. As already noted, Söderlundh (2010), for example, found that Swedish was used to varying extents in university courses offered in English. While we do not know the teaching staff's actual ability to teach in English (with no or little effort), the policy statement certainly demonstrates the belief that the university's teachers can be considered as bilingual or at least very competent second language users of English.

English in the City Streetscape

Linguistic landscaping is a relatively new subdiscipline of sociolinguistics. It involves the documentation of language use in public signs and public writings in urban spaces and seeks to understand the relationships between different languages and their users in multilingual societies (see contributions in Shohamy *et al.*, 2010). Linguistic landscaping can involve any language, but the presence and increased predominance of English in urban spaces is often a part of such documentation (see, for example, Hult, 2003 for a survey of English signs in urban Sweden).

For the purpose of illustrating to what extent English permeates the urban streetscape in Scandinavia, I have documented the use of English in *Gallerian*, a large shopping mall with 80 shops, cafés and restaurants in the centre of Stockholm. On average, four out of five shop windows had signage in English with *sale* being the most frequently used word. The displacement of Swedish *rea* (short for 'realisation') in favour of the English *sale* has been quick and only a few years ago the Swedish word was by far the most common sight. A similar tendency has been reported in a German context with *sale* increasingly replacing the German *Ausverkauf* in Berlin shop windows (Papen, 2012: 66). Papen suggests that this could be explained by the English word carrying more modern connotations and also that *sale* is much shorter than the German counterpart. In the Swedish context, only the former explanation might hold true as the Swedish word for sale involves only three letters.

Only a minority of shops had all their shop window signs in Swedish. Instead, in the majority of cases, the use was mixed with signs including both languages as shown in Figure 1.1. In this case, the use of English is

Figure 1.1 Simultaneous use of English and Swedish in shop signs

limited to a catchy phrase, 'Get the look', followed by a language mixture in *'dagens outfit!'* ('the outfit of the day!' or 'the outfit of today!').

Other similar phrases used include *Get the style!* and *Nine decades of fashion* from two shops selling women's clothing and underwear, respectively. Signs like these serve the purpose of conveying a certain mood, and are emblematic rather than necessary for successful shopping. There are, however, shops in which not only shop frontage signs are in English but where important information about models and sizes, etc., is also in English only, as in the Levi's shop where the following information appears on a placard in the shop (see Figure 1.2):

> Levi's Curve ID is a new fit system created after we listened to women from around the world and analysed more than 60,000 body scans to better understand their shape, proportion and size. Our research team confirmed what we've known all along: one 'fit' does not flatter all women. Levi's* Curve ID are three quintessential fits for women corresponding to three distinct body types: Slight Curve, Demi Curve and Bold Curve. These fits are based on the difference between your seat and hip measurements. This new fit solution gives every woman a pair of jeans that loves her body, based on shape not size.

Figure 1.2 Information sign in English

Companies want to sell their products, and the use of English must be seen in light of this. If the use of English in the shopping mall had been limited to catchy phrases or isolated words in an otherwise Swedish context, the obvious conclusion would be that English served primarily to create a certain mood or feeling, not so different from adolescents code-switching to English as an act of identity. But we are faced with much more far-reaching use of English, which rests on the assumption that shoppers have reasonable command of English – otherwise it would be pointless for companies to promote their wares solely in English. The use of English cannot be explained by the presence of international tourists in the city of Stockholm, as a similar use of English signs is found in shopping malls in other, less central locations. Furthermore, many of the shops in Gallerian belong to large chains and their use of English is uniform across Sweden.

Conclusion

There is a significant tension between contrasting trends of accepting and controlling the role of English in Scandinavia today, as seen in the Swedish examples discussed above. On the one hand, there is the influential debate in language policy quarters about the fear of domain loss, which has formed an important background – albeit implicitly – to the recent Swedish Language Act (2009). The Act and the political debate that preceded legislation (see, for example, Boyd, 2011; Norrby, 2008) have certainly put the linguistic situation and the role of the national language on the agenda. However, official or public statements about safeguarding Swedish against the increased use of English might not have much of an effect on the population at large, as pointed out by Melander (2006) and others (e.g. Boyd & Huss, 2004). In fact, the linguistic reality and attitudes of people in general suggest a much more accepting stance towards English in Scandinavia. The high level of proficiency in English, paired with very positive attitudes, is a factor that promotes further use of English. For example, the high incidence of code-switches to English in conversation, particularly among the young, displays how use of English is an act of identity and a resource for signalling membership in a global (youth) culture (see, for example, Preisler, 2003; Sharp, 2001). Furthermore, the strong presence of English in the linguistic landscape – in shops and restaurants, not just in Stockholm but throughout Scandinavia – shows that English is seen as a positive asset for attracting customers. If shop owners believed that the general public viewed the use of English negatively, they would of course stop such a language practice immediately.

The tension between accepting and controlling perspectives is perhaps never more apparent than in the higher education sector. In courses aimed at the international market, English is not only accepted, but is regarded as a necessary instrument for attracting students from abroad, although the majority of international students in Sweden and other Scandinavian countries do not come from an English language background. The significance of English is obvious from overall statistics on the number of courses and programmes offered in English, as well as from statements in university language policy documents. For the Swedish domestic market the situation is different, however. Here, the tendency is ostensibly towards promoting Swedish and controlling the role of English, such as through university language policy which states that Swedish should be the principal language for teaching in undergraduate courses.

To return to the question posed in the title of this chapter – whether English is monster or mate – the answer is that it depends on whom you ask. There are tensions between different perspectives, on the one hand, of accepting and promoting English, and on the other, of controlling its use through language policy and legislation. However, while English is everywhere in Scandinavia, the national languages are hardly doomed. On the contrary, they are strong languages in the sense that they are highly codified with dictionaries, grammars and a rich national literature, as well as being the languages of officialdom and widely spoken. From such a position, there is hardly reason to believe that English is the monster ready to devour the national languages. It is, however, more likely that we will see more extensive parallel use of languages – a national language side by side with English in a particular domain, rather than domain loss. Such use would promote a higher level of individual bilingualism and counteract 'the monolingual mindset' (Clyne, 2005: 21) that permeates some quarters of national language policy and planning, as seen in the passing of Sweden's Language Act. In other words, it is not a question of, say, Swedish *or* English, Danish *or* English, but of both.

References

Ben-Rafael, E., Shohamy, E. and Barni, M. (2010) Introduction: An approach to an 'ordered disorder'. In E. Shohamy, E. Ben-Rafael and M. Barni (eds) *Linguistic Landscape in the City* (pp. xi–xxviii). Bristol: Multilingual Matters.
Bonnet, G. (ed.) (2002) *The Assessment of Pupils' Skills in English in Eight European Countries*. Paris: European Network of Policy Makers for the Evaluation of Education Systems. See http://www.eva.dk/projekter/2002/evaluering-af-faget-engelsk-i-grundskolen/projekt produkter/assessmentofenglish.pdf.
Boyd, S. (2011) Do national languages need support and protection in legislation? The case of Swedish as the 'principal language' of Sweden. In C. Norrby and J. Hajek (eds) *Uniformity and Diversity in Language Policy: Global Perspectives* (pp. 22–36). Bristol: Multilingual Matters.
Boyd, S. and Dahl, Ö. (2006) Grundlöst om språkdöd [Groundless on language death]. *Språkvård* 4, 36–40.
Boyd, S. and Huss, L. (2004) Do the national languages of Europe need a national language policy? Some reflections on the report of the Committee for the Advancement of Swedish from a multilingual perspective. In A.M. Lorenzo Suárez, F. Ramallo and X. Rodriguez-Yanez (eds) *Proceedings of the Second International Symposium on Bilingualism* (pp. 841–856). Vigo: Servizo de publicacións da universidade de Vigo.

Cabau, B. (2011) Language policy in Swedish higher education. A contextual approach. *European Journal of Language Policy* 3 (1), 37–60.
Clyne, M. (2005) *Australia's Language Potential.* Sydney: University of New South Wales Press.
Delsing, L. and Lundin Åkesson, K. (2005) *Håller språket ihop Norden? En forskningsrapport om ungdomars förståelse av danska, svenska och norska* [*Does language hold the Nordic region together? A research report of adolescents' understanding of Danish, Swedish and Norwegian*]. Copenhagen: TemaNord. See http://www.norden.org/da/publikationer/publikationer/2005-573/.
EC (2006) *Europeans and their Languages.* Special Eurobarometer 243. Brussels: European Commission. See ec.europa.eu/public_opinion/archives/ebs/ebs_243_en.pdf.
Graddol, D. (2006) *English Next. Why Global English May Mean the End of 'English as a Foreign Language'*. London: British Council. See http://www.britishcouncil.org/learning-research-english-next.pdf.
Gunnarsson, B. (2001) Swedish tomorrow – a product of the linguistic dominance of English? In S. Boyd and L. Huss (eds) *Managing Multilingualism in a European Nation-State. Challenges for Sweden* (pp. 51–69). Clevedon: Multilingual Matters.
Haugen, E. (1972) Semicommunication: The language gap in Scandinavia. In S.A. Dil (ed.) *The Ecology of Language. Essays by Einar Haugen* (pp. 215–236). Stanford, CA: Stanford University Press.
Hult, F.M. (2003) English on the streets of Sweden: An ecolinguistic view of two cities and a language policy. *Working Papers in Educational Linguistics* 19 (1), 43–63.
Josephson, O. (2004) Inledning. Engelskan i Sverige. Språkval i utbildning, arbete och kulturliv [Introduction. English in Sweden. Language choice in education, work and culture]. In O. Josephson and K. Jämtlid (eds) *Engelskan i Sverige. Språkval i utbildning, arbete och kulturliv* (Småskrift utgiven av Svenska språknämnden 2004) (pp. 7–24). Stockholm: Norstedts Ordbok.
Melander, B. (2001) Swedish, English and the European Union. In S. Boyd and L. Huss (eds) *Managing Multilingualism in a European Nation-State. Challenges for Sweden* (pp. 13–31). Clevedon: Multilingual Matters.
Melander, B. (2006) Funktion eller kultur – vad ska svensk språkpolitik syfta till? [Function or culture – what are the aims of the Swedish language policy?] In *Språk i Norden* (pp. 43–55). Oslo: Nordic Language Council.
Melander, B. and Thelander, T. (2006) Så tar man livet av ett språk [How to kill a language]. *Språkvård* (2), 39–42.
Norrby, C. (2008) Swedish language policy: Multilingual paradise or utopian dream? In J. Warren and H. Benbow (eds) *Multilingual Europe: Reflections on Language and Identity* (pp. 63–76). Newcastle upon Tyne: Cambridge Scholars Publishing.
Oakes, L. (2001) *Language and National Identity. Comparing France and Sweden.* Amsterdam: John Benjamins.
Papen, U. (2012) Commercial discourses, gentrification and citizens' protest: The linguistic landscape of Prenzlauer Berg, Berlin. *Journal of Sociolinguistics* 16 (1), 56–80.
Preisler, B. (2003) English in Danish and the Dane's English. *International Journal of the Sociology of Language* 159, 109–126.
Rindal, U. (2010) Constructing identity with L2: Pronunciation and attitudes among Norwegian learners of English. *Journal of Sociolinguistics* 14 (2), 240–261.
Salö, L. (2010) *Engelska eller svenska? En kartläggning av språksituationen inom högre utbildning och forskning* [*English or Swedish? A survey of the language situation in higher education and research*]. Stockholm: Språkrådet.
Sharp, H. (2001) *English in Spoken Swedish. A Corpus Study of Two Discourse Domains.* Acta Universitatis Stockholmiensis. Stockholm Studies in English XCV. Stockholm: Almqvist & Wiksell International.
Shohamy, E., Ben-Rafael, E. and Barni, M. (eds) (2010) *Linguistic Landscape in the City.* Bristol: Multilingual Matters.

Söderlundh, H. (2010) *Internationella universitet – lokala språkval: Om bruket av talad svenska i engelskspråkiga kursmiljöer* [*International universities – local language choices: On spoken Swedish in English-medium course environments*]. Skrifter utgivna av Institutionen för nordiska språk vid Uppsala Universitet No. 83. Uppsala: Department of Scandinavian Languages.

Språkrådet (Swedish Language Council) (1998) *Draft Action Programme for the Promotion of the Swedish Language*. Stockholm: Swedish Language Council. See http://www.sprakradet.se/2444.

Språkrådet (Swedish Language Council) (n.d.) New website for living languages and traditions. See http://www.sprakradet.se/international.

Swedish Ministry of Culture (2009) *Swedish Language Act*. Swedish Code of Statutes No. 2009:600. Summary in English. See http://www.eui.eu/Projects/InternationalArt HeritageLaw/Documents/NationalLegislation/Sweden/languageact.pdf.

University of Gothenburg (2010) *Action Plan for Language Issues 2010–2012*. Gothenburg: University of Gothenburg. See http://www.gu.se/english/cooperation/international_ cooperation/international-initiatives/language-initiatives/action-plan-for-language/.

University of Gothenburg (n.d.) *Language Policy for Göteborg University*. See http://www.gu.se/digitalAssets/1340/1340549_language-policy.pdf.

Wächter, B. and Maiworm, F. (2008) *English-Taught Programmes in European Higher Education. The Picture in 2007*. ACA Papers on International Cooperation in Education. Bonn: Lemmens.

Washburn, L. (1997) *English Immersion in Sweden. A Case Study of Röllingby High School 1987–1989*. Stockholm: Department of English, Stockholm University.

Wingstedt, M. (1998) *Language Ideologies and Minority Language Policies in Sweden*. Stockholm: Centre for Research on Bilingualism, Stockholm University.

2 Language in Singapore: From Multilingualism to English Plus

Francesco Cavallaro and Ng Bee Chin

Introduction

With active language planning policies in force since before its independence as a nation in 1965, Singapore's linguistic situation has undergone dramatic change in the last 60 years. As a result of these policies, we have seen the waxing and waning of many languages and an unprecedented transformation of linguistic repertoires for individual Singaporeans. In particular, the last five decades have seen a significant shift to English plus,[1] one of the designated official languages, and the attrition of many other languages, including a diverse array of Chinese vernaculars. This chapter explores language policies and planning in Singapore and their impact, drawing on a number of studies, as well as on census and survey data. The chapter opens with a brief sociolinguistic description of the island state, and discusses the sociohistorical basis for the adoption of the country's language policies, their implementation and impact and language planning. It then evaluates the direct implications of such language policies on the linguistic practices of the different ethnic groups, and turns to the attitudes of Singaporeans towards their varieties of English. Finally, the chapter briefly considers the current and future consequences of language policy and change in Singapore. While Singapore's language policy approach can be associated with positive outcomes, such as Singapore's economic success, there are also negative consequences, including an increasingly reduced multilingualism, official rejection of local creativity in English and communicative dislocation within families and across generations.

Singapore's Multicultural Make-up

Singapore is a multi-ethnic and multilingual society of just over five million people. Of these, 74% are residents and 26% non-residents of Singapore

Table 2.1 Ethnic composition of Singapore residents (%)

	Chinese	Malay	Indian	Others
1957	75.4	13.6	8.6	2.4
1990	77.8	14.0	7.1	1.1
2000	76.8	13.9	7.9	1.4
2010	74.1	13.4	9.2	3.3

Source: Department of Statistics (2001b, 2006, 2011); Kuo (1980a, 1980b).

(Department of Statistics, 2011). Since its independence from the British in 1965, Singapore has maintained the same relative ratio among the main ethnic groups (Department of Statistics, 2001a; Kuo, 1980a, 1980b). Recent figures (Department of Statistics, 2006, 2009, 2011) show that Singapore's society currently has an ethnic mix of 74.1% Chinese, 13.4% Malays, 9.2% Indians and 3.3% so-called 'Others', most of whom are of Eurasian, European or Arab descent (see Table 2.1).

Singapore's Multilingual Composition

In the context of Singapore's colonial history and the politico-pragmatic circumstances before and after independence in 1965, the island nation's language policy has been described as the result of the need to ensure the cohesion of its multi-ethnic fabric (e.g. Bokhorst-Heng, 1998; Gupta, 1998; Wee, 2003). Kuo's (1980b) account of the languages spoken within and across ethnic lines before independence shows Singapore to have been (and to be) linguistically very diverse, with no fewer than 33 mother tongue groups present in the 1950s. Singapore could rightly be taken as an early example of linguistic superdiversity à la Vertovec (2007) – involving a complex and rapidly evolving ethnolinguistic, sociopolitical and economic situation that, for the political leadership of a new nation state/city of only 137 km^2, required clear management (and rationalisation) through official policy and direction.

In the 1950s and 1960s, Hokkien (a Southern Min language of China) and Malay were by far the most widely spoken languages in the small island state. The 1957 census shows that only 1.8% of the population spoke English and only 0.1% spoke Mandarin as mother tongues. In fact, other languages were much better known: 32.5% of the Chinese community, 88.3% of the Indian community and 48% of the total population spoke Malay, and 80% of the Chinese community spoke or understood Hokkien (Kuo, 1980b). Post-independence, the first language of the Singaporean Chinese community was predominantly Hokkien (39%), followed by Teochew, Cantonese, Hainanese and other Chinese languages. The Malay community was more linguistically homogeneous, largely Malay-speaking (85%), with smaller numbers of speakers of languages related to Malay, such as Peranakan Malay and Javanese, while the Indian community predominantly spoke Tamil (59%), Malayalam and other languages. This is a simplification of an even more diverse linguistic setting if we were to include, among others, Bugis, Boyanese, Sinhala, Punjabi, Urdu and other Chinese languages such as Hakka, Hokchia, Hokchew and Shanghainese. Platt (1980) described the linguistic situation in Singapore prior to 1980 as one of 'polyglossia', where the average Singaporean tended to be highly multilingual with a possible linguistic repertoire of six to eight language varieties (albeit not usually English among these; see below). If we take the average adult age of the Singaporean to be 40 at that time, this group of Singaporeans are now in their seventies.

Language Policy and its Impact

Even before formal independence, language was a sensitive and key issue in Singapore's nation building. As observed by other language policy watchers (e.g. Kuo & Jernudd, 1993; Ricento, 2000, 2006), an emergent nation cannot ignore language management as a key factor in its effort to focus and align the resources and potential of its citizens. The more heterogeneous the linguistic context, the more important and controversial such discussions are likely to be. Singapore is no exception. With a highly centralised governance in a small island state, it has been able to implement much of the vision other countries can only debate about. In general, the different language policies through the years have been implemented aggressively through policy statements and through the education system. There have been four main language thrusts that have shaped the Singapore of today:

(a) Official Languages and National Language (1950s)
(b) Bilingualism Policy (1966)
(c) The Speak Mandarin Campaign (1979 to present)
(d) The Speak Good English Movement (2000 to present)

A formal education policy was instituted in the late 1950s in Singapore with an emphasis on four official languages – Mandarin Chinese, English, Malay and Tamil. In its original form, the language policy stated that the four official languages were also the media of instruction. In the time following independence in 1965, while most schools were English medium, there were also a number of Tamil-, Malay- and Mandarin-medium schools. However, by 1987 all of these were closed because of falling student numbers (Tan, 2007). This change reduced Mandarin Chinese, Tamil and Malay to being taught as second languages in primary and secondary schools, and English has since dominated the country's education system (Pakir, 2004; Tan, 2012; Tan & Goh, 2011). This shift to English is in stark contrast to the linguistic situation during the British rule and in the early decades of independence. English was used by the colonial government and then the independent government primarily for administrative purposes. Singaporeans in those days communicated across ethnic lines largely in Bazaar Malay, a form of pidginised Malay (Gupta, 1998), or in a simplified form of Hokkien. For a very brief period, spurred on by the Federation with Malaya in 1963, Malay was also a compulsory language for those who wanted to join the public service until the mid-1970s. This policy has since remained dormant but Malay is still symbolically a national language in Singapore: the national anthem is sung in Malay despite the fact that generations of Singaporeans have sung the anthem every day of their school life with few knowing the meaning of what they are singing.

Although some within a particular ethnic group may not master the group's language, proficiency in it is considered very important socially. The 'mother tongues' are deemed to function as 'an anchor in their [students'] ethnic and cultural traditions' in opposition to the Western values and worldview supposedly imparted through the English language (Gopinathan, 1998: 21). Regardless of how one judges Singapore's efforts at language planning, there is no doubt about the general truth of Pakir's (1991) prediction that postindependence-born Singaporeans today have become 'English-knowing bilinguals', confident in their use of the varieties of Singapore English plus their ethnic language. Yet, as Wee (2003) illustrates, the functional separation between English and the 'mother tongues' in Singapore has been shaken in the wake of economic globalisation, so that the utilitarian value traditionally assigned exclusively to English has now also been extended to Mandarin Chinese. This shift in emphasis has been promoted by government policies and educational reforms. Public initiatives have also been implemented to strengthen the position of Malay and Tamil, so as to preserve the equality between the 'mother tongues'. Wee (2003), however, regards these efforts as futile, due to lack of practicality and bottom-up support.

While Mandarin, Malay and Tamil may well be bona fide mother tongues for many, they were and still are second languages for many others. The only language that can be considered a true mother tongue, given Singapore's location in the Malay Peninsula, is Malay, even though for a long time many of those classified as ethnic Malays in Singapore were in fact mother tongue speakers of other languages such as Boyanese or Javanese, more distantly related to Malay. In effect, however, English is increasingly becoming the mother tongue for more and more Singaporeans, and their ethnic languages are technically more like second languages. Table 2.2 highlights the increase in English as the language most frequently used at home (from 1.8% in 1957 to 32.3% in 2010) as well as Mandarin as the language most frequently used at home (from 0.1% to 35.6%), and a concomitant dramatic decline in the number of speakers of Chinese vernaculars (from 74.4% to 14.3%).

Table 2.2 Speakers of the main languages in Singapore (%)[a]

	English	Mandarin	Chinese vernaculars	Tamil	Malay
1957	1.8	0.1	74.4	5.2	13.5
1980	11.6	10.2	59.5	3.1	13.9
1990	18.8	23.7	39.6	2.9	14.3
2000	23.0	35.0	23.8	3.2	14.1
2010	32.3	35.6	14.3	3.2	12.2

Note: [a]The census figures are based on 'the language most frequently spoken at home'. Figures in this table do not add up to 100%. The remaining speakers speak a variety of more minor languages.
Source: Department of Statistics (2001b, 2006, 2011); Kuo (1980b); Lau (1993).

When we look at the linguistic make-up of the main ethnic groups (see Table 2.3), we can see a dramatic shift in language use within the short space of only 30 years. The Chinese community has shifted to English and Mandarin, at the significant expense of Chinese vernaculars. While the use of Mandarin appears to dominate, its expansion appears to have largely peaked – as a result of the rise of English as home language in this community that continues to gather pace, especially among the youngest Chinese (see also below). In the Indian community, English has now overtaken Tamil as the most widely used language at home, while the Malay community is better at maintaining its language compared to other ethnic groups. However, the increase over 10 years from 7.9% to 17% of Malay Singaporeans claiming to speak English as a first language appears to be the start of a significant trend – lagging behind but still tracking trends in the Chinese and Indian

Table 2.3 A comparison of English and mother tongue use in Singapore, as preferred home language, 1980, 1990, 2000 and 2010[a]

Ethnic group	Language	1980	1990	2000	2010
Chinese	English	10.2	21.4	23.9	32.6
	Mandarin	13.1	30.0	45.1	47.7
	Chinese vernaculars	76.2	48.2	30.7	19.2
Malay	English	2.3	5.7	7.9	17.0
	Malay	96.7	94.1	91.6	82.6
Indian	English	24.3	34.3	35.6	41.6
	Tamil	52.2	43.5	42.9	36.6
	Malay	8.6	14.1	11.6	7.9
	Other Indian languages	14.9	8.1	9.2	13.2

Note: [a]Not all of these figures add up to 100%. The remaining speakers speak a variety of more minor languages.
Source: Department of Statistics (2005, 2011); Lau (1993).

communities. In fact, across the board, we see the increasing use of English and Mandarin Chinese but a reduction in Malay and Tamil. Some care is needed, however, in interpreting the trend data in Tables 2.2 and 2.3: the rise of English is evident across all ethnic communities, while that of Mandarin Chinese is restricted to the ethnic Chinese. Both of these outcomes are the result of official government policy (see below).

The various ethnic groups in Singapore find themselves in many ways in a similar situation to that of immigrant groups in other parts of the world, for example, the Italians in Australia (Cavallaro, 2010; Clyne, 1982, 1991, 2003) or in the US (Carnevale, 2009; Correa-Zoli, 1981; Veltman, 1984). That is, the community is made up of an older, largely monolingual (in their ethnic language, or if multilingual, without English) generation, another largely bilingual generation (in English and their ethnic language) and a younger generation that is increasingly more competent in English than in their ethnic language (see also below). The case of the Chinese community is worth noting briefly here. As pointed out by Platt (1980), elderly Chinese in Singapore are likely to be quite linguistically versatile but many are only multilingual in Chinese vernaculars and in none of the official languages. There is a middle generation of Mandarin and English bilinguals who may also speak some of the vernaculars and then there is a younger generation who barely speak a vernacular and for whom English is clearly more dominant than Mandarin.

Language Shift in Singapore

Singapore has always been a multilingual society. Its population is made up of large numbers of immigrants arriving mainly from India, South East Asia, China and Indonesia. They have all brought their languages with them (see Table 2.4 for the most widely spoken languages).

Chinese Singaporeans are mainly descended from immigrants from South China. Indian Singaporeans are mainly descended from Tamilnadu, but there are also representatives from all over India and Sri Lanka. The Malays were the native inhabitants of Singapore but also include numbers of Boyanese, Javanese and Baba Malay (Peranakan) speakers whose origins are from elsewhere.

Language shift in the Chinese community

As previously noted, the Chinese community makes up 74.1% of the population in Singapore. Mandarin is the official mother tongue attached to this community. However, as also mentioned above, the true cultural and heritage language for the overwhelming majority of Chinese Singaporeans is one of the Chinese vernaculars such as Hokkien, and not Mandarin. With the implementation of language and education policies, however, the use of Chinese vernaculars among the Chinese community has declined

Table 2.4 Most-spoken (local) languages in Singapore

Indian	Chinese	Malay	Others
Tamil	Mandarin	Malay	English
Bengali	Hakka	Javanese	Malaccan Creole
Gujarati	Hainanese	Baba Malay (Peranakan)	Singapore Sign Language
Hindi	Min Nan (Hokkien)	Bazaar Malay	
Malayalam	Teochew	Orang Seletar	
Panjabi, Eastern	Yue (Cantonese)	Boyanese	
Sinhala			

Source: Adapted from Cavallaro and Serwe (2010).

dramatically (Table 2.3). In 1979, the then Prime Minister Lee Kuan Yew launched 'The Speak Mandarin Campaign' (SMC) to encourage the use of Mandarin Chinese as a replacement for all Chinese vernaculars. This campaign has been very successful. As evident in Table 2.3, the latest census reveals that the number of people who report Chinese vernaculars as the language most frequently spoken at home dropped from 76.2% in 1980 to only 19.2% in 2010 (Department of Statistics, 2005, 2011). Most of the shift has been to Mandarin, although there is a significant and rapidly increasing number of Chinese Singaporeans who report speaking English at home. The SMC has made Mandarin the language of solidarity and inter-(Chinese) group communication, especially among younger and middle-aged Chinese adults. Studies also show an increase in positive attitudes toward Mandarin Chinese (e.g. Xu *et al.*, 1998). Given the spread of Mandarin at the expense of other Chinese vernaculars in the home, it is not surprising that it is anecdotally reported to be a key component of Singaporean Chinese identity. This is confirmed by Li *et al.* (1997), who found that young Teochew speakers no longer identify themselves as Teochew but as Singaporean Chinese or simply as Singaporeans.

There have not been many studies carried out on the various Chinese vernaculars in Singapore, but those that do exist confirm the clear shift away from these language varieties to English and Mandarin (see Kuo, 1980a and Kuo & Jernudd, 1993 for an overview of the various censuses; Kwan-Terry, 1989, 2000 and Xu *et al.*, 1998 for the overall Chinese community; Li *et al.*, 1997 for Teochew; and Gupta & Siew, 1995 for Cantonese).

Given that both Mandarin, promoted through the SMC and the bilingual education policy, and English have increasingly displaced the Chinese vernaculars within the Chinese community, there are very few domains that need the use of a vernacular. While the position of Mandarin seems very strong, the fact that it is only taught as a second language at school and not in a true bilingual programme where it would be the medium of instruction or part of the curriculum gives rise to concerns as to whether it can be effectively maintained in the long term (David et al., 2009). On the other hand, Mandarin is unlikely to be entirely eroded due to its increasing international economic value, the increasing population of Mandarin speakers in Singapore and the continuing influx of immigrants from China. The loss of the vernaculars is not without cost within the Chinese community, however. Tan and Ng (2010) documented feelings of loss and alienation by young adult speakers who regretted not being able to speak the vernacular of their grandparents and were therefore unable to forge a meaningful bond with them. These findings were also confirmed in Ng's (2009) study where she interviewed 18 elderly Singapore Chinese who did not speak any of the official languages. In these interviews, they spoke poignantly about their feelings of desolation and dislocation as they were unable to connect with their grandchildren, and their sadness at having to depend on their children for routine tasks such as visits to hospitals; even simple tasks such as catching a train or using the ATM were insurmountable obstacles for them. These issues are often compounded by loneliness, ill-health and poverty.

Language shift in the Indian community

The Indian community makes up 9.2% of the population, and is the smallest of the three main ethnic groups. The official mother tongue for the Indian community is Tamil. As is the case of the Chinese community, however, there are several traditional mother tongues within the Indian community.

With a more recent influx of Indian migrants to Singapore, the government has allowed non-Tamil speakers to choose one of the five non-Tamil Indian languages (NTILs) in lieu of Tamil as the official school-level examination subjects since the 1990s. The number of students studying NTILs (Bengali, Gujarati, Hindi, Panjabi and Urdu) as their second language has grown by about 20% over the past five years to about 4800 students today. Instruction of NTILs is organised by seven South Asian community groups: D.A.V. Hindi School Ltd and Hindi Society Singapore for Hindi; Bangla Language and Literary Society and Bangladesh Language and Cultural Foundation for Bengali; Singapore Gujarati School for Gujarati; Singapore Sikh Education Foundation for Punjabi; and Urdu Development Society for Urdu. These community groups hold classes, employ their own teachers, design their curriculum and set their own assessments. However, the Ministry of Education sets the national school examinations (see Dixon, 2005).

Over the years, the population of North Indians migrating to Singapore has grown steadily. The make-up of these recent migrants has changed as well. Compared to the past, when many Indian migrants took up unskilled jobs, these new immigrants are better educated and skilled professionals.

A large number were – and are – attracted to Singaporean schools for the quality of education they offer. Many have chosen Hindi as the second language/mother tongue at school. Interestingly, many Indian students whose mother tongues may be none of the NTILs mentioned above – nor Hindi or even English – have opted to study Hindi, the main national language of India, instead of Tamil as their second language.

In 2010, 36.6% of the Indian Singaporean population spoke Tamil at home as their primary language – a significant decrease from the 60% reported in 1957. At the same time, 13.2% spoke other Indian languages such as Malayalam, Hindi and Punjabi in 2010. Language shift to English among Indian Singaporeans is significant, as already illustrated in Table 2.3 and confirmed in a series of studies (Gupta & Siew, 1995; Saravanan, 1995, 1999; Schiffman, 1998, 2002). David *et al.* (2009) attributed this shift to two main causes: (1) the notion that a good command of English is tied to economic success and academic accomplishments; and (2) the Tamil variety spoken at home is significantly different from the variety traditionally taught in school, as a result of which students could not make an association between them.

Language shift in the Malay community

The Malay community makes up 13.4% of the population in Singapore. The official ethnic mother tongue of the Malay community is Bahasa Melayu or Malay. The census data point to a situation where the Malay community is more resilient to language shift than the Chinese and Indian communities. Indeed, in the 2010 census, 82.7% of the Malays in Singapore indicated that they use Malay as their preferred home language, and only 17% indicated that the language most frequently used at home is English (Department of Statistics, 2011). There are two things of note in these figures, also shown in Table 2.3. First, that that there was almost a 10% jump in the reporting of English used at home from the 2000 census. This jump is unprecedented compared to previous decades. Secondly, the census does not show the extent of the increase in domains where English has made inroads at the expense of Malay (David *et al.*, 2009). Very few studies have looked into maintenance or shift within the Malay community in Singapore. However, Cavallaro and Serwe's (2010) comprehensive study found that the ages of the speaker and of the interlocutor are the most significant factors determining language choice by Malays, across domains and topics of talk. They found that more English was used among young Malays, while Malays with university degrees and with higher incomes showed the highest use of English overall. Across all these factors, Malay was used among and with community members over 45 years of age. The study also confirms a transfer of domains away from Malay to English, especially among younger Malay Singaporeans.

Language Shift, Attitudes and Identity: Future Prospects

All studies looking into language shift in Singapore point to a situation where traditional languages are losing their grip on younger generations of Singaporeans. Cavallaro and Serwe (2010), Li *et al.* (1997), Pillai (2009) and Ramiah (1991) and all found that their participants aged 18–29 were more comfortable in English. Pillai (2009) even reports that young Singaporean Malayalams are not at all interested in learning Malayalam. For some varieties like Peranakan Malay (or Baba Malay), the shift is drastic, with the language facing imminent endangerment in Singapore.

There is little doubt that the change in Singaporean language practices is due to two main causes: government policies, and people's desire for personal gain and social mobility (Li *et al.*, 1997), with both issues being closely tied to language attitudes and language identity. Singapore has experienced significant social and economic development in the past few decades. These developments have in part been brought about through the government's emphasis on good English language skills. The importance of good English and, to a large extent, a good command of Mandarin – both of which have been actively promoted by the government – has not been lost on the pragmatic Singaporeans. Ng (2008) surveyed parents of Chinese ethnic background in Singapore with young children about their choice of home language. Their responses were overwhelmingly in favour of bringing up the children bilingually in both English and Mandarin Chinese. That said, however, it was striking that, despite the apparent success of official efforts to promote Mandarin for Chinese Singaporeans (as seen in Table 2.3), those who were fluent in Mandarin were also abandoning it in the home in favour of speaking English, their weaker second language.

While it is clear that non-official languages (especially Chinese vernaculars) will always struggle to gain a foothold in the current scenario, a different tension has emerged in the new English-speaking backdrop of Singapore. In the pre-1980s, English was very much associated with the elite and was not widely used as a lingua franca within ethnic groups. In the intervening years, with a concerted push to create a larger base of English-literate bilinguals, the elitism that was associated with speaking English soon lost its lustre. Practically speaking, most Singaporeans who are now 45 years old and below (in 2013) have been educated in English-medium schools. This group of Singaporeans is now expected to be at least bilingual in English and one other official language. As a result, for the last 20–30 years, it has become commonplace for English to be used as a lingua franca among all Singaporeans. This means that, in effect, English has replaced all other languages as a supra-ethnic language. As in all language contact situations, the coexistence of English with other varieties has given rise to a new contact variety of English with substrate influences from other local varieties (Hokkien, Mandarin Chinese and Malay). This variety is sometimes referred to derogatorily or fondly (depending on one's perspective) as 'Singlish' or Singapore Colloquial English (SCE) and exists alongside Standard Singapore English (SSE).

The issue of whether SCE exists as a separate English variety and whether it should be recognised as such is an issue that has polarised the community, much like the debate on standard and non-standard English in the UK or the debate on African American Vernacular English in the US. In surveying the concerns of Singapore's 'Speak Good English Campaign', launched in 2000, one immediately recognises the same reasons put forward for not promoting a non-standard variety. The authorities and critics are concerned about intelligibility, academic achievement, national image and Singapore's economic future, among other issues. On the other hand, proponents of SCE underline the importance of national identity and language rights. As elsewhere, the defenders of SCE are typically the privileged few who have good control of both SSE and SCE. The tension between these two camps is palpable and ongoing. These issues are extremely complex as they involve language attitudes and identity, along with a shift in Singapore's broader linguistic ecology and the loss of some languages. (Given the limited space here, readers are referred to the following for further detail: Bokhorst-Heng & Caleon, 2009; Cavallaro & Ng, 2009; Cavallaro *et al.*, forthcoming; Ng *et al.*, forthcoming; Tan & Tan, 2008).

Discussion

In 50 years or so, a linguistically heterogeneous group living in Singapore has evolved into one with English as an intergroup and intragroup lingua franca. The high levels of English proficiency of Singaporeans have made them an attractive workforce for multinational companies and allow Singaporeans to integrate into the various higher education settings in the English-speaking world with relative ease, as well as giving them a passport to international employment. Locally, the accessibility of education has meant that every Singaporean has a chance to be educated up to at least Year 10. In all international measures of literacy and numeracy skills, Singaporean children are among the most competent in the world. Although an increasing number of Singaporeans are English dominant, they are able to converse in at least two languages. In terms of nurturing a nation of *bilingual* speakers, therefore, the policy has been a resounding success, although the extent to which this officially sanctioned bilingualism can be maintained, or the extent to which it can be balanced, remains to be seen, given the English-medium education system, and the teaching of Malay, Mandarin Chinese and Tamil as second language subjects only.

By the next census in 2020, we expect to see a further increase in the use of English as the preferred home language across the different ethnic groups. In the Chinese community, there will be a further reduction in the number of Chinese vernaculars spoken but also in the use of all the other three official languages in the home, including, for the first time, Mandarin Chinese. In effect, over time, Singaporeans will be even more English dominant in tandem with the rise and spread of English worldwide. This is a formidable market force that is beyond the boundaries of the island state and, as prosaic as it sounds, this 'English tide' will continue to wash over all other languages, with the possible partial exception of Mandarin Chinese outside the home setting if its utilitarian value continues to increase with the economic rise of China. Overall, all this adds up to a situation of increasing linguistic homogeneity at the expense of the more traditional multilingualism practised by many older Singaporeans.

With regard to SSE and SCE, however, it is unclear how the tension between them will be resolved. While official policy still strongly proscribes the use of SCE, its prevalence is clear. While it is relatively easy to sanction against an entire variety (e.g. Hokkien), it is much harder to prohibit a variety that is part of a stylistic continuum, and is an important part of local linguistic creativity and identity. It is clear that both SSE and SCE have their functions. Recently, during a field trip to a Singaporean Supreme Court, the authors observed prosecutors using SCE in their interrogation of their own witnesses but SSE with the defendant. Clearly, these two varieties were being used to both facilitate interaction (in the case of the witnesses for prosecution) and intimidation (in the case of the defendant). Such discourse functions are not unusual and have been documented for other diglossic varieties. Both SSE and SCE have a role to play and these roles are duly exploited by the speakers. In the long run, the best thing may be to encourage speakers to acquire both varieties and to use them in context-appropriate situations. As it stands, Singapore has clearly moved from 'English knowing' to 'English dominant'.

There are other downsides to the rise of English in Singapore that give cause for concern, in particular its social consequences. The 2010 census shows that of the 5,076,700 people in Singapore, 3,771,721 are residents. In terms of literacy, 128,661 people out of the resident population over 15 are non-literate and 887,241 are literate in only one language: 485,511 in Chinese only, 338,221 in English only, 47,278 in Malay only, 10,939 in Tamil only, and 5292 in only one other language. Of these 887,241 residents, 338,387 people are over the age of age of 65, of which 214,778 were born in Singapore and 123,609 were born abroad. Among these senior residents, 283,185 are Chinese, 30,938 are Malay, 19,806 are Indians, and 'Others' comprise the remaining 4458. These elderly residents show the highest use of non-official languages and the lowest use of English. Given these statistics, coupled with a new emerging generation of children who do not speak any of the minority languages or vernaculars, we already have no common language between generations for some groups of speakers. Can the cost of the loss of non-official languages be measured? How does one quantify the sadness of some thousands of elderly people who are cut off from the English-speaking world? What provisions have been made for them to make their last few years a little better? What steps have their children and grandchildren taken to reach out and talk to them and listen to their stories? Official language policy directed at specific outcomes (i.e. language engineering), such as the emphasis on Standard English and on the learning of Mandarin Chinese (and associated shift from traditional vernaculars) by the Chinese community, does not take into consideration any of these social consequences.

The next decade will see the need for Singaporeans to meet and balance three major challenges:

- the harmonious integration of both old and new residents from different cultural and linguistic backgrounds;
- the nurturing and harnessing of the resources of post-independence Singaporeans to meet the needs of the nation's blueprint for success; and
- the management of the ageing population and bridging the language gap between older Singaporeans and the increasingly English-dominant youth.

These challenges are not new, but official policy has always focused on the first two, with scant attention paid to the last. With increasing English plus bilingualism in neighbouring Asian states, Singapore is likely to lose the edge it has always enjoyed in this area. However, by paying careful attention to the transition across generations and across groups, it can lead the way in responding to the market forces of globalisation while nurturing the varieties that create meaningful and harmonious bonding within the community – including within families and across generations.

Note

(1) 'English Plus' is a term used by Michael Clyne in his video *Growing up with English Plus* (Beligan et al., 1999) about bilingualism in Australia. Although the situations in Australia and Singapore are vastly different, we will show how this term now aptly applies to Singaporeans today.

References

Beligan, A., Clyne, M. and Lotherington, H. (1999) *Growing Up with English Plus*. DVD. Melbourne: Language and Society Centre, Monash University.

Bokhorst-Heng, W. (1998) Language planning and management in Singapore. In J.A. Foley, T. Kandiah , B. Zhiming, A.F. Gupta, L. Alsagoff, Ho Chee Lick, L. Wee, I.S. Talib and W. Bokhorst-Heng (eds) *English in New Cultural Contexts: Reflections from Singapore* (pp. 287–309). Singapore: Oxford University Press.

Bokhorst-Heng, W. and Caleon, I.S. (2009) The language attitudes of bilingual youth in multilingual Singapore. *Journal of Multilingual and Multicultural Development* 30 (3), 235–251.

Carnevale, N.C.A. (2009) *New Language: A New World: Italian Immigrants in the United States, 1890–1945*. Chicago, IL: University of Illinois Press.

Cavallaro, F. (2010) *Transgenerational Language Shift: From Sicilian and Italian to Australian English*. Melbourne: Italian Australian Institute.

Cavallaro, F. and Ng, B.C. (2009) Between status and solidarity in Singapore. *World Englishes* 28 (2), 143–159.

Cavallaro, F. and Serwe, S. (2010) Language use and shift among the Malays in Singapore. *Applied Linguistics Review* 1 (1), 129–170.

Cavallaro, F., Seilhamer, M. and Ng, B.C. (forthcoming) Singapore Colloquial English: Issues of prestige and identity. In *English and Identity in Contemporary Singapore (Special Issue for World Englishes)*.

Clyne, M. (1982) *Multilingual Australia*. Melbourne: River Seine.

Clyne, M. (1991) *Community Languages: The Australian Experience*. Cambridge: Cambridge University Press.

Clyne, M. (2003) *Dynamics of Language Contact*. Cambridge: Cambridge University Press.

Correa-Zoli, Y. (1981) The language of Italian Americans. In C.A. Ferguson and S.B. Heath (eds) *Language in the USA* (pp. 239–256). Cambridge: Cambridge University Press.

David, M.K., Cavallaro, F. and Coluzzi, P. (2009) Language policies – impact on language maintenance and teaching: Focus on Malaysia, Singapore, Brunei and the Philippines. In F. Cavallaro, A. Milde and P. Sercombe (eds) *Language, Culture and Identity in Asia* (pp. 155–191). Special issue of *The Linguistics Journal*.

Department of Statistics (2001a) *Census of Population 2000 Statistical Release 2: Education, Language and Religion*. Singapore: Department of Statistics, Ministry of Trade and Industry. See http://www.singstat.gov.sg/.

Department of Statistics (2001b) *Census of Population 2000 Statistical Release 5: Households and Housing*. Singapore: Department of Statistics, Ministry of Trade and Industry. See http://www.singstat.gov.sg/.

Department of Statistics (2005) *General Household Survey 2005*. Singapore: Department of Statistics, Ministry of Trade and Industry. See http://www.singstat.gov.sg/.

Department of Statistics (2006) *General Household Survey Statistical Release 1: Sociodemographic and Economic Characteristics*. Singapore: Department of Statistics, Ministry of Trade and Industry. See http://www.singstat.gov.sg/.

Department of Statistics (2009) *Monthly Digest of Statistics Singapore: May 2009*. Singapore: Department of Statistics, Ministry of Trade and Industry. See http://www.singstat.gov.sg/.

Department of Statistics (2011) *Monthly Digest of Statistics Singapore: April 2011*. Singapore: Department of Statistics, Ministry of Trade and Industry. See http://www.singstat.gov.sg/.

Dixon, L.Q. (2005) Bilingual education policy in Singapore: An analysis of its sociohistorical roots and current academic outcomes. *International Journal of Bilingual Education and Bilingualism* 8 (1), 25–47.

Gopinathan, S. (1998) Language policy changes 1979–1997: Politics and pedagogy. In S. Gopinathan, A. Pakir, Ho Wah Kam and V. Saravanan (eds) *Language, Society, and Education in Singapore: Issues and Trends* (2nd edn) (pp. 19–44). Singapore: Times Academic Press.

Gupta, A.F. (1998) The situation of English in Singapore. In J.A. Foley, T. Kandiah, L. Wee, B. Zhiming and A. Fraser Gupta (eds) *English in New Cultural Contexts: Reflections from Singapore* (pp. 106–126). Oxford: Oxford University Press.

Gupta, A.F. and Siew, P.Y. (1995) Language shift in a Singapore family. *Journal of Multilingual and Multicultural Development* 16 (4), 301–314.

Kuo, E. (1980a) Population ratio, intermarriage and mother tongue retention. In E.A. Afendras and E. Kuo (eds) *Language and Society in Singapore* (pp. 254–264). Singapore: Singapore University Press.

Kuo, E. (1980b) The sociolinguistic situation in Singapore: Unity in diversity. In A.E. Afendras and E. Kuo (eds) *Language and Society in Singapore* (pp. 39–62). Singapore: NUS Press.

Kuo, E. and Jernudd, B.H. (1993) Balancing macro and micro sociolinguistic perspectives in language management: The case of Singapore. Reprinted in J. Lindsay and Y.Y. Tan (eds) (2003) *Babel or Behemoth: Language Trends in Asia* (pp. 103–123). Singapore: Asia Research Institute, National University of Singapore.

Kwan-Terry, A. (1989) Education and the pattern of language use among ethnic Chinese school children in Singapore. *International Journal of the Sociology of Language* 80, 5–31.

Kwan-Terry, A. (2000) Language shift, mother tongue, and identity in Singapore. *International Journal of the Sociology of Language* 143, 85–106.

Lau, K.E. (1993) *Singapore Census of Population 1990*. Singapore: Department of Statistics.

Li, W., Saravanan, V. and Ng, L.H.J. (1997) Language shift in the Teochew community in Singapore: A family domain analysis. *Journal of Multilingual and Multicultural Development* 18 (5), 364–384.

Ng, B.C. (2008) Linguistic pragmatism, globalization and the impact on the patterns of input in Singaporean Chinese homes. In P. Tan and R. Rubdy (eds) *Language as Commodity: Global Structures, Local Marketplaces* (pp. 71–88). London and New York: Continuum Press.

Ng, B.C. (2009) 'Where do the old folks go?' Evolving multilingual contexts, language displacement and elderly Singaporeans. Paper presented at the *7th International Symposium on Bilingualism,* 8–11 July, Utrecht, The Netherlands.

Ng, B.C., Cavallaro, F., and Koh, S.P.D. (forthcoming) Singlish can: Speech accommodation in Singapore English. Special Issue for World Englishes. *English and Identity in Contemporary Singapore.*

Pakir, A. (1991) The range and depth of English-knowing bilinguals in Singapore. *World Englishes* 10, 167–179.

Pakir, A. (2004) Medium-of-instruction policy in Singapore. In J.W. Tollefson and A.B.M. Tsui (eds) *Medium of Instruction Policies: Which Agenda? Whose Agenda?* (pp. 117–133). Mahwah, NJ: Lawrence Erlbaum.

Pillai, A.D. (2009) Language shift among Singaporean Malayalee families. *Language in India 9* (1). See http://www.languageinindia.com/jan2009/singaporemalayalee.pdf (accessed 14 May 2011).

Platt, J. (1980) Multilingualism, polyglossia and code selection in Singapore. In E.A. Afendras and E.C.Y. Kuo (eds) *Language and Society in Singapore*. Singapore: NUS Press.

Ramiah, K. (1991) The pattern of Tamil language use among primary school Tamil pupils in Singapore. *Asia Pacific Journal of Education* 11 (2), 45–53.

Ricento, T. (2000) Historical and theoretical perspectives in language policy and planning. In T. Ricento (ed.) *Ideology, Politics, and Language Policies: Focus on English* (pp. 9–24). Amsterdam: John Benjamins.

Ricento, T. (2006) Topical areas in language policy: An overview. In T. Ricento (ed.) *An Introduction to Language Policy: Theory and Method* (pp. 231–237). Oxford: Blackwell.

Saravanan, V. (1995) Linguistic and cultural maintenance through education for minority groups in Singapore. In M.L. Tickoo (ed.) *Language and Culture in Multilingual Societies: Viewpoints and Visions*. Pathology Series No. 56. Singapore: SEAMO Regional Language Centre.

Saravanan, V. (1999) Bilingual Chinese, Malay and Tamil children's language choices in a multilingual society. *Early Child Development and Care* 152, 43–54.

Schiffman, H.F. (1998) Standardization or restandardization: The case for 'Standard' spoken Tamil. *Language in Society* 27, 359–385.

Schiffman, H.F. (2002) Tongue tied in Singapore: A language policy for Tamil? *Journal of Language, Identity and Education* 2 (2), 105–125.
Tan, J. (2007) Schooling in Singapore. In G.A. Postiglione and J. Tan (eds) *Going to School in East Asia* (pp. 301–319). Westport, CT: Greenwood Publishing Group.
Tan, P.K.W. and Tan, D.K.H. (2008) Attitudes toward non-standard English in Singapore. *World Englishes* 27 (3–4), 465–479.
Tan, S. and Ng, B.C. (2010) Three generations under one roof: A study of the influence of the presence of grandparents on language shift, identity and attitudes. *TRANEL (Travaux neuchâtelois de linguistique)* 52, 69–92.
Tan, Y.Y. (2012) To r or not to r: Social correlates of /ɹ/ in Singapore English. *International Journal of the Sociology of Language* 218, 1–24.
Tan, Y.Y. and Goh, I. (2011) Politics of language in contemporary Singapore cinema: The films of Jack Neo, or politics by cinematic means. *Interventions: Journal of Postcolonial Studies* 13 (4), 610–626.
Veltman, C. (1984) *Language Shift in the United States*. Berlin: Mouton.
Vertovec, S. (2007) Super-diversity and its implications. *Ethnic and Racial Studies* 29 (6), 1024–1054.
Wee, L. (2003) Linguistic instrumentalism in Singapore. *Journal of Multilingual & Multicultural Development* 24 (3), 211–224.
Xu, D., Chew, C. and Chen, S. (1998) Language use and language attitudes in the Singapore Chinese community. In S. Gopinathan, A. Pakir, Ho Wah Kam and V. Saravanan (eds) *Language, Society and Education in Singapore* (pp. 133–155). Singapore: Times Academic Press.

3 English as an International Language: A Multilingual and Pluricentric Perspective

Farzad Sharifian

The rapid global spread of the English language and the strengthening of its role as a major language of international communication raise the question of whether or not English stands in opposition to bilingualism and multilingualism (e.g. Clyne & Sharifian, 2008; House, 2003). In this context, the thesis of 'linguistic imperialism' associates the pre-eminence of English in the world with certain hegemonic forces, and rightly argues that the continued dominance of English has led to and will continue to lead to the demise of other languages (e.g. Pennycook, 1994; Phillipson, 1992). There are, however, scholars who take a more positive outlook towards the spread of English and do not view it as a threat to multilingualism. For example, Hoffmann (2000: 2) argues that 'the presence of and need for English have become so widespread, and access to and provision for it so varied, that it is now possible to talk about "bilingualism with English", rather than just the use of English as a foreign language'. This chapter explores the interaction of the internationalisation and global spread of English with bi/multilingualism. It argues that the globalisation of English does not appear to pose a threat to bi/multilingualism, but in fact increases the pluricentricity of the language. In other words, it offers a view of English as a pluricentric language, and its implications for teaching English as first (L1) or second (L2) language.

The chapter begins by discussing the internationalisation of English and the influence of globalisation on the language in recent years, followed by a consideration of the positioning of English vis-à-vis bilingualism and multilingualism. It will then explore the pluricentricity of English from the perspective of the framework of *language and cultural conceptualisations* (Sharifian, 2011), finally presenting examples of cultural conceptualisations in newer varieties of English. The latter part of the chapter focuses on the inclusion of cross-cultural communication skills in teaching English as an L1 and L2.

Internationalisation and Globalisation of English

The fact that English has gained the status of an international language is nothing new, dating back to colonial times and the migration of English-speaking people to different parts of the world, including new continents such as the Americas and Australia. However, recent decades have witnessed some radical changes to the English language as a result of new forces that have impacted upon it, including globalisation and communication through new technology. Graddol (1997) observes a complex relationship developing between the English language and globalisation. He argues that economic globalisation has encouraged the global spread of English, while at the same time the worldwide spread of English has encouraged globalisation. More recently he observes that 'English is now redefining national and individual identities worldwide, shifting political fault lines, creating new global patterns of wealth and social exclusion, and suggesting new notions of human rights and responsibilities of citizenship' (Graddol, 2006: 12).

The global spread of English has entailed important demographic changes in the use of the language (e.g. Sharifian, 2009). It is now widely adopted as a means of communication by communities of speakers who have traditionally been identified as non-native speakers of the language. This has led to further diversification of the language and the development of more world Englishes (Kachru, 1986), such as Chinese English (Xu, 2010a). In its journey across the *globe*, English has become increasingly *localised* by many communities of speakers around the world, a process which may be called *glocalisation* of the language (Sharifian, 2010a).

At the end of the 20th century, Crystal (1997) observed that more than 80% of communication in English was between non-native speakers of the language, and this observation is undoubtedly already out of date. The startling figures on the use of English internationally are also related to international travel. Graddol observes that:

> [t]here were around 763 million international travellers in 2004, but nearly three-quarters of visits involved visitors from a non-English-speaking country travelling to a non-English-speaking destination. This demonstrates the scale of need for face-to-face international communication and a growing role for global English. (Graddol, 2006: 29)

Graddol (2006: 11) maintains that English, in its global form, is now 'a new phenomenon, and if it represents any kind of triumph it is probably not a cause for celebration by native speakers [of English]'. Moreover, global access to new technology, including the internet, for communication across national borders has not only sizably increased the use of international languages, but has also changed the nature of such communication, for example through the use of *netspeak* (Crystal, 2006).

Where are bilingualism and multilingualism placed in this changing landscape of the globalisation of the English language? The next section focuses on this question.

Bilingualism, Multilingualism and the Global Spread of English

The global spread of English as a language for international communication does not logically, in itself, threaten bilingualism and multilingualism. The very fact that the majority of English use is now by non-native speakers of the language means that the majority of English language speakers today are bilingual and multilingual. Some scholars have even recommended the use of the term 'bilingual users of English' (e.g. McKay, 2002) instead of 'non-native speaker', on the grounds that 'non-native' is rather pejorative: it labels the speakers for what they are not, rather than for their skills and what they know. House (2003) maintains that in many contexts today, English is being used as a language of *communication*, whereas local languages are used as the language of *identification*. She argues that individuals' first languages 'are likely to be the main determinants of their identity, which means holding a stake in the collective linguistic-cultural capital that defines the L1 group and its members' (House, 2003: 560). Some writers, however, have felt that they can fully express their local identity and culture in English (e.g. Achebe, 1975). The issue of identity and English is a complicated one. For example, some learners of English as an L2 aspire to learn particular accents, such as that of American English, to project certain identities that are often associated with images of native speakers of that variety of English in ELT materials. Within the context of the argument that English poses a threat for local languages, House argues that the spread of English may boost the maintenance of local languages, noting:

> [p]aradoxical as it may seem, the very spread of ELF [English as a lingua franca] may stimulate members of minority languages to insist on their own local languages for emotional binding to their own culture, history and tradition, and there is, indeed, a strong countercurrent to the spread of ELF in that local varieties and cultural practices are often strengthened. (House, 2003: 561)

Historically, some scholars have viewed the spread of English as a threat to the ecology of other languages (e.g. Phillipson, 1992), causing the death of languages. Some have even called it a 'killer language' (e.g. McMahon, 1994; Skutnabb-Kangas, 2000). While in certain contexts this is a valid observation, it does not mean that the spread of English as an international language, and the spread of other languages for international communication, are necessarily in conflict with learning and speaking two or more languages.

In fact, in some contexts, it is the *national* lingua franca that can be viewed as posing a threat to the life of local languages, such as the case of Bahasa Indonesia in Indonesia. Many people learn Bahasa Indonesia, the official language of the country, as their second language, and they may also learn English as a language for international communication. This 'new' trend in bilingualism, that is, national language/local lingua franca, plus English, seems to restrict multilingualism in certain contexts (e.g. Kirkpatrick, 2012). Thus, in such contexts, the demise of certain local languages may not necessarily be caused by the international language, nor does it necessarily lead to monolingualism, but in many cases it can lead to becoming bilingual in two lingua francas only – one for use within national borders and one beyond.

Participation in global citizenship increasingly requires the learning and use of more than one language, although few L1 English speakers are aware of this. An often-heard view is that 'English is not enough' and this is not just for non-native speakers of the language. Nevertheless, Graddol (2006: 118) observes that the 'slogan "English is not enough" applies as strongly to native speakers of English as for those who speak it as a second language'. The rise of new economic powers, in particular China and India, has already provided a strong need for many to learn the languages of these countries. It would probably be more effective to engage in business, for example, with the giant economic powers of the future, without the intermediary of English. In fact, Graddol (2006) predicts a bleak economic future for monolinguals, as the global market increasingly requires global citizens, fluent in more than one language. As he puts it:

> The familiar 'story of English' provides a historical narrative which represents the emergence of global English as 'triumph' for native speakers. The reality is that there are much wider and more complex changes in the world language system now taking place. English is not the 'big' language in the world, and its position as a global language is now in the care of multilingual speakers. (Graddol, 2006: 57)

Many companies and businesses now prefer to recruit multilingual speakers who can act as their international liaison officers (see, for example, Hollister, 2007). Many international providers, such as international airlines, boast that their staff can speak different languages, to appeal to an international market. In multilingual societies such as Australia, many businesses – real estate agencies and health clinics, for example – showcase their linguistic capital by listing the languages that their staff can speak, as exemplified in Figure 3.1.

Thus, the rise of English as an international language within the context of globalisation does not necessarily seem to force other languages off the scene. If anything, it seems that globalisation calls for the use of more than one language. In fact, many scholars use the phrases 'the spread of English' and 'multilingualism' in conjunction with each other. For instance, Graddol

Figure 3.1 Brochure for a medical clinic in Victoria, Australia

(2006: 116) observes that 'in response to the spread of English and increased multilingualism arising from immigration, many countries have introduced language laws in the last decade.' Crystal maintains that:

> [t]here are no precedents in human history for what happens to languages, in such circumstances of rapid change. There has never been a time when so many nations were needing to talk to each other so much. There has never been a time when so many people wished to travel to so many places. There has never been such a strain placed on the conventional resources of translating and interpreting. Never has the need for more widespread bilingualism been greater, to ease the burden placed on the professional few. And never has there been a more urgent need for a global language. (Crystal, 2003: 14)

Although Crystal duly acknowledges the growth in international communication, and in particular the demand for bilingualism, his use of the term 'global language' seems to present a limited view of international communication, as the world is in fact moving towards needing and using more than one global language. Languages such as Mandarin, Spanish and Arabic are the world's fastest-growing languages and have arguably begun to pose a threat to the international status of English. Graddol (2006: 62) observes that 'English is no longer the "only show in town". Other languages now challenge the dominance of English in some regions. Mandarin and Spanish, especially, have become sufficiently important to be influencing national policy priorities in some countries'.

Not only does the global spread of English not seem to be posing a threat to multilingualism, it also increases the pluricentricity of English. This occurs through contact with cultural conceptualisations that have traditionally been associated with other languages, a phenomenon that is leading to the development of an increasing number of World Englishes. This theme is elaborated on in the following sections.

English as a Pluricentric Language

The term 'pluricentric' refers to languages that have multiple centres which interact with each other, each serving as a national variety with its own norms. As Clyne (1992: 1) put it: 'pluricentric languages are both unifiers and dividers of peoples. They unify people through the use of the language and separate them through the use of national norms and indices and linguistic variables with which the speakers identify.' English is perhaps the most diversified language that the world has ever seen, given its geographical reach and thanks to its global spread. It is a pluricentric language par excellence. Examples of other pluricentric languages include Chinese (Putonghua), German, Spanish, Arabic, Bahasa Indonesia, and French.

English is currently spoken in more than 70 territories as a first language or as an official (second) language. Communities of speakers in these territories have localised English to suit their communicative needs. New varieties of English are also fast developing in what Kachru (1986) termed 'Expanding Circle' countries, that is, countries in which English has had no official role, and was traditionally just learned as a foreign language. These include countries such as China, Japan, Korea, Saudi Arabia and nations of the former USSR. A number of scholars have been documenting the development of China English, for example, which is likely to become a major variety of English in the future, partly due to the rise of China as a world economic power (Hu, 2004, 2005; Xu, 2010a, 2010b). In 2004 Hu argued that:

> [t]he huge population of China, the country's recent entry into the World Trade Organization, and the ensuing international cultural and business contacts may all mean that China will be using English more and more, providing a basis from which its own variety of the language may very well dominate, due – if nothing else – to the sheer numbers of Chinese speakers and foreigners' new contacts with China. (Hu, 2004: 26)

The diversification of English takes place at different levels of the language, from the sound system to the deeper layers of cultural conceptualisations (Sharifian, 2011). Although it is, in my view, the sound system that is most noticeable when communities of speakers localise English, it is largely the localisation at the level of cultural conceptualisations that makes the speech of these communities into new varieties of English. Traditionally people have extensively relied on the emergence of systematic changes at the level of phonology and grammar (and to a lesser extent lexicon) as the criteria for the recognition of a new variety. However, I argue that changes at the level of conceptualisation are more significant in terms of the development and existence of a new variety and pluricentricity of the language. It is at this level that culture substantially interacts with language. I will elaborate on this theme in the following section.

Cultural Conceptualisations

Cultural conceptualisations are the building blocks of cultural cognition, which is the collective cognition of a cultural group (Sharifian, 2011). Cultural cognition emerges from interactions between the members of a cultural group across time and space, and is constantly negotiated and renegotiated across generations of speakers. Cultural cognition is largely, but not solely, transmitted through language. Therefore, it is also instantiated into the content and the use of language.

Examples of cultural conceptualisations are cultural schemas, cultural categories and prototypes and cultural-conceptual metaphors. Cultural schemas are conceptual structures (or pools of knowledge shared by the members of a cultural group) that enable us to interpret and communicate cultural knowledge and experiences. Cultural categories arise out of our tendency to categorise every single entity around us, for example, as 'food', 'furniture', 'stationery' and 'groceries'. We tend to associate certain prototypes with such categories. These categories and their associated prototypes may differ across different cultures. What is categorised as 'food' and what is prototypically evoked in our mind when we hear the word 'food' is to a large extent culturally constructed. Conceptual metaphors are defined as cognitive structures that allow us to understand one conceptual domain in terms of another (e.g. Lakoff & Johnson, 1980). The English metaphorical expression, 'You broke my heart', reflects the conceptual metaphor of heart as THE SEAT OF EMOTION. Many conceptual metaphors are culturally constructed. For example, some conceptual metaphors that use the human body as the source domain appear to have their origin in ethnomedical and other cultural traditions (e.g. Sharifian *et al.*, 2008; Yu, 2009).

Cultural Conceptualisations in Varieties of English

Diversification of English in the form of newer varieties may be observed at various levels of the language, from the phonological to the grammatical and discourse structure (Kirkpatrick, 2007). As mentioned earlier, diversification, and an increase in the pluricentricity of the language, also takes place at the conceptual level, that is, through particular features of the English language being associated with cultural conceptualisations of various communities of speakers, which serve as repositories of meaning at the semantic and pragmatic levels (e.g. Sharifian, 2006, 2010b; Wolf & Polzenhagen, 2009).

Here I present a few examples from the variety of English that is emerging in Hong Kong, referred to as 'Hong Kong English' (e.g. Bolton, 2002). In Hong Kong English the word 'gift' is associated with certain cultural conceptualisations, for example that of the GIFT GIVING schema and the cultural category of GIFT. People in Hong Kong often talk about what is not appropriate to be given as GIFT. For instance, according to the Hong Kong schema of GIFT, clocks are usually considered inappropriate as gifts, as they connote death. There are also elements of this cultural schema relating to what is appropriate to take as a gift when people are invited to one other's homes, depending on the occasion. The cultural schema of GIFT in Hong Kong encourages people, for example, to accept gifts with both hands, and discourages them from unwrapping the gift in front of the giver. It is to be noted that in Hong Kong the word 'gift' may also be used to refer to a bribe, to avoid the latter's negative connotation.

A common cultural category in Hong Kong is SPIRIT MONEY (Cummings & Wolf, 2011), also referred to as 'paper money', 'hell money', 'ghost money' and 'hell bank notes'. 'Spirit money' refers to fake banknotes that are burned in rituals, offering them to the dead. Cummings and Wolf (2011) maintain that this usage is based on the underlying cultural conceptualisations of A SUPERNATURAL BEING IS A HUMAN BEING, A PAPER MODEL IS A REAL OBJECT IN THE SUPERNATURAL WORLD, which originate from Buddhist tradition.

An example of a cultural-conceptual metaphor from Hong Kong English would be the use of kinship terms such as 'auntie' and 'uncle' as terms of address for a member of society, which reflects conceptualisations of A MEMBER OF SOCIETY IS A MEMBER OF THE FAMILY (Cummings & Wolf, 2011). Here the domain of family serves as the source domain, which is mapped onto the domain of member of society. Such usage is usually associated with respect and closeness and is reserved for people who are considered as belonging to one's parents' generation. The use of this metaphor reflects a cultural norm and is also common in many other varieties of English such as Singaporean English, Malaysian English and Chinese English (also known as China English). Another metaphor from Hong Kong English is the use of the expression 'golden rice bowl' to refer to a secure high-paying job. This metaphor is based on the conceptualisation of A JOB IS A FOOD CONTAINER (Cummings & Wolf, 2011) and WEALTH AND PROSPERITY ARE GOLD. In Hong Kong the common cultural food is rice, which is usually served in a bowl and thus the use of 'golden rice bowl' reflects a cultural artefact.

These brief examples should suffice in showing how the global spread of English may accompany conceptual diversity in the sense that features of

English are used to encode cultural conceptualisations that were not originally associated with this language. It should be added here that the descriptions that have been provided so far of the examples of cultural conceptualisations should not be interpreted as characterising *people*, but *conceptualisations*. As mentioned earlier, cultural conceptualisations emerge from interactions between speakers across time and space and are constantly negotiated and renegotiated across generations of speakers. The ways in which individual members of a cultural group internalise elements of cultural conceptualisations is far from being unified, and hence my use of the notion of *heterogeneously distributed cultural conceptualisations* (see Sharifian, 2011). Thus, for example, the degree to which, in Hong Kong, people's practices in terms of gift giving and so on conform to the cultural conceptualisations described here vary according to their life experiences.

In the following section I elaborate on the view that a linguistic response to globalisation requires 'instruction in both English as a Second Language and English as a First Language, which focuses on cross-cultural/intercultural communication, especially in pragmatic, discourse, and conceptual variation' (Clyne & Sharifian, 2008: 28.12).

Instruction in English as an International Language

Traditionally, English language teaching (ELT) has been used in the contexts of learning English as either a foreign language or a second language, and the aim of such language learning was viewed as enabling learners to communicate with the so-called 'native speakers of the language' (e.g. Bhatt, 2002). English classes focused on improving learner pronunciation to approximate that of native speakers, narrowly conceptualised mainly as those who speak 'standard' forms of American and British English. Learners would also receive lessons in the grammar of such varieties as well as improving the skills of reading, writing and listening, again of English as spoken by native speakers of these varieties.

As I have discussed in this chapter, recent decades, thanks to forces such as globalisation, have seen significant demographic changes in the use of English around the world, and in the nature of the language itself. As mentioned earlier, most international travel has increasingly been between non-English-speaking countries and a common language is needed, predominantly English, for communication to take place. For example, many people travel and migrate for work and study to countries such as Australia, South Africa and New Zealand, where people speak varieties of English other than American or British English. Many students now prefer to go to countries and regions such as Singapore, Malaysia or Hong Kong to study, as these countries now offer higher education in English, and because living conditions in such countries have become more attractive (for example, due to the lower cost of living and tuition fees) to international students. Changes in global mobility, due to factors such as these, have radically changed the aim of learning English to communicate with native speakers of American or British English. In general, the majority of learners of English now use English to communicate with non-native speakers of English, including speakers of varieties of English such as China English, Indian English and Malaysian English. Alongside this development, the notion of the 'native speaker' is no longer clear-cut. There are now native speakers of such varieties as Singaporean English, Malaysian English and Aboriginal English. Many people also learn English as their second language but use it as their dominant language in their everyday lives. Often, whether or not these speakers identify themselves as native speakers is related to questions of identity rather than language competence (Brutt-Griffler & Samimy, 2001).

The demographic changes discussed so far have had significant implications for teaching English as an international language (e.g. McKay, 2002; Sharifian, 2009). As early as 1983, Larry Smith (1983: v) observed that 'in today's world non-native speakers use English quite frequently with other non-native speakers and they need specific training for that'. He added that 'native English speakers should study English as an international language if they plan to interact in English with non-native or with other native speakers who use a different national variety'. Thus, it cannot be taken for granted that native speakers of English will have no difficulty in communicating in English wherever they go in the world. Also, learners of English need to be exposed to more than just one or two varieties of English, to achieve the flexibility that is required to handle the degree of variation that is currently associated with English. In general, the diversification that has characterised English at various levels of the language calls for new concepts of 'fluency' and 'competence' in the teaching of English as an international language. For example, Canagarajah (2006: 233) maintains that '[i]n a context where we have to constantly shuttle between different varieties [of English] and communities, proficiency becomes complex. ... One needs the capacity to negotiate diverse varieties to facilitate communication'. To some extent this involves what he calls 'multidialectal competence', part of which is 'passive competence to understand new varieties [of English]'.

Instances of communication in English in today's world, including L1 English-speaking countries, are becoming ever more intercultural and multicultural in nature, requiring speakers to be equipped with intercultural communication skills, whether or not they are native speakers of the language. Several scholars have referred to competencies that are called for in the context of an ever-increasing complexity of communication in the global era. These include 'intercultural competence' (see Rathje, 2007 for a critical review of different definitions), 'intercultural communicative competence' (e.g. Byram, 1997) and 'symbolic competence' (e.g. Kramsch, 2006). Kramsch describes symbolic competence as follows:

> Social actors in multilingual settings, even if they are non-native speakers of the languages they use, seem to activate more than a communicative competence that would enable them to communicate accurately, effectively and appropriately with one another. They seem to display a particularly acute ability to play with various linguistic codes and with the various spatial and temporal resonances of these codes. (Kramsch, 2008: 400)

As mentioned earlier in this chapter, the heightened degree of contact between people from around the globe, as part of the process of globalisation, has led to an increase in multilingualism, and symbolic competence is a result of frequent contact between interlocutors speaking multiple languages in multilingual contexts.

I have also referred to another notion of competence, which I have called *metacultural competence* (Sharifian, 2013), which seems to be of use in the context of observations made earlier about the diversity in the systems of cultural conceptualisations coming into contact with one other as a result of intercultural communication. Metacultural competence enables interlocutors participating in intercultural communication to communicate and negotiate their cultural conceptualisations. This competence develops as a result of familiarity with cultural conceptualisations that form part of cultural cognitions of different speech communities and the awareness that one language can be used by different communities of speakers to express their cultural conceptualisations. This awareness may be referred to as 'conceptual variation awareness' (Sharifian, 2013). Metacultural competence enables speakers to make use of strategies such as 'conceptual explication' – the effort to explicate the cultural conceptualisations that a speaker draws upon and that he/she thinks other interlocutors may not be familiar with. For example, a speaker of Hong Kong English may attempt to elaborate on his/her use of the word 'gift' in English and on the cultural schema of gift. Such an elaboration may take the form of describing what would usually be common gifts for which occasions, and from whom to whom.

Metacultural competence is also reflected in a speaker's use of 'conceptual negotiation strategies', such as 'seeking conceptual clarification'. For example, the speaker is aware that even everyday words, such as 'family', may be associated with different cultural conceptualisations among different speech communities and may thus seek clarification for the use of certain words from other speakers, as appropriate, during intercultural communication.

In general, the competencies that are discussed here, and that are deemed as requisite in the context of the complexity of communication in the new era, would develop naturally if ELT curricula provided learners with exposure to the diversity that characterises the sociolinguistic reality of the use of languages, including the use of English as a global lingua franca. Also, as argued by Clyne and Sharifian (2008), instruction in English in today's world needs to place a significant degree of emphasis on developing intercultural communication skills among speakers of English, whether or not they are native speakers of the language. Graddol (2006: 87) observes that '[r]esearch is also beginning to show how bad some native speakers are at using English for international communication. It may be that elements of an ELF [English as a lingua franca] syllabus could usefully be taught within a mother tongue curriculum.' The elements that Graddol refers to here are the pragmatic strategies required for successful intercultural communication skills. I would add to this the inclusion of exposure to some degree of conceptual variation that characterises the use of English in the world today, through presenting some systematic accounts of cultural conceptualisations of different speech communities.

Concluding Remarks

This chapter has explored the relationship between English as a global language and bi/multilingualism from several perspectives. It has examined the implications of the global spread of English for bi/multilingualism and argues that the worldwide spread of English does not inherently pose a threat to bi/multilingualism. This is partly because the majority of those who learn and use English at the global level speak other languages, for intranational, and in some cases for international communication. It also argues that the global spread of English is in fact increasing this language's pluricentricity, through contact between the language and cultural conceptualisations that have not traditionally been associated with it. This phenomenon has significant implications for the teaching and learning of English, including for those who speak it as their L1. In general, this chapter argues that the globalisation of English is leading to, and is accompanied by, an increase in both bi/multilingualism and pluricentricity of the language.

Acknowledgements

The author would like to thank Professor James D'Angelo and Dr Zhichang Xu, as well as the reviewers and the editors of the volume, for their helpful comments on an earlier draft of this chapter.

References

Achebe, C. (1975) The African writer and the English language. In C. Achebe (ed.) *Morning Yet on Creation Day: Essays* (pp. 55–62). New York: Anchor.
Bhatt, R.M. (2002) Experts, dialects, and discourse. *International Journal of Applied Linguistics* 12 (1), 74–109.
Bolton, K. (ed.) (2002) *Hong Kong English: Autonomy and Creativity.* Hong Kong: Hong Kong University Press.

Brutt-Griffler, J. and Samimy, K.K. (2001) Transcending the nativeness paradigm. *World Englishes* 20 (1), 99–106.

Byram, M. (1997) *Teaching and Assessing Intercultural Communicative Competence*. Clevedon: Multilingual Matters.

Canagarajah, S. (2006) Changing communicative needs, revised assessment objectives: Testing English as an international language. *Language Assessment Quarterly* 3 (3), 229–242.

Clyne, M. (ed.) (1992) *Pluricentric Languages: Differing Norms in Different Nations*. Berlin: Mouton de Gruyter.

Clyne, M. and Sharifian, F. (2008) English as an international language: Challenges and possibilities. In F. Sharifian and M. Clyne (eds) Special Forum Issue: International Forum on English as an International Language. *Australian Review of Applied Linguistics* 31 (3), 28.1–28.16.

Crystal, D. (1997) *English as a Global Language*. Cambridge: Cambridge University Press.

Crystal, D. (2003) *English as a Global Language* (2nd edn). Cambridge: Cambridge University Press.

Crystal, D. (2006) *Language and the Internet*. Cambridge: Cambridge University Press.

Cummings, P.J. and Wolf, H.G. (2011) *A Dictionary of Hong Kong English: Words from the Fragrant Harbor*. Hong Kong: Hong Kong University Press.

Graddol, D. (1997) *The Future of English*. London: British Council.

Graddol, D. (2006) *English Next*. London: British Council.

Hoffmann, C. (2000) The spread of English and the growth of multilingualism with English in Europe. In J. Cenoz and U. Jessner (eds) *English in Europe. The Acquisition of a Third Language* (pp. 1–21). Clevedon: Multilingual Matters.

Hollister, J. (2007) Business potential boosts demand for bilingual applicants. *Job Journal*, 22 April. See http://www.jobjournal.com/article_full_text.asp?artid = 1989 (accessed 11 December 2012).

House, J. (2003) English as a lingua franca: A threat to multilingualism? *Journal of Sociolinguistics* 7 (4), 556–578.

Hu, X.Q. (2004) Why China English should stand alongside British, American, and the other world Englishes. *English Today* 78 (2), 26–33.

Hu, X.Q. (2005) China English, at home and in the world. *English Today* 21 (3), 27–38.

Kachru, B.B. (1986) *The Alchemy of English: The Spread, Functions and Models of Non-native English*. Oxford: Pergamon.

Kirkpatrick, A. (2007) *World Englishes: Implications for International Communication and English Language Teaching*. Cambridge: Cambridge University Press.

Kirkpatrick, A. (2012) English in ASEAN: Implications for regional multilingualism. *Journal of Multilingual and Multicultural Development* 33 (4), 331–344.

Kramsch, C. (2006) From communicative competence to symbolic competence. *Modern Language Journal* 90 (2), 249–252.

Kramsch, C. (2008) Ecological perspectives on foreign language education. *Language Teaching* 41, 389–408.

Lakoff, G. and Johnson, M. (1980) *Metaphors We Live By*. Chicago, IL and London: University of Chicago Press.

McKay, S.L. (2002) *Teaching English as an International Language: Rethinking Goals and Approaches*. Oxford: Oxford University Press.

McMahon, A.M.S. (1994) *Understanding Language Change*. Cambridge: Cambridge University Press.

Pennycook, A. (1994) *The Cultural Politics of English as an International Language*. London: Longman.

Phillipson, R. (1992) *Linguistic Imperialism*. Oxford: Oxford University Press.

Rathje, S. (2007) Intercultural competence: The status and future of a controversial concept. *Language and Intercultural Communication* 7 (4), 254–266.

Sharifian, F. (2006) A cultural-conceptual approach and world Englishes: The case of Aboriginal English. *World Englishes* 25 (1), 11–22.
Sharifian, F. (ed.) (2009) *English as an International Language: Theoretical Framework and Applications*. Bristol: Multilingual Matters.
Sharifian, F. (2010a) Glocalization of English in World Englishes: An emerging variety among Persian speakers of English. In T. Omoniyi and M. Saxena (eds) *Contending with Globalisation in World Englishes* (pp. 137–158). Bristol: Multilingual Matters.
Sharifian, F. (2010b) Semantic and pragmatic conceptualisations in an emerging variety: Persian English. In A. Kirkpatrick (ed.) *Routledge Handbook of World Englishes* (pp. 442–457). New York and London: Routledge.
Sharifian, F. (2011) *Cultural Conceptualisations and Language: Theoretical Framework and Applications*. Amsterdam and Philadelphia, PA: John Benjamins.
Sharifian, F. (2013) Cultural linguistics and intercultural communication. In F. Sharifian and M. Jamarani (eds) *Language and Intercultural Communication in the New Era* (pp. 60–79). New York: Routledge/Taylor and Francis.
Sharifian, F., Dirven, R., Yu, N. and Neiemier, S. (eds) (2008) *Culture, Body, and Language: Conceptualizations of Internal Body Organs Across Cultures and Languages*. Berlin and New York: Mouton De Gruyter.
Skutnabb-Kangas, T. (2000) *Linguistic Genocide in Education – or Worldwide Diversity and Human Rights?* Mahwah, NJ: Lawrence Erlbaum.
Smith, L.E. (ed.) (1983) *Readings in English as an International Language*. Oxford: Pergamon Press.
Wolf, H.G. and Polzenhagen, F. (2009) *World Englishes: A Cognitive Sociolinguistic Approach*. Berlin: Mouton de Gruyter.
Xu, Z. (2010a) *Chinese English: Features and Implications*. Hong Kong: Open University of Hong Kong Press.
Xu, Z. (2010b) Chinese English: A future power? In A. Kirkpatrick (ed.) *The Routledge Handbook of World Englishes* (pp. 282–298). New York and London: Routledge.
Yu, N. (2009) *The Chinese HEART in a Cognitive Perspective: Culture, Body, and Language*. Berlin and New York: Mouton de Gruyter.

4 German or Swiss? Address and Other Routinised Formulas in German-speaking Switzerland

Doris Schüpbach

Switzerland, with its four official languages – German, French, Italian, Romansh – and many immigrant languages, provides a rich environment for researching address and linguistic politeness in a variety of contexts. However, relatively little research into these issues is actually available. Manno's (2005) study, based on findings from the German- and French-speaking parts of the country, suggests that there seems to be a specifically Swiss politeness, characterised by a culture of distance which values privacy and individualism and generally prefers negative politeness strategies. With regard to the ways in which politeness practices in Switzerland differ from those in the 'dominant' nations of the respective pluricentric languages, i.e. in Germany, France and Italy, Manno (2005: 101) concludes that while there is some influence from the dominant countries, 'differences [across borders] are as numerous as the similarities deriving from common cultural and linguistic backgrounds'.

In this chapter, I will focus on the German-speaking part of the country and address whether and in what ways current Swiss practices and perceptions of address and linguistic politeness differ from those seen as representative of Germany. It is thus a contrastive study within the frame of German as a pluricentric language, following House (2005: 19) who posits that 'through contrast, linguistic and cultural characteristics of politeness can be better described and explained'. Pronominal address will be the focus, while nominal address and other formulaic routines, in particular greetings and leave-taking formulas, will also be considered. These aspects were chosen (a) because they 'are prominent opportunities to express politeness, presumably because they explicitly acknowledge rank and pay respect' (Haumann *et al.*, 2005: 85); and (b) because greetings and leave-taking formulas often conventionally co-occur with certain address pronouns (Kretzenbacher, 2011).

A considerable proportion of early studies on address and other politeness practices in German-speaking Switzerland were conducted within the discipline of *Volkskunde* [European ethnology] rather than in sociolinguistics or pragmatics. In addition, dialectology has contributed to the study of address and greetings – most prominently through the *Sprachatlas der deutschen Schweiz* (Hotzenköcherle, 1962–1997, summarised in Christen *et al.*, 2010) – focusing on internal regional variation.

Previous contrasting studies of linguistic politeness in German concentrated on Germany and Austria and the respective national varieties of German (e.g. Clyne & Norrby, 2011; Clyne *et al.*, 2009; Kretzenbacher, 2011), the only exception being Elter (2009) who analysed pronominal address, the use of titles and greeting and leave-taking formulas in the German, Austrian and Swiss varieties of German. She established that – apart from lexical differences in greeting and leave-taking formulas – divergent conventions of politeness are apparent, characterised by a rather direct style of communication in Germany, widespread T-address in Switzerland and frequent use of titles in Austria. She argues that these may be due to different *Kulturstandards* [cultural standards] influencing the linguistic realisation of politeness in the three countries.

Background and Data

Although not a member of the EU, Switzerland has entered into a number of bilateral agreements with the EU, one of them concerning the free movement of people which took effect on 1 June 2002. This agreement made it much easier for citizens of the 15 'core' EU countries to live and work in Switzerland. It has led to increased immigration from these countries, most prominently from Germany. The total number of German citizens living in Switzerland rose from 116,649 at the end of 2001 to 276,828 on 31 December 2011, most of whom settled in the German-speaking part of the country. In 2001 Germans made up 8.2% of all non-Swiss living in Switzerland. By 2011, this had increased to 15.6%, which made them the second largest group of foreign citizens behind the Italians (16.4%) (Bundesamt für Migration, 2012).

This influx has not gone unnoticed in Switzerland. It has been reported extensively in the media and has sparked vigorous discussion. Furthermore, many Germans have been quite surprised by the communication difficulties they have encountered in Switzerland, a neighbouring country supposedly sharing a language. These difficulties have led to the publication of a wide range of advice literature and of blogs reflecting on experiences and observations, as well as to the establishment of clubs and special interest groups

Address and Other Routinised Formulas in German-speaking Switzerland   65

for Germans in Switzerland. In addition, issues relating to politeness, particularly terms of address, are topics that are regularly discussed in the Swiss print media.

These books, newspaper articles, blogs, online discussion forums and websites (listed in the Appendix) constitute the folklinguistic corpus on which I draw in this chapter. It complements the relatively scarce scholarly literature on linguistic politeness practices from a Swiss, as well as from a pluricentric perspective. While anecdotal and relaying individual perceptions, such folklinguistic sources provide an insight into how Germans, as well as Swiss, perceive predominant politeness practices in Switzerland. Online contributions, in particular, are often confirmed or contested by other participants and thus corroborated (or not).

Despite the diglossic situation in German-speaking Switzerland – the Swiss variety of Standard German is used for most writing and orally in very formal contexts and the local dialect for most oral interaction and for some informal written communication (e.g. text messaging) – neither the folklinguistic corpus nor some of the scholarly literature is explicit about the language variety discussed. It can be deduced, though, that the main focus is on oral interaction and therefore on Swiss-German dialects for interactions between German-speaking Swiss and, for interactions between Germans and Swiss, on either the German and Swiss varieties of Standard German or, if the Germans understand the local dialect, on German Standard German and the Swiss German dialect. Overall, however, it seems that the language variety used is not the main issue.

Address in German-speaking Switzerland

In this section, I first consider pronominal address – its historical development, current usage and the V-form 'Ihr' specific to certain dialects – and then briefly discuss nominal address.

Pronominal address

Address between individual interlocutors is the focus here. In all national varieties of Standard German 'du' (2nd person singular) is the informal T-form; first 'Ihr' (grammatically 2nd person plural) and later 'Sie' (3rd person plural), which now prevails, appeared as formal V-forms. For multiple addressees, the T-form is 'ihr' (2nd person plural), the V-form originally 'Ihr', then 'Sie'. 'Ihr' (V singular or plural) and 'ihr' (T plural) can only be distinguished in writing: the V-form is conventionally spelled with an upper case initial.

Historical development
Pronominal address in German-speaking Switzerland developed, overall, in parallel with the rest of the German-speaking world. Changes spread from

what today is Germany and were taken up in Switzerland with some delay. Reciprocal T/'du' was generally used between individuals of the same social standing. From the late Middle Ages the V-form 'Ihr' appeared and was used to address interlocutors of superior rank, who would address inferiors with T/'du'. This non-reciprocal address also entered the home domain with children using 'Ihr' to address their parents, while being addressed as 'du'. Over time mutual 'Ihr' became the preferred address within social groups in urban areas, while reciprocal 'du' remained strong in rural contexts, where everyone except the doctor, the pastor/priest and sometimes the teacher was addressed as 'du'.

From the end of the 18th century – again originating in Germany – the V-form 'Sie' began to spread, albeit much more slowly than in other German-speaking areas (Hauser, 1998). Initially 'Sie' was used in addition to the existing dichotomy of 'du' and 'Ihr', relegating 'Ihr' to an intermediate level of address. Considered backward, uncultured and boorish (Trümpy, 1963), 'Ihr' began to disappear during the late 19th century from the urban areas of eastern Switzerland, while in rural contexts it remained strong for a considerable time. Dialects in particular maintained V/'Ihr' for much longer (Besch, 2003), some even until today (see below).

In the course of further democratisation and the blurring of previously rigid social hierarchies (Hauser, 1998), non-reciprocal address all but disappeared during the first half of the 20th century (with the exception of the interaction between children and adult non-family members). So did the general use of 'du' towards strangers in rural areas (Hotzenköcherle, 1993: Vol. 7, p. 117), whereas mutual T remained common among locals (Trümpy, 1977c).

Based on observational data, Trümpy (1977a, 1977b, 1977c) provides an inventory of groups and situations where, in the 1970s, automatic reciprocal 'du' was the norm. These included sports clubs (particularly team sports), trade unions, left-wing parties and among university students. In workplaces involving a uniform (e.g. public transport, police force) or specific workwear (e.g. on a building site) the general 'du' only excluded the highest level of the hierarchy (e.g. the station master). Less automatic 'du' was reported from mixed-gender groups as well as among women, centrist and right-wing political parties and clubs involving individual sports; in these contexts the address terms were individually negotiated.

From the 1960s onwards, mutual 'du' increased considerably and entered all domains. Hauser (1998) posits that this development – yet again – originated in and spread from Germany. However, Trümpy (1977b) reports that university students in Zürich were on 'du'-terms as early as 1946 and literary critic Gunhild Kübler (in Altwegg & de Weck, 2003) recalls her surprise in finding general automatic 'du' among all students in Zürich when she arrived for a semester abroad in the late 1960s. At her home university in Berlin – even during the nascent student revolt – 'Sie' was used among students in the lecture theatres and tutorials. Such instances, anecdotal as they may be, suggest that the changes may not all have originated in Germany.

T and V today

Scholars do not agree on the degree of 'informality' in Switzerland (compared to Germany) as apparent in the extent of 'du' use, although these evaluations are generally presented without much supporting evidence or data. Manno (2005: 102) claims that German-speaking Switzerland is 'less "progressive" than Germany' – presumably implying higher incidence of V – and Rash (1998: 276) posits that T- and V-forms are used in a similar way to Germany but that 'the [German-speaking] Swiss are, if anything, stricter in their application of the "rules", using "du" for friends, family, children under 15, people who share a club membership, sport or hobby'. Elter (2009: 210), on the other hand, maintains that 'du' is more widespread in Switzerland than in Austria (where, in turn, it is more widespread than in Germany) and that the transition from V to T is done quickly and more casually. This contradictory picture is mirrored by the inconsistent perceptions of Germans and Austrians of address patterns in Switzerland, which are based on impressions, anecdotes and possibly stereotypes (Kretzenbacher, 2011).

Contributors to blogs and discussion forums agree that, overall, mutual 'du' is more prevalent in Switzerland than in Germany. In the following contribution, the writer lists various domains where, in his view, such quick transition to T would be unusual in Germany:

Also ich war anfangs auch ziemlich verwundert wie schnell man sich hier duzt. Bei uns im Haus eh, nach einem halben Jahr den Chef und mittlerweile sogar die Klassenlehrerin vom Sohn meiner Frau. (Hallo Schweiz, sfera72, 30 August 2007)

[Well, at first I was pretty amazed at how quickly one moves to 'du' here. In the apartment block of course, the boss after six months and now even my wife's son's teacher.]

The advice literature on living and working in Switzerland mirrors this view:

In der Regel gelten in der Schweiz dieselben Regeln betreffend Sie und Du wie in Deutschland, wobei die Barriere für eine (sic) Wechsel zum vertraulicheren Du in der Schweiz sehr viel niedriger ist. (Reihl, 2009: 25)

[As a rule, Switzerland follows the same rules regarding Sie and Du as Germany, whereby the barriers for a change to the more intimate Du are much lower in Switzerland.]

Most sources in my folklinguistic corpus concentrate on address practices in the workplace, which may indicate that this is the domain where the difference between German and Swiss usage is most marked and most consistent. In the workplace, mutual 'du' is often the unmarked form of address between people on the same hierarchical level, while mutual V may remain in place with superiors, particularly senior management, unless individually negotiated. General 'du' across the whole company has been introduced in some companies (e.g. McDonald's) following popular management models which claim that it fosters identification with the company and thus increases efficiency (Hafner, 2003). More recent examples are the telecommunications company Swisscom and the Federal Office of Information Technology which introduced general 'du' across all levels in 2008 and 2011, respectively (Aebi, 2011; Elter, 2009).

Many statements, particularly in the advice literature on living in Switzerland, draw implicit or explicit connections between address and the prevalent understanding of the role of workplace hierarchies. Address terms are thus often seen as reflective of the corporate culture: V emphasises hierarchy and power and coincides with a top-down communication style; T emphasises equality, solidarity, a flat hierarchical structure and a cooperative communication style. For instance, Sitzler (2007: 74) links 'du' in the workplace to the comparatively flat hierarchical structures of many Swiss companies and the expectation that co-workers and superiors treat each other as equal partners in a respectful way. Thus *'ein Schweizer fühlt sich sehr ungern als Befehlsempfänger, darum teilt er auch nicht gern Befehle aus'* [a Swiss does not like to feel ordered about, therefore he does not like to give orders]. This is in line with Elter's (2009) interpretation of widespread use of T in Swiss workplaces which she attributes to the cultural standard *Gruppenbildung* [orientation towards groups] as opposed to the workplace cultures of Germany and Austria which are more oriented towards hierarchy.

Address practices in service encounters are discussed in contemporary popular descriptions but not in blogs and discussion forums so that no comparative perspective is available for this domain. Addressing customers with T has become common in businesses catering mainly for younger people (e.g. fashion) or for groups associated with a 'du' culture (e.g. fitness centres, suppliers of outdoor equipment). Anecdotal evidence suggests that customer complaints about the general T use are increasing; it is unclear, however, whether this is a backlash against 'du'. Many businesses react by introducing more flexible guidelines. The fashion retailer H&M, for instance, which used to have a T policy, now leaves it to the customer by starting the interaction with a 'neutral' greeting such as 'Hallo' (Zumoberhaus, 2006).

Ikea is a case in point for the variability and change in pronoun use in service encounters. The company opened its first shop outside Scandinavia in Switzerland in 1973, introducing the Swedish address practice (mutual T). In the 1970s, customers were handed out buttons stating *Sag mir du* [Say you (T) to me] and reportedly only a fraction objected to this *'unschweizerische Zumutung'* [un-Swiss imposition] (Trümpy, 1977b: 58). In the 1990s Ikea reacted to increased customer complaints and changed its policy in Switzerland (but not in Germany and Austria where 'du' prevailed), addressing customers with V. According to Norrby and Hajek (2011), in March 2010 Ikea's Swiss websites in German, French and Italian used the V-form except when addressing prospective job applicants. In July 2012, individual customers were again being addressed as 'du'. However, sections of the website aimed at the media and at business customers use 'Sie'.

The 'Ihr'-form

'Ihr' – grammatically the 2nd person plural pronoun – fulfils various functions, depending on the language variety and the context. Firstly, and in all varieties of German used in Switzerland, it is the plural form of the T pronoun, used to address a group of people with whom one is on T terms (e.g. a teacher addressing a group of primary school students). Secondly, it remains the (singular) V-form in the dialects of the western part of German-speaking Switzerland (the cantons of Valais, Fribourg, parts of Solothurn and Lucerne but particularly associated with the canton of Bern). And thirdly, it seems to re-emerge to some extent as an intermediate form in other varieties. It is the second and third functions that I will discuss here.

'Ihr' takes a different form depending on the local dialect and the case (e.g. Iir or Diir in nominative, Öich or Üüch in accusative and dative). In the following, I will use the standard German form 'Ihr' to refer to the various dialectal forms.

As mentioned earlier, 'Ihr' is a historic V-form which survived longest in German dialects, as opposed to Standard German, but has disappeared from many of them. For Switzerland, Simon (2003: 125–126) mentions the dialects of Zurich where 'Sie' is prevalent and of Lucerne where mixed forms ('Sie' and 'Ihr') were observed in the 1960s. This pattern is in line with data collected between 1939 and 1958 (Hotzenköcherle, 1993: 117): 'Ihr' was used as the only pronoun of address for a stranger in the western cantons of German-speaking Switzerland; either 'Ihr' or 'Sie' was used in rural areas of central Switzerland and in Alpine valleys, and 'Sie' in the remaining areas. This distribution illustrates the spread of the form from the northeast and from urban to rural areas. The current boundary between 'Sie' and 'Ihr' areas has been quite stable for some time (Simon, 2003: 126). Whether increased internal migration and urbanisation will lead to a further spread of 'Sie' remains to be seen.

Why did the change from V/'Ihr' to V/'Sie' not take place in the western part of German-speaking Switzerland? Several hypotheses are proposed. Firstly, 'Ihr' is in line with practice in French, where the 2nd person plural pronoun ('vous') is the V-form. The areas concerned are bordering on the French-speaking part of Switzerland and the bourgeoisie of Bern used to speak French as their prestige language. Secondly, 'Sie' may have been consciously refused as being 'German' (not Swiss), when the new form appeared during the later 19th century, the era of German unification and increasing nationalism. Hauser (1998: 69) quotes a popular poem by Gottfried Strasser

(1854–1912), written in the local dialect – *'Mir Bärner sage "Dihr"'* [We Bernese say 'Dihr']. Strasser rejects 'Sie' as *'frömde Plunder'* [foreign rubbish] but simultaneously evokes French and English with their 2nd person plural V-forms to support his argument. This leads to a third hypothesis with conservatism contributing to the non-uptake of the new form, connected to what Trümpy (1963: 166) calls *'ausgeprägtes sprachliches und damit auch kulturelles Sonderbewusstsein'* [a pronounced awareness of being special in linguistic and therefore also in cultural terms]. This view is also apparent in Simon's (2003: 126) statement that for the Bernese dialect, 'Ihr' seems to have become some sort of Shibboleth to identify (and be identified) as a speaker of this dialect.

The usage conventions for T/'du' and V/'Ihr' are generally the same as for 'du' and 'Sie' in other parts of Switzerland. In areas where 'Ihr' is the V-form, 'Sie' is only used when speaking or writing in Standard German or – very rarely – in encounters with speakers from other parts of Switzerland to avoid misunderstandings. Such situations mentioned by Swiss blog contributors include a service encounter where a salesperson does not trust customers from eastern Switzerland to know about this Bernese peculiarity (Blogwiese, HPZ, 2 January 2010) and a writer from Appenzell (eastern Switzerland) who reports using 'Ihr' in a rural context, 'Sie' in a town or when talking to non-locals *'damit sie nicht beleidigt sind'* [so that they're not offended] (Blogwiese, Marischi, 12 May 2006).

Anecdotal evidence suggests a resurgence of 'Ihr' in central and eastern Switzerland to address one person. Rash (1998: 276) reports students addressing a teacher with 'Ihr' and Siegenthaler (2003) relates the increased use of 'Ihr' in service encounters to address the – often female and/or elderly – customer and often in encounters involving technical support. Many addressees regard this as condescending and as *'verstecktes Duzen'* [thinly veiled 'du']. It seems that some of the German bloggers living in eastern Switzerland (e.g. Blogwiese, 22 May 2012) are mistaking the 'Bernese' V/'Ihr' as such an intermediate form of address.

In summary, the three functions of 'Ihr' express different levels of distance: from maximum distance in its function as V address to minimum distance in its function as the plural T pronoun, with possibly re-emerging functions in eastern Switzerland as an intermediate form of address in the singular.

Nominal address

The typical co-occurrence of pronominal and nominal address – honorific, name, title – in all German-speaking areas is as follows (Rash, 1998: 276):

```
T (du)        +         first name
V (Sie/Ihr)   +         {honorific + last name} or {honorific + title} or
                        {title + last name}
              e.g.      {Herr Meier} or {Herr Professor} or {Professor Meier}
```

Mixed forms are rather unusual in Switzerland. V + first name may be used – as in Germany and Austria – by teachers addressing their students over 16 years of age or by older neighbours or friends of parents addressing adults they have known since childhood. According to Elspaß and Möller (2003), both V + first name and T + last name are rather uncommon in Swiss workplaces, as opposed to northern Germany where V + first name is reported to occur 'now and again'.

There is general consensus in scholarly literature (Manno, 2005; Rash, 1998) as well as in my corpus that professional and academic titles are not considered particularly important in Switzerland. With the exception of medical doctors, titles are only used in very formal academic settings and in formal letters. The fact that blogs and online discussion forums do not mention titles at all may indicate that the situation is similar to Germany but not Austria (see Elter, 2009).

Greeting and Leave-taking Formulas

Overall, more research is available on greetings than on forms of address in German-speaking Switzerland. Hauser (1998) explores historical developments, Bruckner (1939) and Zollinger-Escher (1925) take an ethnographic perspective, and the *Sprachatlas der deutschen Schweiz* (Christen et al., 2010; Hotzenköcherle, 1993) takes a dialectological perspective. These studies focus on regional variation in Swiss German and consider so-called *Zeitgrüsse* (i.e. greetings depending on the time of the day), as well as *Arbeitsgrüsse* (greetings related to specific tasks), many of which are related to traditional rural tasks and are therefore no longer in use.

More recently, Rash (2004) surveyed current greeting practices and the importance assigned to them by 80 participants mainly from the centrally located canton of Aargau. She found that 'greeting is the minimum token of politeness that most germanophone Swiss expect to give and receive at the beginning and end of a communicative act [...] greeting rituals are a vital aspect of human communication' (Rash, 2004: 70). That is, they are not just an empty convention in the Swiss German context.

I will focus here on greeting and leave-taking formulas in conjunction with pronominal and nominal address and on a selection of issues that Germans now resident in Switzerland perceive as different. As Kretzenbacher (2011: 72) posits, many greetings 'are perceived as appropriate or inappropriate in combination with specific address forms'. Table 4.1 gives an overview of common greeting and leave-taking formulas in German-speaking Switzerland and the pronominal address associated with them. It lists the singular forms; the plural can be expressed by adding 'mitenand' or 'zäme' [together] to most formulas. These greetings are in use throughout German-speaking Switzerland, although some comments point to 'hoi' being more

Table 4.1 Common greeting and leave-taking formulas in German-speaking Switzerland

Greeting	+ T/V	Leave-taking	+ T/V
grüezi/grüessech	V(T)	adieu	V
guete Morge; guete Tag; guete Abe	T/V	uf Wiederluege/uf Wiedersee	V(T)
hallo	T/V	adee	T/V
grüess di	T	guet Nacht	T/V
hoi	T	ä Guete	T/V
salü/sali	T	ä schöne; schöne Abe; …	T/V
ciao/tschau/tschou	T	bis später	T/V
hey/hi	T	salü/sali	T
		ciao/tschau/tschou	T
		tschüss	T

Notes: T = associated with T; V = associated with V; T/V = used with T and V; V(T) = used with T and V but generally associated with V.

common in eastern parts and the French-origin 'salü'/'sali' and 'adieu' in western parts.

'Grüezi'/'Grüessech' mirrors the 'Sie'/'Ihr'-divide discussed above, where 'Grüezi' is associated with 'Sie' and 'Grüessech' with 'Ihr'. This is also reflected in the folklinguistic etymology (see, for example, Hallo Schweiz, Myy, 20 February 2008; Sitzler, 2008) which interprets 'Grüezi' as a short form of 'ich grüsse Sie' [I greet you (V)]. It originates, however, in the old greeting 'Gott grüez-i', where -i is the unstressed pronoun *öi* (euch) (Christen *et al.*, 2010; Zollinger-Escher, 1925) and is thus equal to 'Grüessech'. 'Grüezi'/'Grüessech' is the most neutral and most typically Swiss greeting and can be used without limitations in terms of time, context or social situation (Christen *et al.*, 2010). Kühntopf (2010: 261) even terms it an *'Allerweltsgruss'* [all-purpose greeting]. It is frequently discussed in blogs and online forums, clearly not because of its usage but due to the pronunciation difficulties the 'üe'-diphthong poses to most Germans.

Some Swiss-German greetings are transfers from French ('salü', 'adieu') and Italian ('ciao'). Currently English greetings like 'hi' seem to be becoming popular. In addition, in the second half of the 20th century, the German expressions 'tschüss' and 'hallo' have been adopted. To the surprise of many Germans in Switzerland, however, the northern German leave-taking formula 'tschüss' is occasionally also used as a greeting (similar to 'ciao' and 'salü') and is seen as associated with 'du'. Bloggers term the German use of 'tschüss' + 'Sie' as the classic faux pas of Germans in Switzerland (e.g. Blogwiese, 9 November 2005), although the German use is making inroads. 'Hallo' is seen by some as a neutral greeting that can be used with T or V, indeed to avoid direct address or to postpone *'die heikle Entscheidung'* [the tricky decision] (Blogwiese, MikkiS, 11 May 2006). Others, however, consider 'hallo' just as casual as 'tschüss' (Hallo Schweiz, Anja Sara, 1 January 2007).

Beyond specific formulas, Germans in Switzerland notice the frequency and extent of greetings and the frequent use of names with greetings. Sitzler (2008: 57) gives the following succinct advice:

Grüßen ist in der Schweiz sehr wichtig. [...] Gegrüßt wird auch die Kassiererin im Supermarkt. Sobald Schweizer den Namen einer Person erfahren, wird dieser Name dem Gruss angehängt.

[Greeting is very important in Switzerland. [...] The supermarket checkout person is also greeted. As soon as the Swiss know the name of a person, they attach it to the greeting.]

The extensive use of names in connection with greetings, leave-taking and other formulas (e.g. when toasting) is discussed frequently in the blogs and confirmed by Rash (2004: 55). The following exchange from 'Hallo Schweiz' (27 May 2011) illustrates not only the contrast with Germany but also the perceived difficulties associated with it:

Meine Freundinnen [in Deutschland] finden es immer wieder lustig, wenn ich sie am Telefon mit einem lebhaften 'Hoi XY' begrüsse statt mit 'Hallo' ohne Namen. Dass hier grundsätzlich mit Namen begrüsst und verabschiedet wird habe ich so langsam auch im Blut. (Schubradina)
Wohl wahr, aber schwierig wird es, wenn man sich nicht mehr an den Namen erinnern kann. (Tante Tilly)
Dann kann man sich – je nach 'Bekanntheitsgrad' – immer noch mit einem Ciao Bella, Sali Duuuuuu oder Jähalloscholangnümgseh retten. (Nobody)

[My friends [in Germany] think it's funny when I greet them on the phone with a lively 'Hi XY' instead of 'Hello' without a name. By now I'm used to the general practice of greeting and leave-talking with names. (Schubradina)
True, but it gets difficult if you can't remember the names. (Tante Tilly)
Depending on how well acquainted you are – you can save yourself with a 'Ciao Bella', 'Hello youuuuu' or 'Ahhellohaven'tseenyouforages'. (Nobody)]

The occurrence of greetings in circumstances where it may be uncommon in Germany is echoed in many contributions to the online forums, for example:

Was für mich auch recht neu war, ist, dass man auch beim Einkaufen immer freundlich begrüsst wird [...]: Ein kurzes 'Grüezi' beim ersten Blickkontakt und ein 'Ufwiederluege' zusammen mit dem Wechselgeld. Wer den Abschiedsguss erwidert, bekommt dafür ein noch längeres 'Merci vielmal, schöns Tägli, ade....'

zurück. Kaum eine Chance, dabei das letzte Wort zu behalten. (Hallo Schweiz, Alexandre, 27 February 2003)

[What was quite new for me too, were the friendly greetings when shopping [...]: a brief *'Grüezi'* with the first eye contact and a *'Ufwiederluege'* with the change. Those who reciprocate the leave-taking formula will get a longer *'Merci vielmal, schöns Tägli, ade. ...'* back. Hardly a chance to have the last word.]

This contribution also points to the extensive exchange of formulas, particularly during leave-taking, in service encounters and in telephone conversations, which has been observed by many (e.g. Rash, 2008; Willmeroth & Hämmerli, 2009). Thus, while Germany and Switzerland both value negative politeness, greetings constitute the outstanding example of positive politeness in German-speaking Switzerland (Manno, 2005).

Not adhering to these conventions – greetings, use of names, ritualistic exchanges and so on – more than smaller hiccups like using 'tschüss' with the V-form – may contribute to the view held by many Swiss that Germans are rude and impolite (see, for example, House, 2005; Manno, 2005). Another contributing factor not discussed here is a different communicative style exemplified by German directness and Swiss indirectness.

Swiss Versus German Politeness?

In summary, address practices in German-speaking Switzerland are perceived as including the following: more T use than in Germany, particularly in the workplace; continued use of the V-form 'Ihr' in some areas, obsolete in most other German-speaking areas; the widespread use of names in conjunction with greetings (but hardly any titles); and extensive exchanges of formulaic routines particularly when taking leave.

While most German bloggers and commentators appreciate the widespread 'du', some see it as not carrying the same weight as in Germany:

Deutsch und direkt formuliert: Das Schweizer Duzi-Machen schafft keine wirkliche Nähe. (Blogwiese, Neuromat, 28 May 2008)

[In German and bluntly put: the Swiss 'du' does not create real closeness.]

Similar comments also arise about other politeness practices (e.g. greetings) once the initial surprise has evaporated. Terms like *lästig* [annoying and cumbersome], *aufgesetzt* [superficial], *übertrieben* [exaggerated] and *unverbindlich* [uncommitted] are used. By applying German norms, i.e. evaluating it from an etic perspective (House, 2005), Germans in Switzerland sometimes perceive Swiss behaviour as artificial, not quite sincere, hiding reserve and even mistrust. On the other hand, what some Germans initially interpret as friendliness, cordiality or warmth is simply thought of as appropriate polite behaviour by the Swiss. Politeness rituals such as greetings are at the core of polite behaviour and maintaining them is seen as essential by Swiss Germans (Rash, 2004).

In this chapter, I have identified some divergences between German and Swiss politeness patterns. This lends support to Manno's (2005) claim that, at least in the case of Switzerland, the sociocultural context overrides shared language in influencing politeness practices. It also highlights the phenomenon that speakers of supposedly the same language who have been socialised in different sociocultural contexts are less prepared for communicative problems. As Elter (2009) rightly points out, issues of cross-cultural communication thus become relevant: interlocutors from different backgrounds refer to different cultural standards, which in turn leads to variation in the linguistic realisation of politeness. Interpreting my findings in terms of the dimensions of cross-cultural differences that House (2005) identified for German and English interaction patterns, the Swiss seem to value verbal routines and reciprocal phatic moves more than Germans (although nowhere near as much as Anglophones), and seem less oriented towards the self than Germans by balancing the rights of speaker and addressee more evenly (Manno, 2005). Similarly, group orientation, a cultural standard typical for Switzerland (Elter, 2009), can explain flatter hierarchies and resultant higher T use in many Swiss workplaces. Reasons for such divergent cultural standards in neighbouring countries lie in divergent historical, political and cultural developments such as Switzerland's development as a small, federal, more democratic, less hierarchical entity and its more frequent contact with other languages, French in particular.

Appendix: Bibliography

Online sources and blogs

Blogwiese: Erlebnisse und sprachliche Beobachtungen als Deutscher in der Schweiz (Jens-Rainer Wiese). See http://www.blogwiese.ch (accessed 28 May 2012).
Deutscher Club Zürich. See http://www.deutscher-club.ch (accessed 26 July 2012).
Hallo Schweiz Forum. Alles rund um Aufenthalt und Leben in der Schweiz. See http://www.hallo-schweiz.ch/forum (accessed 28 May 2012).
Swissinfo-Blog. Die Schweizer und die Deutschen: Was beschäftigt Sie als Deutsche in der Schweiz? See http://deutscheinderschweiz.swissinfo.ch (accessed 8 April 2012). (Blog no longer online; copy on file).
Swissinfo-Blog. Leben in der Schweiz. See http://deutscheinderschweiz.swissinfo.ch (accessed 8 April 2012). (Blog no longer online; copy on file).
XING Group. Deutsche in der Schweiz. See http://www.xing.com/net/germanyswitzerland (accessed 12 July 2012).
XING Group. Deutsche leben in der Schweiz. See http://www.xing.com/net/dls (accessed 12 July 2012).

Books and newspaper articles

Aebi, M. (2011) Warum der Direktor einfach Giovanni sein will. *Berner Zeitung*, 2 November.
Altwegg, J. and de Weck, R. (eds) (2003) *Kuhschweizer und Sauschwaben. Schweizer, Deutsche und ihre Hassliebe*. Zurich: Nagel & Kimche.
Dürscheid, C. (2009) Vom 'Duzis-Machen' und Dankesagen. *Der Tagesspiegel*, 31 July.
Dürscheid, C. (2012) Duzis oder Siezen? *Tagblatt der Stadt Zürich*, 23 May.
Hafner, K. (2003) Ein täglicher Stress: Duzen oder Siezen? *Tages-Anzeiger*, 25 September.
Hark, U. (1998) Sag ganz einfach und ganz locker du. *Tages-Anzeiger*, 29 September.
Kühntopf, M. (2010) *Alltag in der Schweiz: Leben und Arbeiten in der Eidgenossenschaft: ein praktischer Ratgeber für alle Neuankömmlinge*. Meerbusch: Conbook.
Küng, T. (2008) *Gebrauchsanweisung für die Schweiz*. Munich and Zurich: Piper.
Lacour, J. (2010) *Deutsche in der Schweiz: vom Leben und Arbeiten im Nachbarland: Geschichten und Tipps*. Paderborn: Lektora.
Reihl, B. (2009) *Der feine Unterschied: ein Handbuch für Deutsche in der Schweiz*. St Gallen and Zurich: Midas Management Verlag.
Siegenthaler, M. (2003) Siezen oder Duzen? *Brückenbauer*, 3 June, 23.
Sitzler, S. (2007) *Grüezi und Willkommen: Die Schweiz für Deutsche* (4th edn). Berlin: Ch. Links.
Sitzler, S. (2008) *Aus dem Chuchichäschtli geplaudert: das ultimative Sprachlexikon für die Schweiz*. Munich and Zurich: Pendo Verlag.
Willmeroth, S. and Hämmerli, F. (2009) *Exgüsi: ein Knigge für Deutsche und Schweizer zur Vermeidung grober Missverständnisse*. Zurich: Orell Füssli.
Ziauddin, B. (2008) *Grüezi Gummihälse: Warum uns die Deutschen manchmal auf die Nerven gehen*. Reinbek: Rowohlt.
Zumoberhaus, D. (2006) Lieber ein Grüezi als ein Du. *Tages-Anzeiger*, 5 January.

References

Besch, W. (2003) Anrede. In W. Besch, A. Betten, O. Reichmann and S. Sonderegger (eds) *Sprachgeschichte: Ein Handbuch zur Geschichte der deutschen Sprache und ihrer Erforschung* (pp. 2599–2628). Berlin: Mouton de Gruyter.
Bruckner, W. (1939) Sprachliches vom Grüssen. *Schweizerisches Archiv für Volkskunde* 37 (2), 65–86.
Bundesamt für Migration (2012) *Ausländerstatistik*. Bern-Wabern: Swiss Federal Office for Migration. See https://www.bfm.admin.ch/content/bfm/de/home/dokumentation/zahlen_und_fakten/auslaenderstatistik.html.
Christen, H., Glaser, E. and Friedli, M. (eds) (2010) *Kleiner Sprachatlas der deutschen Schweiz*. Frauenfeld: Huber.
Clyne, M. and Norrby, C. (2011) Address in pluricentric languages – the case of German and Swedish. In A. Soares da Silva, A. Torres and M. Gonçalves (eds) *Línguas Pluricêntricas: Variação Linguística e Dimensões Sociocognitivas/Pluricentric Languages: Linguistic Variation and Sociocognitive Dimensions* (pp. 147–160). Braga: Aletheia.
Clyne, M., Norrby, C. and Warren, J. (2009) *Language and Human Relations: Styles of Address in Contemporary Language*. Cambridge: Cambridge University Press.
Elspaß, S. and Möller, R. (2003) *Atlas zur deutschen Alltagssprache*. Salzburg: University of Salzburg and Liège: University of Liège. See http://www.atlas-alltagssprache.de.
Elter, I. (2009) Höflichkeit in den nationalen Varietäten des Deutschen: Am Beispiel der Anrede. In C. Ehrhardt and E. Neuland (eds) *Sprachliche Höflichkeit in interkultureller Kommunikation und im DaF-Unterricht* (pp. 201–216). Frankfurt: Lang.

Haumann, S., Koch, U. and Sornig, K. (2005) Politeness in Austria: Politeness and impoliteness. In L. Hickey and M. Stewart (eds) *Politeness in Europe* (pp. 82–99). Clevedon: Multilingual Matters.
Hauser, A. (1998) *Grüezi und Adieu. Gruss- und Umgangsformen vom 17. Jahrhundert bis zur Gegenwart*. Zurich: Verlag NZZ.
Hotzenköcherle, R. (ed.) (1962–1997) *Sprachatlas der deutschen Schweiz* (8 vols). Berne and Basle: Francke.
House, J. (2005) Politeness in Germany: Politeness in GERMANY? In L. Hickey and M. Stewart (eds) *Politeness in Europe* (pp. 13–28). Clevedon: Multilingual Matters.
Kretzenbacher, H.L. (2011) Perceptions of national and regional standards of addressing in Germany and Austria. *Pragmatics* 21 (1), 69–81.
Manno, G. (2005) Politeness in Switzerland: Between respect and acceptance. In L. Hickey and M. Stewart (eds) *Politeness in Europe* (pp. 100–115). Clevedon: Multilingual Matters.
Norrby, C. and Hajek, J. (2011) Language policy in practice: What happens when Swedish IKEA and H&M take 'you' on? In C. Norrby and J. Hajek (eds) *Uniformity and Diversity in Language Policy* (pp. 242–257). Bristol: Multilingual Matters.
Rash, F. (1998) *The German Language in Switzerland: Multilingualism, Diglossia and Variation*. Berne: Peter Lang.
Rash, F. (2004) Linguistic politeness and greeting rituals in German-speaking Switzerland. *Linguistik Online* 20, 47–72.
Simon, H.J. (2003) *Für eine grammatische Kategorie 'Respekt' im Deutschen: Synchronie, Diachronie und Typologie der deutschen Anredepronomina*. Tübingen: Niemeyer.
Trümpy, H. (1963) Die Formen der Anrede im älteren Schweizerdeutschen. In P. Zinsli and O. Banle (eds) *Sprachleben der Schweiz. Sprachwissenschaft, Namenforschung, Volkskunde* (pp. 157–166). Berne: Francke.
Trümpy, H. (1977a) Das Duzen im Vormarsch. *Schweizer Volkskunde* 67 (2), 18–21.
Trümpy, H. (1977b) Ergebnisse unserer Umfragen im 2. Heft. *Schweizer Volkskunde* 67 (4), 56–60.
Trümpy, H. (1977c) Nochmals: Anredeformen. *Schweizer Volkskunde* 67 (4), 79–84.
Zollinger-Escher, A. (1925) *Die Grussformeln der deutschen Schweiz*. Freiburg: Wagner.

5 Meet and Greet: Nominal Address and Introductions in Intercultural Communication at International Conferences

Heinz Kretzenbacher, Michael Clyne†, John Hajek, Catrin Norrby and Jane Warren

Introduction

The way we address one another – nominal address such as first names, last names and titles, or pronominal address, the use of informal (T) versus formal (V) 2nd person pronouns such as the French *tu* and *vous* 'you', respectively – is fundamental in marking social relations and encodes human relationships. This pilot study examines nominal address in intercultural communication among academics, focusing specifically on address and introduction practices at international conferences. Address here encompasses use of titles (Ti), first names (FN), last names (LN), and combinations of these in the introduction of self and of another person as well as introduction of self by another.

International conferences present a valuable research site for research on intercultural pragmatics given the unique combination of potentially countervailing factors at play. Such factors include the identity of who is being introduced, the conference as formal activity, the potential for status differences among participants who are at the same time also academic peers, as well as the effect of differences in linguistic and cultural background, and in age. Here we consider the effect of some of these factors, both in the first language and in English as conference lingua franca. We use existing intracultural models of address and politeness to better understand our results in an important intercultural context.

Overview and Issues

The overwhelming majority of published research on address practices has been on intracultural address, i.e. within the same language or cultural community, while studies of intercultural address are rare, e.g. Schüpbach et al. (2007) and Clyne (2009). The international conference has become a key site for intercultural contact and exchanges among academics from around the globe. On meeting, they necessarily take part in introductions – of themselves and others – and have to decide how to do so, whether in their own language or, as is increasingly common, in English.

Every language offers a variety of linguistic means for the expression of a speaker's personal and social orientation to others through address, including the appropriate use of nominal address terms. The nominal terms that we focus on here, e.g. first names and titles, can be put on a scale of 'social distance', considered as the overarching principle that guides speakers in their choice of address forms (Clyne et al., 2009). Social distance is a multidimensional concept involving degrees of affect, solidarity and familiarity (cf. Clyne et al., 2009: 35; Svennevig, 1999).

In any interaction, interlocutors position themselves in relation to the other. We can consider the self as a social construction which is performed or presented. The presentation of self can be regarded as 'a claim to a particular social position', and the speaker seeks to meet the expectations of the position they have claimed (Svennevig, 1999: 23). Participants in a conversation should act so as to project their preferred face, or self-image, and to ensure that the face of other participants is not threatened (Goffman, 1967). In positioning themselves in relation to one another, individuals use positive and negative politeness strategies which enhance the interlocutors' positive or negative face. Brown and Levinson (1987) differentiate between negative face, the 'want' not to be imposed upon by others, and positive face, the 'want' to be approved of by others.

In an encounter, a choice of address mode is made, or a transition to another address mode is initiated, on the basis of a set of six principles, as first established by Clyne et al. (2009). The address model they developed is considered here as providing a useful framework for understanding the results of our investigation of intercultural communication in the academic conference setting. The model was formulated as a result of a comparative project on variation and change in intracultural modes of address in French, German, Swedish and English, based on focus groups, interviews, chat groups and participant observation, while also taking into account national variation for all of the languages (except French). Below we set out the principles and a series of questions that illustrate how they work:

P1. *Familiarity principle:*
Do I know this person?

P2. *Maturity principle:*
Do I perceive this person to be an adult?
P3. *Relative age principle:*
Do I perceive this person to be considerably older than me? Or younger?
P4. *Network membership principle:*
Is this person a regular and accepted member within a group I belong to?
P5. *Social identification principle:*
Do I perceive this person to be similar to or different from me?
P6. *Address mode accommodation principle:*
If this person uses T (or V), or a T-like (or V-like) address with me, will I do the same? (Clyne *et al.*, 2009: 158)

The principles relate to absolute assessment of the interlocutor (PP1, 2 and 4), to assessment of the interlocutor in relation to oneself (PP3 and 5), or to address mode per se (P6). Most of the address data collected and analysed here concern the principles of Network membership (P4) and Social identification (P5) and to a lesser extent Relative age (P3).

Among the factors influencing the operation of these principles are the specific address rules of a particular language or culture, the address preferences of a specific social network and/or the individual, as well as contextual factors such as domains, institutions and medium of communication. Together, principles, factors and scales (see below, for example) provide a useful framework for deciding where to place an interlocutor on the social distance continuum in relation to oneself and thus which address form(s) to use.

Nominal address terms can be placed on a social distance scale (or scale of relative formality), ranging from more formal V-like forms, i.e. those that mark high social distance between interlocutors, to more informal T-like forms, i.e. those that mark low social distance between interlocutors. On such a scale, use of title and last name would, for instance, mark [+ social distance], and use of first name would mark [− social distance]. English, for example, unlike French, does not have T and V pronouns, and uses T-like nominal forms, such as first name, 'mate' and 'dear', and V-like forms such as title + last name, 'Sir' or 'Madam' to express lower and higher social distance, respectively (Clyne *et al.*, 2009: 157).

Data and Overall Results

The database for this pilot study consists of 195 questionnaires collected at three international conferences held in Hamburg in Germany (bilingualism conference, 97 respondents), in Gothenburg in Sweden (pragmatics conference, 65 respondents) and Melbourne in Australia (medical conference, 33 respondents). A comparison of different academic disciplines is not possible here given the relatively small number of responses from the medical conference. The 195 delegates who responded to our questionnaire come from over 40 countries and represent close to 50 different language backgrounds, including mother tongue bilinguals (here referring to those who have entered more than one first language on the questionnaire). In the first instance, we make a distinction between first (L1) and second (L2) language speakers of English in order to identify any general differences in behaviour. However, given the high degree of linguistic variability in our sample, we decided to focus our analysis on the more language-specific behaviour of some of our respondents at a macro level according to three regional cultural groupings (see below for specific detail). There are also approximately three times as many women as men (141 and 52, respectively, with two unidentified), but initial surveying of results found little difference between genders. For this reason, gender is not treated as a variable here. Consideration is, however, given to the effect of age on introduction patterns, and its potential interaction with language and cultural background. Slightly more than half (109) are aged between 30 and 50 years. The two other age groups are (a) under 30 and (b) over 50 (45 and 41 respondents, respectively).

The questionnaire was designed to gather information about the respondents' age, sex, country of origin and of residence, and language experience. It also contained specific questions about introductions in conference settings. We were interested in collecting information about everyone's experience in English, and for second language speakers of English, we also asked about their experience in their first language. Three basic questions (concerning Principles 3, 4 and 5 above) were asked about conference interactions where English is the common language or where the speakers use their first language: How do you introduce yourself to others? How do you introduce others? How do others introduce you? For each question, four choices, including three address options, were given: (a) 'by first name'; (b) 'by first and last name'; (c) 'by title and last name'; and (d) 'other' (with a space for comments). We also provided further space at the bottom of the page for extra comments elaborating on the three questions.

While most of our respondents chose one of the three address forms indicated, the answers to 'other' and the open questions provided us with a wide scope of different and combined address alternatives as well as some very interesting additional information. For the purposes of this study, however, and in order to provide a clearer picture in the figures below, all answers were collated as summarised in Table 5.1, following Hook (1984): any answer that mentioned first name only (FN), at least as a possibility, was coded as 'close' in terms of social distance, any that mentioned last name in any way but without title ('FN + LN' or 'FN + LN or other') were coded as 'neutral', and all answers that mentioned Title at least as a possibility were coded as 'distant'. Answers which did not fit in this scheme, e.g. were left blank, were coded as 'not applicable' (n/a).

Table 5.1 Coding of relative social distance

Address form	Relative social distance
FN-only	Close
FN + LN, FN + LN or other	Neutral
Title in any combination	Distant
All other possibilities	Not applicable

Overall, where English is the common language, the most frequent type of introduction in all three situations is a combination of FN and LN. However, as is evident in Figure 5.1, respondents tend to be more distant or formal when introducing others compared to how they introduce themselves, or how they expect to be introduced by a colleague. The clearest asymmetry occurs between how people introduce themselves and how they would introduce a colleague in the same context. In the first situation, use of FN-only (25%), is relatively common, while titles are almost always avoided. In the latter situation, titles can be used, and use of FN-only is much less likely. The third situation, how respondents expect others to introduce them, falls in between the other two in terms of closeness–distance.

The following quotations, from an Australian and a British informant, respectively, illustrate the asymmetry between how respondents introduce others and how they expect to be introduced by others, and point to the fact that informants do not seem to be overly concerned if introductory

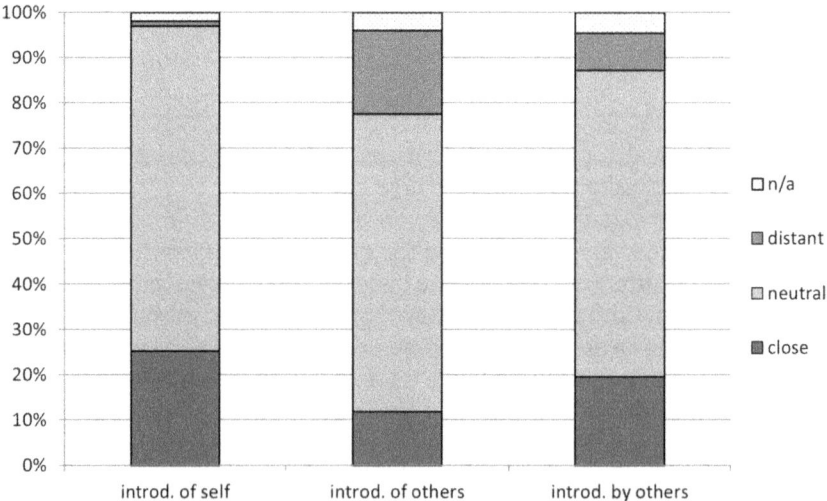

Figure 5.1 Patterns of introductions: First meeting, in English, regardless of first language (195 respondents)

patterns are non-reciprocal. (In each quotation, the informant is identified with the following details: country of birth, sequence number, gender, age group, first language [L1] – in the case of multilinguals more than one L1 is indicated.)

> I tend to refer to one's title when introducing others, but I don't expect others to do the same with me. (Au2, Male, 30–50, English)

> Have no strong 'expectations' as to how I'd be introduced, don't really mind being addressed differently [from how he would address others]. (UK3, Male, under 30, English)

Linguistic and Regional Macrocultural Effects on Nominal Address in Introductions

Introductions when English is used in a conference context

The study also investigated whether there are differences in preferred introductions depending on the respondents' linguistic and cultural background. As already noted, given the very large number of countries and first languages identified by the respondents, we decided to group as many as possible into specific regional macrocultural groupings and analyse the results for those informants accordingly. While such groupings may contain many different languages, longstanding linguistic and cultural contact and areal diffusion favours shared linguistic structures and practices within them. Three such groupings of approximately even size were identified for our purposes: (a) English-speaking with 39 respondents; (b) Central Europe with 45 respondents; and (c) Northern Europe with 34 respondents. In total, 118 of 195 subjects were included in the macroregional analysis (the remaining 77 who did not come from any of these regions were excluded). These three groupings were inspired by Galtung's (1985) work on intellectual styles based on such linguistic practices as turn-taking patterns (including turn maintenance and turn appropriation), turn length (including clustering of speech acts), degree of directness in speech act realisations, and predominance of positive or negative politeness. This approach, with the same set of groupings, had previously proved meaningful in a study of English as a lingua franca in the workplace (Clyne, 1994), where the issue of central and peripheral macrocultural membership also arose. We follow this approach here, without further discussion.

Figure 5.2 shows the results of our responses for the three macrocultural groupings. Central Europe includes as core Croatia, Hungary, Austria, Slovenia, Czech Republic, Slovakia and on the periphery Switzerland and Germany, while Northern Europe includes the Netherlands, Denmark,

84 Part 1: Language Use and Policy in the International Context

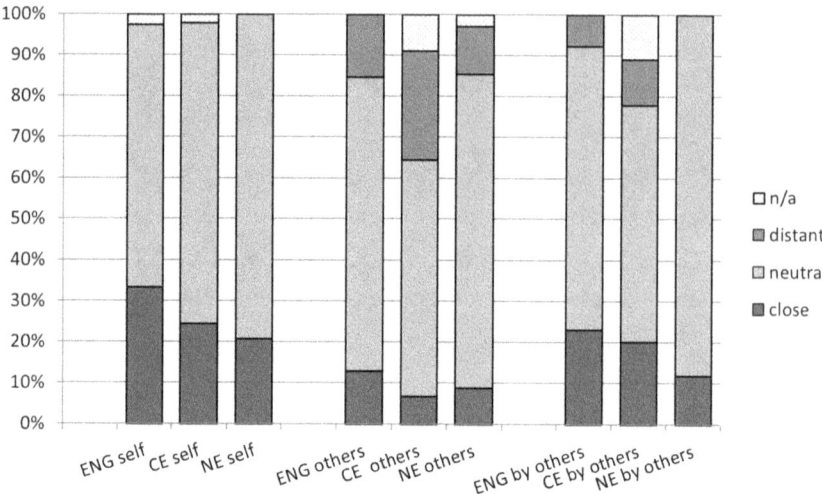

Figure 5.2 Distribution of introductions (%) in English, according to macrocultural group (118 respondents)

Norway, Sweden, Finland and the Dutch-speaking parts of Belgium. The results for subjects of English-speaking background include the following countries: UK, Ireland, USA, Canada and Australia.

Figure 5.2 indicates that the tendency to use FN-only, at least sometimes, in self-introductions in English is greatest among L1 speakers of English (ENG, 33%). When introducing others, results for all three groups show an increased degree of distance or formality, with the Central Europeans (CE) being the most formal; 27% of them report potential use of titles in this context. The English L1 speakers remain the most informal when introducing others in the sense that they employ a higher level of FN, but the Northern Europeans (NE) report the lowest incidence of title use here (12%), and even then almost always only as an option alongside title-less introductions. With respect to how respondents expect to be introduced by others, the Central Europeans again remain the most formal, seen in the greatest expectation of a title (11%).

Use of FN is predominantly a practice that can be linked to interactions in English (cf. Figure 5.3, below), and is in particular favoured by native speakers of English. Comments from our informants – below from a German and an American – lend qualitative support to the notion that use of FN is more typical of English language interactions and of L1 English speakers:

> I am often surprised that many colleagues from English-speaking countries introduce themselves by their first name only, although they

are much superior than I am, as they have many important titles, have published many papers and books etc. To them it does not seem to make a difference whether you are 'just' a student or already a famous researcher. They always see you as an important member of research and if you are young often as someone bringing in new ideas. (G30, Female, 30–50, German)

In English, I will sometimes also introduce others by first name only. (US1, Male, 30–50, German/English, lives in Germany)

Introductions when informant's first language is used in a conference context

Turning to the responses of the entire sample (195 subjects) in relation to the respondents' reported use in their first language (including English as L1), there is an overall tendency towards more formality and distance than in English as shared conference language. While FN + LN remains by far the most common pattern (ranging from 74% in self-introduction to 59% for the introduction of others), there is a tendency to use FN less (ranging from 6% for introducing others to 11% when being introduced by others) and titles more, as seen in Figure 5.3, when compared to the results in Figure 5.1.

We note the greater frequency of other ('n/a') answers in L1 introductions, as compared to English as a lingua franca (see Figure 5.1): it appears that in the former there is greater likelihood that the respondent does not explicitly introduce her/himself or others and does not expect to be introduced

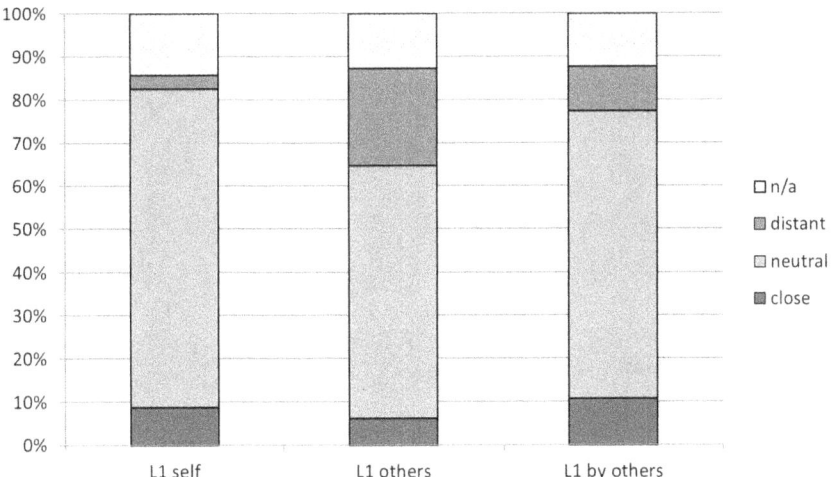

Figure 5.3 Patterns of introductions in L1 (195 respondents)

explicitly by others. Such behaviour can be understood as a kind of face-saving strategy that avoids marking relative status or uncertainty. Instead, other means are used, such as showing the conference name tag (which was not explicitly investigated in our questionnaire, but commented upon by some respondents) or by using vague introductions without direct naming, e.g. 'This is my colleague'.

In a preliminary test of differences in the effect of more specific linguistic/cultural background, in Figure 5.4 we have singled out L1 introductions in the two European macrocultural regional groupings under consideration (comparable results for the L1 English-speaking grouping can be seen in Figure 5.2). The results below confirm a clear tendency towards more formality and distance among the Central Europeans (CE) when interacting in their L1 – compared to L1 Northern Europeans (and L1 English in Figure 5.2) – seen in increased use of titles and a general unwillingness to use FN-only introductions. Northern Europeans (NE), by way of contrast, make some limited use of FN in all three contexts, and generally avoid titles, especially in introductions involving the self. Moreover, there appears to be little difference in behaviour or expectation for Northern Europeans when the self is involved – either in self-introduction or in introduction of self by another. For Central Europeans (as well as for L1 English speakers and for L2 English speakers overall), self-introduction is clearly less formal than introduction of self by another, while for both groupings (and English L1) the introduction of another involves the greatest degree of formal behaviour.

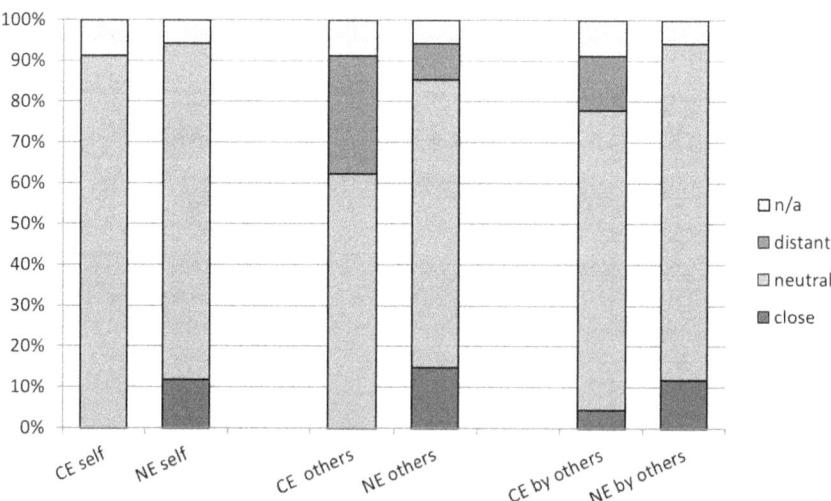

Figure 5.4 Distribution of introductions (%) in L1 (central and northern Europeans only)

Macrocultural and linguistic background, individual awareness and practice

The following comments from a Belgian and an Australian respondent clearly show that the linguistic and cultural background of the colleague is taken into account when introducing him/her:

> This depends on the other person. I would introduce him/her with title and last name when s/he is German. (B1, Female, 30–50, Dutch)

> I worry about how to address people in English. It seems too pompous to me to use titles but I also know this is more acceptable in Europe, so I just avoid address terms or code-switch into German and use 'Sie' and titles. (Au1, Female, under 30, English)

Here the speaker's sensitivity to an interlocutor's L1 and cultural background enables her to adopt different strategies, such as code-switching, to resolve a potential intercultural problem. While the differences in expressed level of formality between introductions in English and in other languages can be accounted for by an awareness of cultural differences – a variant of Principle 5 (Social identification) – our qualitative data also demonstrate that the choice of introductions is governed by a number of interacting concerns, such as the age and status of the other person, the situational context, and personal relationships already established between interlocutors. In addition, there is a tendency towards mirroring the behaviour of the interlocutor, as is illustrated by the following quotations from a Canadian and a Belgian respondent, respectively:

> My usage depends in part on my perception of norms used by the others. (C3, Female, over 50, English)

> I generally try to pick up/mirror the strategies used by other people, e.g. try to 'copy' the way in which someone introduced him-herself when introducing him/her to others. (B7, Female, under 30, Dutch)

Not all informants, however, avoid a mode of address or wish to mirror patterns used by their interlocutor. The following comments from a Dutch and an Italian respondent reveal that introductions (of self and other) can for some also be guided by personal choice, being a specifically 'T(-like)' or a 'V(-like)' person, and are non-negotiable:

> I never never use title (+last name). (Nl5, Female, 30–50, Dutch)

> I don't like using title when addressing people (except for seniors) and I don't like to be addressed by title by others. (It3, Female, age not disclosed, Italian)

88 Part 1: Language Use and Policy in the International Context

Comments such as these demonstrate that at least some informants dislike being addressed in a certain way, in contrast to those L1 speakers of English quoted in the Data section who comment that they do not mind if there are address asymmetries.

The Effect of Respondents' Age on Nominal Address Patterns in Introductions

Introductions when English is used in a conference context

The results in Figure 5.5 present the impact across the entire sample (195 subjects) of respondents' age, regardless of first language, on the use of FN or FN + LN or combinations involving a title in English. When we compare self-introduction and introduction of self by others with introduction of others, we see that respondents, regardless of age, are more willing to expect FN-only for themselves. At the same time, the decreasing age of the respondent is clearly inversely correlated with increased use of FN-only – in the introduction of others or of self by others. But interestingly those in the 30–50 group (28%) are just as likely as those below 30 (29%) to use FN-only in self-introductions – a sign that this informal pattern has been acceptable in English (as first or second language) for some time – in contrast to other languages (see below). The use of FN by those over 50 in any context is well below overall average results. Conversely, this same group is much more

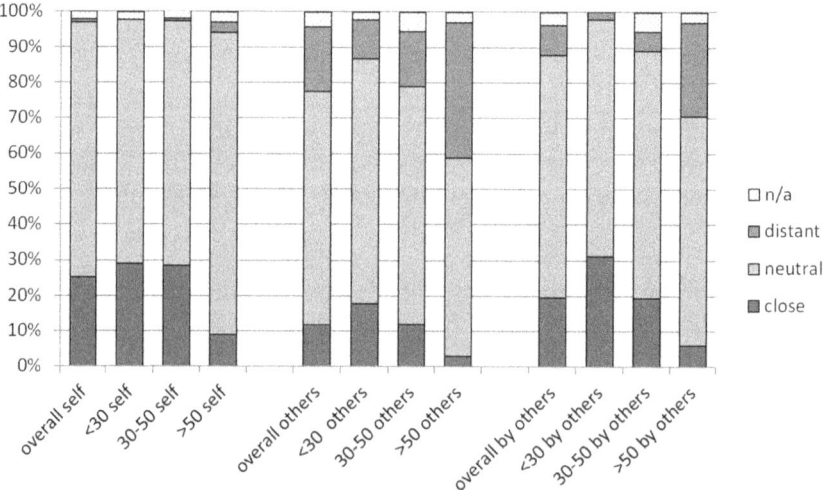

Figure 5.5 Patterns of introductions in English, according to age, regardless of first language (195 respondents)

likely (85%) to insist on using FN + LN in self-introductions, well above the sample average (72%).

With respect to the use of titles in introductions, there is a large divide between respondents over 50 and those below that age cut-off, with the former showing much greater propensity to both use and expect titles. Overall, titles are used very little for self-introductions. On the other hand, the use of title combinations is notable for its frequency when introducing others (19% overall) – especially as respondents' age increases. The frequency is 11% among the under 30s, 16% among the 30–50 year olds and 38% in the over-50 age group. With respect to introduction by others, titles are rarely reported by respondents under 30 (2%) or between 30 and 50 (6%). By contrast, more than a quarter of the 50+ group (27%) report the use of titles in the same context. Such a difference is not unexpected and reflects two different trends: (1) more traditional address patterns that favour more formal introductions associated with titles are more likely to be maintained by older respondents; and (2) younger respondents still on their way to establishing their careers are much less likely to have formal titles themselves and have less experience of using them.

Introductions when respondents' first language is used in a conference context

When we consider the same types of age-related interactions given in Figure 5.5, the effect of L1 is marked (see Figure 5.6) – in particular on the reduced use of FN-only when compared to introductions in English as shared

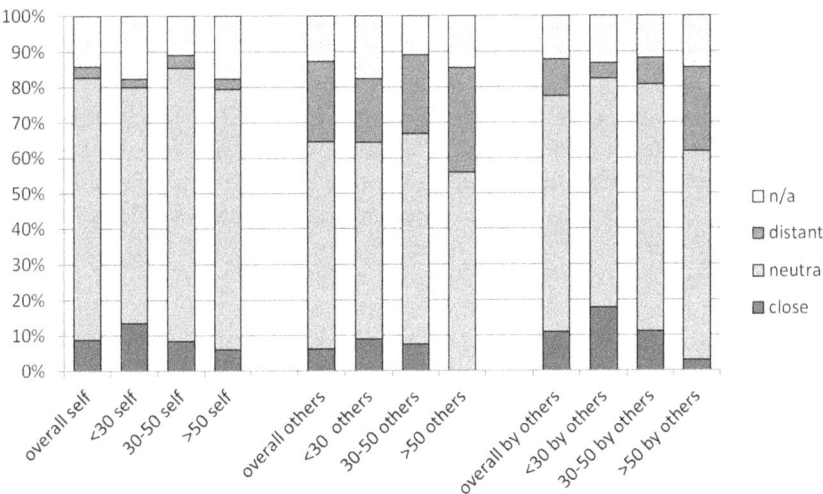

Figure 5.6 Patterns of introductions in L1 according to age (195 respondents)

language (see Figure 5.5). An age-related effect on FN use is discernible, but the differences between generations are much less marked in L1 than in English only. Moreover the generational divide here is earlier – at 30 – which suggests that a shift to more informal address through FN-only is more recent and less developed in languages other than English. Such a finding is consistent with previously noted observations by respondents about the greater informality and more limited use of titles in English compared to many other languages (although not all: titles are used even less in the Scandinavian languages, as confirmed by our findings here for Northern European and by Clyne *et al.*, 2009: 98–99).

In Figure 5.6 we see that the youngest respondents (those under 30) are also less likely to introduce themselves with FN + LN (67%) than those aged 30–50 (77%) or over 50 (74%). On the other hand, when compared to the 50+ group, they are as likely to use it when introducing others (<30: 56%; >50: 56%), and more likely to accept it when being introduced (<30: 64%; 30–50: 70%; >50: 59%). These differences correlate with the increased use of titles in introductions as age increases, especially evident again among those over 50. In contrast to the two other age groups, the under-30 age group also shows a greater willingness to be identified by FN-only when being introduced by others, rather than in self-introduction. We consider this to be a sign of sensitivity to reduced relative status marked by such things as a lesser likelihood of having a formal title or doctoral qualification (e.g. as postgraduate students compared to professors).

Discussion

Predictable variation and patterning across the three introduction scenarios

The overall differences in address practices for introducing self and others, and expectations about how to be addressed by others, indicate that respondents are concerned about protecting the other person's integrity and negative face needs in the context of international conferences. They achieve this through the use of more formal patterns, e.g. titles, that highlight a certain degree of social distance, thereby not imposing on the other. When introducing themselves, however, they are much more likely to signal low social distance and invite a closer relationship through more informal address. In other words, the reported asymmetries in self and other introductions display a concern for the negative face of the other and positive face of self.

Titles are mentioned most often in questions relating to the introduction of others – a sign of acceptable status marking. They are least likely in self-introductions (see Data section) – a sign that the speaker should be modest and avoid marking potential status differences. This pattern is irrespective of whether the introduction is done in English as a conference language or in the informant's L1. However, our results indicate that non-native speakers of English tend to reduce the use and expectation of titles in English – a clear indication of their own acquired sensitivity to the less distancing and more informal address norms in English than those that occur in many other languages, or cultural areas, such as Central Europe.

Despite consistent differences across our three macrocultural groupings, such as the very obvious shift in the Central European group towards more formality through increased title use when asked to report on introductions in their L1, the overall differences across the three address scenarios remain largely the same, regardless of grouping and use of L1 and/or English: as already noted, respondents tend to be the least formal when they introduce themselves, clearly more formal when introducing others, while the introductions by others generally fall in between these two. This regular patterning across categories highlights that the same type of politeness concerns are also at play when the interaction takes place in the respondent's L1. The only partial exception to this patterning is found among the Northern Europeans, for whom introduction of self by another is very similar to self-introduction in terms of relative formality. In addition, the fact that the Northern European group does not display a particularly marked shift as compared to their reported behaviour in English when interacting in their L1 towards greater formality, e.g. through greater title use, is an illustration of the relatively informal to neutral address practices that characterise Scandinavians in particular and, to a somewhat lesser degree, the Dutch.

With respect to age of respondent, our results show a strong correlation for the entire sample: increased age involves increased formality overall; older subjects (>50) are more likely to employ and expect more formal modes of address, including titles, regardless of language used (English as conference language or L1). However, with respect specifically to self-introduction, there is a marked difference in behaviour among 30–50 year olds according to language type: they are just as likely as those under 30 to use FN in English, in stark contrast to L1 – a sign of accommodation to perceived norms in English in favour of such use in that specific context.

Pluricentricity

While the macroregional groupings we use here have been found to be reliable markers of shared linguistic practice (e.g. Clyne, 1994; Galtung, 1985), we are aware that they can also contain within them considerable variation in address routines between nations using the same pluricentric language (see also Kretzenbacher et al., 2013). The main example referred to in the questionnaires is the greater use of titles in Austria compared to Germany (cf. Clyne et al., 2009: 139–141; Kretzenbacher, 2011: 77–78), as shown in the following quotations from a German and a Polish/Austrian respondent:

> I am living in Austria since February 2007 and there is something different which may be important to your topic. In Austria, the titles are much more important than in Germany and the mentioning of titles in public is very common. 'Herr Professor X', 'Herr Magister X' [Magister = person with four-year degree]. I am not familiar with Austrian conferences but it could be that this style is somewhat reflected in academia too. (G32, Male, 30–50, German)

> In Austria, we often introduce ourselves with title + FN + LN, whereas in Germany (less-status conscious) only the name is used. (P5, Female, over 50, Polish, Polish-Austrian origin, living in Austria)

Contextual factors and principles

The academic conference can be regarded as an institution providing its own contextual rules for address. As noted briefly in the introduction, on the one hand, the conference is a formal academic activity. There are status differences between the participants, who vary in age, institutional seniority and international reputation. On the other hand, all conference participants can be considered as peers with an underlying sense of solidarity and even egalitarianism.

The results presented here enable us to see how contextual factors can influence the use of the particular principles described in the Overview and Issues section. According to the Social identification principle (P5), the consideration of all conference participants as peers makes the use of titles inappropriate, as the following Belgian respondent makes clear:

> I perceive conference colleagues as equals, which means I don't need to signal status differences, I would use title and name when presenting a colleague to students. (B4, Male, 30–50, French + Dutch)

The Social identification principle (P5) appears, however, to be modified by issues of seniority. For instance, a recently acquired title can be used to introduce its bearer, thus signifying increased seniority:

> If somebody had just received their title, I might introduce them with the title. (UK8, Female, 30–50, English)

The informant CZ2 (Female, under 30, Czech speaker) comments that, both in English and in Czech, she would introduce colleagues her own age by FN + LN, but 'older/more respectable people' by Ti + LN.

Conclusion: Contribution of this Study

There is no doubt that international academic conferences are particularly valuable sites for address research, given the solidary and yet formal context, and the underlying importance of status and hierarchy in academia (even in English-speaking countries). These same conferences are also noteworthy because of the opportunities for intercultural contact and communication. As a consequence, we have also been able to consider the role of face and to apply a set of principles arising from a previous comparative study of intra-cultural address to better understand reported behaviour in this intercultural institutional context – in respondents' first language as well as in English as the conference lingua franca.

Overall, the results of our pilot study have usefully cast light on the effects of and interactions between: (a) English as L1 and conference language, (b) different cultural backgrounds and first languages, and (c) age, on perceived and expected modes of address in the conference setting. All these elements are seen to have an effect on address in introductions. In particular, the results presented here highlight the potential – among non-native speakers of English – for English language routines and patterns to be influenced by differing cultural norms operating in other languages and cultural areas. At the same time, our results also show some sensitivity to English L1 norms – particularly the heightened use of first name-only address, when academics from different cultural backgrounds meet at international conferences. Our restricted macrocultural analysis is seen to be useful in confirming that L1 speakers of languages other than English do not behave uniformly in their first language or in English. Finally, regardless of language, age is seen to be a useful marker of the relative status of respondents and their interlocutors as expressed through address patterns: the oldest respondents, most likely to achieve higher academic standing over an extended career, are least likely to use FN-only but most likely to use and expect formal titles.

References

Brown, P. and Levinson, S.C. (1987) *Politeness: Some Universals in Language Usage*. Cambridge: Cambridge University Press.
Clyne, M. (1994) *Inter-Cultural Communication at Work: Cultural Values in Discourse*. Cambridge: Cambridge University Press.
Clyne, M. (2009) Address in *intercultural* communication across languages. *Intercultural Pragmatics* 6 (3), 395–409.
Clyne, M., Norrby, C. and Warren, J. (2009) *Language and Human Relations: Styles of Address in Contemporary Language*. Cambridge: Cambridge University Press.
Galtung, J. (1985) Struktur, Kultur und Intellektueller Stil. In A. Wierlacher (ed.) *Das Fremde und das Eigene* (pp. 151–193). Munich: Iudicium.
Goffman, E. (1967) *Interaction Ritual: Essays on Face-To-Face Behavior*. Garden City, NY: Anchor Books.

Hook, D.D. (1984) First names and titles as solidarity and power semantics in English. *IRAL, International Review of Applied Linguistics in Language Teaching* 22 (3), 183–189.
Kretzenbacher, H.L. (2011) Perceptions of national and regional standards of addressing in Germany and Austria. *Pragmatics* 21 (1), 69–83.
Kretzenbacher, H.L., Hajek, J. and Norrby, C. (2013) Address and introductions across two pluricentric languages in intercultural communication. In C. Amorós Negre, R. Muhr, C. Fernández Juncal, K. Zimmermann, E. Prieto and N. Hernández (eds) *Exploring Linguistic Standards in Non-dominant Varieties of Pluricentric Languages/ Explorando estándares lingüísticos en variedades no dominantes de lenguas pluricéntricas* (pp. 259–274). Vienna: Peter Lang.
Schüpbach, D., Hajek, J., Warren, J., Clyne, M., Kretzenbacher, H.L. and Norrby, C. (2007) A cross-linguistic comparison of address pronoun use in four European languages: Intralinguistic and interlinguistic dimensions. In: I. Mushin and M. Laughren (eds) *Selected Papers from the 2006 Annual Meeting of the Australian Linguistic Society. Brisbane, 7–9 July.* UQ eSpace, University of Queensland's Institutional Digital Repository 2007. See http://espace.library.uq.edu.au/view.php?pid = UQ:13126.
Svennevig, J. (1999) *Getting Acquainted in Conversation: A Study of Initial Interactions.* Amsterdam: John Benjamins.

Part 2

Immigrant Languages in Australia: Understanding and Advancing Multilingualism

6 L1 and L2 Chinese, German and Spanish Speakers in Action: Stancetaking in Intergenerational and Intercultural Encounters

Marisa Cordella and Hui Huang

Background

The Australian population is culturally and linguistically diverse, with over 400 languages identified in the 2011 national census. Nationally, 18.2% of Australians predominantly speak a language other than English at home, while in the state of Victoria, where this study was conducted, two or more languages are used in 25.7% of households, with 23.1% of individuals predominantly speaking a language other than English at home (ABS, 2012). Some of these languages are spoken mainly by older migrants, whose level of English may be poor. This latter fact can limit opportunities for social participation, leading to feelings of isolation and disengagement (Angel & Angel, 1992; Kritz *et al.*, 2000; Lee & Crittenden, 1996; Litwin, 1995). This isolation, in turn, may become a predictor of poor general health. In contrast, active social participation has been shown to enhance older people's health and wellbeing (Newman & Brummel, 1998; Seeman & Crimmins, 2001). Further, the opportunity to share their language and cultural heritage with young people in their adopted country can give older migrants a renewed purpose in life (Clyne *et al.*, 2013).

Migrant human resources remain underutilised in Australia and yet reports from secondary education sectors (e.g. Liddicoat *et al.*, 2007) lament that second language (L2) students are seldom able to interact with native speakers in a natural setting (Clyne, 2005). This is seen as an obstacle to their motivation and development to continue learning the language at school. Liddicoat *et al.* (2007) report low levels of participation, achievement and retention rates in language learning programmes in Australian schools.

Michael Clyne, in his book *Australia's Language Potential* (Clyne, 2005), vividly highlighted the social, cultural and economic benefits of utilising the language resources within Australian migrant communities. Considering that nearly a quarter of the Australian population was either born in a non-English-speaking country or has parents from a non-English-speaking country, it would seem sensible to offer older migrants the opportunity to engage in social activities where they could share their language and cultural knowledge with other generations. Apart from the direct social and psychological benefits accruing to the elderly, the language skills and intergenerational understanding of young people would also be enhanced by such an intergenerational experience. This approach to learning could serve as a model from which to foster a stronger plurilingual Australia. This idea led us, with Michael Clyne and others, to undertake the present study, which connected L2 learners with mother tongue (L1) older migrant speakers in order to investigate how the participants engaged in and responded to a series of intercultural and intergenerational encounters.

The theoretical framework that we used draws on the concept of *stance* in discourse (Du Bois, 2007; Englebretson, 2007; Jaffe, 2009), with additional interpretations provided by the concepts of positioning, alignment and footing (e.g. Goffman, 1981). In his introduction, Englebretson (2007: 2) states that having a clear definition of stance would 'border on academic imperialism', as 'definitions and conceptions of stance are as broad and varied as the individual backgrounds and interests of the researchers themselves' (Englebretson, 2007: 1). Although leaving the 'door' open for alternative definitions may have its advantages, there is a need to situate our study within a clear theoretical framework.

The *stance triangle* proposed by Du Bois (2007) serves as a starting point for understanding *stancetaking*. In Du Bois' model the dialogical dynamics are performed by social actors who assign value to the object of interest, position themselves and others in relation to the object, and establish a scalar alignment between stancetakers in relation to central sociocultural elements.

Following a sociolinguistic approach, Jaffe (2009: 8) distinguishes stances within a dialogical dimension. These are 'mobilized interactionally across turns', allowing fluid expressions of social identities to be manifested within a sociocultural matrix. The positioning of participants and their relationships with each other are enacted and negotiated throughout the conversation, and the contextualisation cues serve as a guide to understand speakers' stance attribution to themselves and others.

As an example, we may observe how a language teacher and a student interact in a classroom situation. Both participants individually position themselves in the event and by doing so they also position the other (teacher versus student). In the scenario of a language exercise being conducted in class, students' responses are likely to align to the teachers' questions. Language teachers in turn may provide cues that signal students' language proficiency through their feedback.

In our study we are also interested in *positionality* (alignment or disalignment with the stance of the interlocutor), and *indexicalisation* (the link between individual performance and social meaning) (Jaffe, 2009: 4–5).

The sociolinguistic approach we adopt in this study understands the speaker's linguistic choices as being a representation of both the local interaction and the wider sociocultural coordinates within which the discourse emerges. Contexts, linguistic forms, content and identities (Fox, 2001; Johnstone, 2007; Ochs, 1992) are all at play, signalling the subject's positions and relationships that can be represented in the discourse and changed during the course of the interaction. Jaffe (2007: 56) writes:

> Linguistic treatments of stance focus on how speakers deploy linguistic resources (such as modals or evidentials) to display moral or epistemological positions... Stance thus acts as a guide for interpretation: it is a kind of contextualization cue that instructs interlocutors on the nature of the relationship the speaker wishes to project with respect to the form and content of his or her utterance.

In this study, the migration experience, language proficiency, sociocultural knowledge and age of the participants are the fundamental elements that we considered in our analysis of the interactions between L2 learners and L1 speakers.

Research Site and Participants

Students involved in this study were learning a foreign language at VCE level in Year 11 or Year 12 (the final two years of secondary schooling) at three secondary schools located in southeastern Melbourne, Australia. Their language proficiency at the start of the project was due mainly to the instruction they had received at school, consisting of approximately 90–120 hours a year.[1] The total number of participants was 56, comprising 28 pairs divided into eight Chinese pairs, 10 German pairs and 10 Spanish pairs (one L1 migrant and one L2 student in each pair). The languages were chosen taking into consideration the older migrant population in the area and also the international standing of the languages in question. Approximately 28 hours of recorded material were fully transcribed using the audio transcription software ELAN for maximum precision.

The L1 migrant speakers ranged in age from 60 to 93 years and were recruited from community centres, clubs and churches. The meetings were organised fortnightly during the first three school terms – corresponding roughly to 30–32 weeks taught in periods of 10–12 weeks with a break of two weeks between terms. Conversations were recorded at the beginning, middle and end of the year, but for the purpose of this study we examined only the first and last exchanges. The pairs conversed in the target language for approximately 50 minutes at each meeting.

All of the Chinese seniors were late immigrants, having lived in Australia for approximately five years. They came from Mainland China or Hong Kong and spoke Mandarin and also dialects at home; their English language proficiency was limited. The German-speaking group came from Germany and had firm social networks in Melbourne where they had been living for over 30 years, and were mostly bilingual. Spanish-speaking seniors came from Argentina, Chile, Colombia and El Salvador. The majority had been living in Australia for between 20 and 40 years, with one senior having been resident in Australia for only five years. Generally, the Spanish group was not fluent in English.

In order to ascertain that the positioning of the participants was categorised correctly, one researcher analysed in detail the conversations in one language (see Cordella & Huang, 2012), identifying the prominent stances that the subjects took up in the encounters. This categorisation then served as the basis for the analysis of the dataset across all three languages – Chinese, German and Spanish.

Research Questions

Given the space limitations, here we mainly focus on the older speakers' stancetaking and the responses of the L2 learners. The following questions are addressed in this study:

(1) What stances did L1 speakers take up in the exchange?
(2) How did L2 speakers respond to the positioning of L1 speakers?
(3) What can we learn about Chinese, German and Spanish speakers' sociocultural values and norms from their taking up of stances?

Results and Interpretation

Although the older migrants were not told to take a particular stance in the conversations but to speak naturally with VCE language learners, it was remarkable to see the high degree of similarity across language groups in the stances that they predominantly used, albeit with some interesting differences in relative weight. Positionality was in full display as the participants engaged with their interlocutors.

Table 6.1 L1 and L2 stances during the oral exchanges

L1/Older speaker's stance	Directions	L2/Learner's stance
L2 language instructor	↔	L2 language learner
English learner		English language instructor
Sociocultural guide	↔	Sociocultural guide
Ethical–moral adviser	→	L2 no response

Both groups of participants (seniors and learners) indexed their language proficiency, sociocultural knowledge, and ethical and moral values through the display of contextualisation cues. They positioned themselves in relation to the interaction and broader cultural ideologies (Bucholtz, 2009), projecting three main stances: (1) language instructor, (2) sociocultural guide and (3) ethical–moral adviser.

Table 6.1 indicates that both L2 and L1 speakers may position themselves as language instructors and/or sociocultural guides. While seniors help students develop their language skills in the target language, students may also provide, albeit to a lesser degree, input on the seniors' English expression. Similarly, students and older participants may contribute to the discourse by providing sociocultural knowledge. What appears not to flow in both directions, however, is the stance of 'ethical-moral adviser' which only the senior participants projected in their talk.

The stance of the language instructor

The stance of the language instructor was taken frequently in the conversations. Chinese, German and Latin American seniors all adopted this stance in every exchange, with a frequency of 78–90% (more than three times as high as the other two stances). In contrast, the L2 learners aligned themselves with a non-expert or novice stance (Jaffe, 2009).

The elders as 'expert-knowledge-in-action' (Sarangi, 2001) did not always provide a satisfactory response to the students' queries, but they contributed by assisting the students' language development and confidence when speaking the language (Clyne *et al.*, 2013).

As language instructor, older speakers predominantly led the conversations, asked questions of the L2 learners, explained (new) lexicon and negotiated meaning using a set of linguistic strategies to facilitate the flow of the conversation and assist the students with their language development. Some examples are presented below.

In Example 6.1 (488) the senior asks the student to frame the time of a past event he is referring to. Following the L2 interjection 'Ah', which could index either a failure to understand the question or an inability to answer it, L1 provides multiple choice alternatives (490), repeating the syntactical

Example 6.1 Asking questions
Conversation E4 S4; E: Elder, S: Student (German)[a]

488	E	*Wieviele Jahre ist das her?*
		How many years ago is that?
489	S	*Ah*
		Ah
490	E	*War das voriges Jahr oder vor zwei Jahren oder vor drei Jahren?*
		Was that last year or two years ago or three years ago?
491	S	*Ah, fünf Wochen – Woche*
		Ah, five weeks – week
492	E	*Fünf Wochen*
		Five weeks

Note: [a]Unpolished transcripts are reproduced in the text. See transcript symbols in the Appendix.

structure. L2 then adopts the stance of a learner by attempting her own answer (491) while disaligning herself from the model given in 490. In doing so, L2 presents herself as an active learner who, in spite of her uncertainty as to the plural of 'Woche', still attempts to provide her own answer. This positive attitude favours L2 language development and self-confidence in the target language (Bandura, 1997; Hsieh & Schallert, 2008) and concomitantly reinforces the relationship that both L2 and L1 have been shaping throughout the interaction. This is consistent with Long's (1980) view that interactions not only facilitate language learning but lead to the building up of interpersonal relationships between experts and learners (i.e. teachers and more advanced learners).

In Example 6.2 the Spanish word 'librería' (bookstore) is introduced and the senior provides the contextual framework that the store sells books, notebooks and pens (274) for school children (275). The explanation of the word 'librería' as a way of preventing the L2 learner from using it when referring to its false cognate (library) may have been prompted by their attributed stances (language instructor versus language learner). Concomitantly, the use of the imperative 'sabé' (you -informal- know) and 'entendé' (you -informal- understand) affirms the asymmetrical relationship of the discourse, reinforced by the use of the verb form of vos^2 directed to a much younger interlocutor to mark difference in status and age.

When it came to negotiating meaning, seniors mostly achieved this by modelling, repeating words or utterances, rephrasing for clarification, using English to facilitate understanding, and mirroring the students' contribution. Example 6.3 illustrates one instance of this type. Helping the L2 learner produce a well-formed utterance is at the heart of the conversation. The senior states the correct form of the answer ('Ich habe nicht vor nach Amerika zu fahren' (443)), asks the student to repeat the correct syntactical

Example 6.2 Explaining the lexicon
Conversation E2 S2; E: Elder, S: Student (Spanish)

271	E	...un negocio grande (1) de (.) de librería (.)
		...(.) a big shop (1) a (.) a bookstore (.)
272		sabé – librería/ librería (.) es este el negocio (1) local entendé – local
		you know – bookstore/ bookstore(.) this is a shop (1) a local do you understand – a local shop
273	S	um sí <EyepE>
		uhm yes <EyepE>
274	E	sí (..) donde venden libros (..) cuadernos (..) [lápices] (1) para chicos
		yes (..) where books are sold (..) notebooks (..) [pens] (1)
275		de la escuela
		for school children

Example 6.3 Negotiating meaning
Conversation E4 S4; E: Elder, S: Student (German)

441	E	Und wann fährst du nach Amerika?
		And when are you going to America?
442	S	Ah, ich habe nicht nach Amerika gefahren
		Ah, I have not gone to America.
443	E	Ich habe nicht vor nach Amerika zu fahren
		I don't intend going to America.
444	S	Aha
		Aha
445	E	Ja, sagste das nochmal? Ich habe nicht vor nach Amerika zu fahren. Zu fahren
		Yes, say that again? I don't intend going to America. To go
446	S	Ich habe nicht vor Amerika ge – zu gefahren
		I don't intend America go – to go
447	E	Ich habe nicht vor nach Amerika zu fahren
		I don't intend going to America
448	S	Zu fahren. Ich habe nicht vor nach Amerika zu fahren
		To go. I don't intend going to America
449	E	Ja
		Yes

structure ('Ja, sagste das nochmal? Ich habe nicht vor nach Amerika zu fahren' (445)) and again provides the model (Long, 1996; Schmidt, 2001) for the student to repeat (447).

Saville-Troike (1988) identifies a number of linguistic strategies that assist communicative interactions in a classroom situation. The use of repetition, paraphrasing, expansion and elaboration, sentence completion, comprehension check and request for clarification are some of the strategies she identifies. All of these strategies were employed by the L1 participants to assist their interpersonal exchange with the student.

The students also sought to improve their language skills by asking their L1 instructors for assistance either directly or indirectly (e.g. 'How do you say X in Y language?'). The Chinese students were the most assertive in this regard (77% of their questions), followed by Spanish and German students with 55% and 44% of questions, respectively. In contrast, questions which were not related to language (e.g. 'What are your views on X?') accounted for less than 27% of questions by German students and 21% of Spanish students, while the Chinese L2 learners did not ask any questions of this kind.

Students also took up the stance of a language instructor by correcting the seniors' sporadic introduction of English terms into their discourse. Our data suggest that both seniors and students positioned themselves as L2 language instructors and as learners, although such positioning was asymmetrical – students being mainly learners and elders mainly instructors.

The stance of the sociocultural guide

The elders also positioned themselves as sociocultural guides, and in doing so they revealed some of their past and shared their life experiences with the students. In their reflections they expressed their views about their countries of origin as well as about those places they had gained knowledge from. The disclosure of the sociocultural guide allowed the past to be reformulated and given a new meaning in the present.

The stance of the sociocultural guide also exposed the students to the migrants' outlook and cultural background. For some of the students this was the first time they had been introduced to such knowledge and information. It provided a unique opportunity for them to begin to conceptualise the migrant experience and to shape their views about sociocultural diversity.

The case of the Spanish speakers is of particular interest here because this group found political refuge in Australia, in contrast to German speakers who migrated after WWII in search of better job opportunities, and Chinese speakers from Mainland China and Hong Kong who migrated to Australia only recently to join family members.

The views of the L1 group from Latin America tended to be associated with elements based on the time of migration. Many of them fled Argentina, Chile or Uruguay in the 1970s because of political turmoil and financial instability. They left behind their homeland, establishing themselves in a new cultural and linguistic environment which gave their children the opportunity to flourish in their professional careers.

In the process of recounting the past, members of the Latin American group positioned themselves and evaluated the object (Du Bois, 2007) from a migrant point of view, aligning with feelings of sadness that their own country had failed them. In Example 6.4 the country in question is Argentina in the 1970s. Financial and political problems prevented parents from providing a future for their families (17–24). In Latin America, education is appreciated as a social value that breaks the poverty cycle. Seeing his adult children complete tertiary education and obtain a professional job, the senior positively evaluated his decision to migrate to Australia.

Following Rauniomaa (2003: 1, quoted in Damari, 2010) we could argue that the Latin American migrants may have acquired 'stance accretion', in which

> particular stances are likely to be accumulated in the run of a conversation or several conversations. Stances can be seen to accrue, which gives them the potential to become attached to the identities that they help to evoke.

Example 6.4 Migration to Australia
Conversation E5 S5; E: Elder, S: Student (Spanish)

16	S	¿por qué imigraron a Australia?
		Why have you migrated to Australia?
17	E	() la::: emigré a Australia por la situación económica ()
		() the::: (I) migrated to Australia because of the financial situation
18		e:::() el gobie::rno/ había ()problemas de gobierno/ () e:::m::: () <l> el
		e:::() the government/had () problems the government/() e:::m::: () <l> the
19		dinero o la plata/ e::: no alcanzaba para vivir/ () tenía () tengo dos hijos
		the money or cash/ e::: wasn't enough to meet the needs/ () I had () I've two children
20		a la cual() no le podía dar un estudio/ () no podían ir
		to whom I couldn't give an education/() they couldn't go
21		a un::: () i::: () ir a un::: <als e::> a la <E High eschool E >
		ahm::: () g::: () attend the:: <to the::> the <E High eschool E >
22		a la:: *esto:: la secundaria/como se dice allá/ () (H)
		a *the:: the secondary school /as it is called there/ () (H)
23		y::: () entonces no había posibilidad de darle un futuro
		and ::: () so there wasn't a chance to give them a future
24		< otre> () que siguieran estudiando () 'tonce emigré () a Australia
		< other> () unless they could study () so I migrated () to Australia
25		/ () e::: () bueno mi hijo () es maestro de escuela primaria/(H)
		/ () e::: () well my son () is a primary teacher/(H)
26		y CLAUdia mi hija es e::: <est> trabaja () e:::m <E marke^ting E >
		and CLAUdia my daughter is e::: <eh> works() e:::m <E marke^ting E >
27	S5	() hm

In other words, the migration experience and the reasons for migration may have emerged regularly in their conversations and the stance of opening up a discussion about the overall situation in the southern cone of South America (Argentina, Chile and Uruguay) in the 1970s had become accreted and embedded. Certainly the topic was also raised frequently in conversations among students and researchers, signalling the impact these events had had on people's lives.

With respect to the German elders, we found that the most prevalent themes for L1 speakers were language learning experiences and sociocultural features of Germany and Australia. Other topics such as family in Australia, the reunification of Germany, travelling experiences, and youth and schooling in Germany emerged less frequently and were mainly associated with the topic of discussion assigned for the week.

In the Chinese data, the most prevalent themes were the Chinese social system, including the economy, school management and education, in addition to sightseeing in China. Seniors also introduced topics such as food, weather, life and people in China, but their frequency of appearance in the discourse was lower than that of the topics identified above.

Students also contributed to the stance of the sociocultural guide by aligning with the topics the elders had chosen and evaluating the experiences they had gained themselves through personal exposure, interactions with others or knowledge accrued by any other means.

The L2 learner in Example 6.5 introduces the weather of India which she asserts is very hot (378 and 380). The senior echoes the student's laugh and agrees with her. A few seconds later in the conversation the student refers to the interesting people that live in countries such as Sri Lanka (where her family comes from), Australia and India (388), connecting them with the culture they represent.

The stance of the ethical–moral adviser

The stance of the ethical–moral adviser tends to set the social and cultural expectations of a given group. In the case of the Chinese the value of education was prominent in the dataset. Education is understood as a critical social value and students are expected to work hard and responsibly to obtain a job at the end of their studies, not only for themselves but for their families' pride as well. Fifty-seven percent of Chinese seniors raised the importance of education with L2 learners. Markers indexing the stance of the ethical–moral adviser included imperative forms like 'don't do drugs', 'save money' and 'study hard, your parents are working hard for you' in the Chinese dataset. Example 6.6 illustrates the social value of education.

From the traditional Chinese perspective, such learning is expected to lead to harmony within the hierarchical organisation of society. The process of learning is guided by the five virtues of Confucianism: benevolence,

Example 6.5 Student developing the stance of sociocultural guide
Conversation E3 S3; E: Elder, S: Student (Spanish)

378	S	(3.3) *sí* (1) la (..) en <Aus> en ah India (1) la clima es muy <@calien[te]@>
		(3.3) *yes* (1) the (..) in <Aus> in ah India (1) the weather is very <@ho[t]@>
379	E	[< @@>] (.) sí =
		[<@@>] (.) yes =
380	S	=muy caliente...
		=very hot...
...		
388	S	(1) el <Aus> (.) en el Sri <Lan> [oh] en el Australia India (1.8) es muy::
		(1) in <Aus> (.) in Sri <Lan> [oh] in Australia India (1.8) it's very::
389	E	[m:::]
		[m:::]
390	S	(2.3) personas:::
		(2.3) people:::
391	E	(.) mhm:::
		(.) mhm:::
392	S	(..) *personas* (2.2) pero (1.6) pero (.) muy interesante sí por (.) porque (.) cultura/
		(..) *people* (2.2) but (1.6) but (.) very interesting yes beca (.) because (.) culture/

Example 6.6 Education
Conversation E2 S2; E: Elder, S: Student (Chinese)

888	E	因为为什么(.) 这个这个这个你们要生活好的话\
		Because why (.)this this this if you want to have a good life\
889		要生活很快乐的话\那你要就学习好[(.)] =学习好将来有工作
		If (you) want to live very happily\then you must study well [(.)] studying well and then (you) will have jobs in future
890		干[对吧] 哎\你没技术那你就: 你不什么都不会干[什么都]不
		[yeah\]m\ you don't have any skills and then you, you not cannot do anything
891		知道(.)那你怎么生活啊对不对啊\[(.)]那你那你就找不到工作
		You don't know [anything] (.) then how you lead a life, is that right \ [(..)]then you then you cannot find a job
892		(.)哎\你首先要解决工作((emphasis)) 对不对e\
		(.)mm\Your priority is to find a job ((emphasis)) Is that right e\

righteousness, propriety, intelligence and honesty. Learning objectives are expected to be fulfilled in class and disappointment may ensue whenever Chinese students believe that they are not advancing in their knowledge (Hui, 2005; see also Yu-lan Fung, 1948).

In contrast, the German and Spanish elders frequently appeared to offer a range of recommendations without highlighting any one in particular. The ethical–moral adviser stance of the Spanish seniors outlined the value of friendship and family, of learning the language of the host country and of speaking more than one language as positive traits that will open opportunities in life. The Germans recommended that young learners enjoy what they do in life, use their personal talents, save money for their retirement, keep up to date with their finances, have some professional goals, acquire a broad general knowledge and stay active.

We could argue that the variability in seniors' recommendations in these two groups may reflect their own life experience. Spanish speakers' English proficiency was limited and the recommendation of speaking the language of the host country may be indicative of what they had missed. Most Spanish speakers openly disclosed to us their limited English proficiency and commented on the difficulties they faced and are still facing. Family members and friends provide pivotal social support and at times they also assist seniors with their English expression, for example when accompanying them on medical visits. German speakers instead are fully bilingual and well integrated into Australian society. Their recommendations are varied and centred on the individual's enjoyment, finances, knowledge and health.

In their position as ethical–moral advisers the seniors reflected their own individual life experiences. In contrast, the students' alignment did not go further than listening and paying attention to the elders' viewpoint. They remained silent, probably as a sign of respect, as one student commented to us in the focus group.

Concluding Remarks

By studying stances, seniors' and students' positions and stance attributions became clearer and revealed how each person portrayed himself or herself in relation to the context, the speaker's diverse L1 and L2 language proficiency, life experience, and age. Through the use of stances, individuals projected qualities of themselves, informing each other about their attributes and viewpoints that would assist in closing the gap between generations.

There are many benefits to be gained by pairing young language students with older migrants for a series of conversations in the migrant's native language, as can be seen in the results of our study. Both L1 elders and L2 learners engaged dialogically, intersubjectively and sequentially throughout the exchanges. Seniors engaged with upper secondary L2 learners using three main stances: language instructor, sociocultural guide and ethical–moral adviser. In contrast, language learners used both the stance of the language instructor and the sociocultural guide to a much lesser degree than L1 migrants and did not introduce the ethical–moral adviser stance in the discourse. The seniors became language and cultural ambassadors who also took on the role of 'grandparents', building up a positive relationship with the much younger L2 learners from which knowledge, wisdom, advice and life experiences could be shared through the stances.

A high percentage of seniors in all three language groups adopted the language instructor stance, positioning themselves as being 'responsible' for imparting knowledge about language and culture to the L2 learners. In doing so they utilised many of the strategies that language teachers employ in the classroom (Long, 1996; Lynch, 1990; Saville-Troike, 1988) and that grandparents use when they are transmitting the language to their grandchildren (Lambert, 2008). The strategies of negotiating meaning, asking questions and explaining the lexicon were commonly employed by the L1 seniors to prevent communication failure and assist students with their language performance. Students also adopted the stance of language instructor, although to a lesser degree, correcting mispronounced English words that were introduced sporadically into the elders' discourse.

The seniors also positioned themselves as sociocultural guides, sharing with the students stories of their homeland and other places they had visited, their reasons for migrating, the opportunities they have had in Australia, and the relationships they have experienced, all of which have contributed to shaping their views about themselves, others and their surroundings.

The time older people have spent in the host country and the degree to which they have engaged in the local community have influenced their perception of the world and the position they took in the stance of the sociocultural guide. Spanish speakers fled their countries for political reasons and had little opportunity to participate in the Australian community, German speakers had more easily established networks in Australia, presumably due to their English proficiency, while Chinese speakers showed the least engagement with Australian society due to their recent migration.

To the students, this sociocultural sharing by the elders offered a valuable insight into the migrant experience and the way other cultural groups function. The students also responded to the migrants' stories with their own thoughts and experiences, positioning themselves, in turn, as sociocultural guides.

As we have noted, while both L1 and L2 participants adopted the stance of language instructor and sociocultural guide in the exchange, the seniors also adopted the stance of ethical–moral adviser, drawing on their life experiences to encourage the young learners to follow certain precepts. The students appeared to show respect for the elders by adopting a listening stance during these utterances.

In our view, a programme of regular intergenerational and intercultural encounters is not only mutually beneficial for second language learners and ageing migrants, but would also assist in breaking down stereotypes between generations and improve social cohesion, in Australia and elsewhere. Such a programme would offer 'mutually beneficial relationships needed to underpin a fair and equitable society in the future' (Hatton-Yeo, 2011: 321). The results of this study and others (Clyne *et al.*, 2013; Cordella & Huang, 2012; Cordella *et al.*, 2012) have shown that when students are given the opportunity to improve language skills with native speakers, greater understanding and respect between generations and cultures are also achieved.

Appendix: Transcription Symbols

Unit	Event	Symbol
	Truncated syllable (first)	'
	Truncated syllable (middle and final)	–
Speakers	Speaker identity/turn start	:
	Overlapping talk begins	[
	Overlapping talk ends	]
	Latching (No silence left between first speaker and second speaker's turn)	=
Tone	Low falling tone	\
	Rising tone	/
Pause/silence	Silence timed in seconds	(1)
	Pause of less than half a second	(`)
	Pause longer than half a second	(``)
Vocal noises	Inhalation	(H)
	Exhalation	(Hx)
Quality of voice	Emphasis (perceived change based on volume or pitch change)	EMPHASIS
	Lower in volume than the rest of the talk	**
	Laugh quality	<@@>
Lengthening	Vowel/consonant elongation	:::
Transcribers' perspective	Researcher's comment	(())
	Uncertain hearing	<XX>

Acknowledgements

The authors' most sincere thanks go to all the students and seniors who agreed to become involved in the project. They also thank their research assistants Brigitte Lambert, Cecilia Kokubu and Yanying Lu for their valuable contribution to the data analysis and Meredith Sherlock for her fruitful feedback.

This project is being financed by the Australian Research Council in conjunction with four partner organisations: Department of Education and Early Childhood Development; Independent Schools Victoria; Department of Premier and Cabinet, Office of Multicultural Affairs and Citizenship; and the Council on the Ageing.

Notes

(1) The Victorian Curriculum Assessment Authority (VCAA) notes that there are three streams of Mandarin learners at VCE level. These are: (i) second language regular; (ii) second language advanced; and (iii) first language. The Mandarin students in this study were in the stream 'VCE second language regular' since they were born in Australia, did not receive any formal classroom teaching in Chinese before Year 7, and did not speak Mandarin at home. Some of the students had been exposed to dialects (e.g. Cantonese) in the home, but were not excluded on that account.
(2) A pronominal system employed in Argentina and other Latin American countries that indexes informal speech (see *tuteo* and *voseo*). The younger speaker in the context under investigation here would be expected to use the more formal form in response.

References

ABS (2012) *Data Analysis of 2011 Census*. Online database. Canberra: Australian Bureau of Statistics. See http://www.abs.gov.au/websitedbs/censushome.nsf/home/Data.
Angel, J. and Angel, R. (1992) Age at migration, social connections, and well-being among elderly Hispanics. *Journal of Aging and Health* 4, 480–499.
Bandura, A. (1997) *Self-Efficacy: The Exercise of Control*. New York: Freeman.
Bucholtz, M. (2009) From stance to style. In A. Jaffe (ed.) *Stance: Sociolinguistic Perspectives* (pp. 146–170). Oxford: Oxford University Press.
Clyne, M. (2005) *Australia's Language Potential*. Sydney: University of New South Wales Press.
Clyne, M., Cordella, M., Schüpbach, D. and Maher, B. (2013) Connecting younger second language learners and older bilinguals: Interconnectedness and social inclusion. *International Journal of Multilingualism* 10 (4), 375–393.
Cordella, M. and Huang, H. (2012) Encuentros intergeneracionales e interculturales en Australia: Los roles participativos del adulto mayor y el estudiante de EL2. *Signo y Seña* 22, 13–33.
Cordella, M., Radermacher, H., Huang, H., Browning, C., Baumgartner, R., De Soysa, T. and Feldman, S. (2012) Intergenerational and intercultural encounters: Connecting students and older people through language learning. *Journal for Intergenerational Relationships* 10 (1), 80–85.
Damari, R.R. (2010) Intertextual stancetaking and the local negotiation of cultural identities by a binational couple. *Journal of Sociolinguistics* 14 (5), 609–629.
Du Bois, J.W. (2007) The stance triangle. In R. Englebretson (ed.) *Stancetaking in Discourse: Subjectivity, Evaluation, Interaction* (pp. 137–182). Amsterdam: John Benjamins.
Englebretson, R. (ed.) (2007) *Stancetaking in Discourse: Subjectivity, Evaluation, Interaction*. Amsterdam: John Benjamins.
Fox, B. (2001) Evidentiality: Authority, responsibility, and entitlement in English conversation. *Journal of Linguistic Anthropology* 11, 167–192.
Goffman, E. (1981) [1979] *Forms of Talk*. Philadelphia, PA: University of Pennsylvania Press.
Hatton-Yeo, A. (2011) Looking back, looking forward: Reflections on the 10th anniversary of the Beth Foundation Centre for Intergenerational Practice. *Journal of Intergenerational Relations* 9 (3), 318–321.

Hsieh, P.S.P. and Schallert, D.L. (2008) Implications from self-efficacy and attribution theories for an understanding of undergraduates' motivation in a foreign language course. *Contemporary Educational Psychology* 33, 513–532.

Hui, L. (2005) Chinese cultural schema of education: Implications for communication between Chinese students and Australian educators. *Issues in Educational Research* 15 (1), 17–36.

Jaffe, A. (2007) Codeswitching and stance: Issues in interpretation. *Journal of Language, Identity and Education* 6 (1), 53–77.

Jaffe, A. (ed.) (2009) *Stance: Sociolinguistic Perspectives*. Oxford: Oxford University Press.

Johnstone, B. (2007) Linking identity and dialect through stancetaking. In R. Englebretson (ed.) *Stancetaking in Discourse: Subjectivity, Evaluation, Interaction* (pp. 49–68). Amsterdam: John Benjamins.

Kritz, M., Gurak, D. and Likwang, C. (2000) Elderly immigrants: Their composition and living arrangements. *Journal of Sociology and Social Welfare* 27 (1), 85–114.

Lambert, B. (2008) *Family Language Transmission: Actors, Issues, Outcomes*. Frankfurt: Peter Lang.

Lee, M.S. and Crittenden, K.S. (1996) Social support and depression among elderly Korean immigrants in the United States. *International Journal of Aging and Human Development* 42 (4), 313–327.

Liddicoat, A., Scarino, A., Curnow, T., Kohler, M., Scrimgeour, A. and Morgan, A. (2007) *An Investigation of the State and Nature of Languages in Australian Schools*. Canberra: Department of Education, Employment and Workplace Relations.

Litwin, H. (1995) The social networks of elderly immigrants: An analytical typology. *Journal of Aging Studies* 9 (2), 155–174.

Long, M.H. (1980) Input, interaction and second language acquisition. PhD dissertation, University of California, Los Angeles, CA.

Long, M.H. (1996) The role of the linguistic environment in second language acquisition. In W.C. Ritchie and T.K. Bhatia (eds) *Handbook of Second Language Acquisition* (pp. 413–468). New York: Academic Press.

Lynch, T. (1990) Researching teachers: Behaviour and belief. In C. Brumfit and R. Mitchell (eds) *Research in the Language Classroom* (pp. 117–143). Hong Kong: Modern English Publications.

Newman, S. and Brummel, S. (1998) *Intergenerational Programs: Imperatives, Strategies, Impacts, Trends*. New York: Haworth Press.

Ochs, E. (1992) Indexing gender. In A. Duranti and C. Goodwin (eds) *Rethinking Context* (pp. 325–358). Cambridge: Cambridge University Press.

Sarangi, S. (2001) Editorial. On demarcating the space between 'lay expertise' and 'expert laity'. *Text* 21 (1/2), 3–11.

Saville-Troike, M. (1988) Private speech: Evidence for second language learning strategies during the 'silent' period. *Journal of Child Language* 15, 567–590.

Schmidt, R. (2001) Attention. In P. Robinson (ed.) *Cognition and Second Language Instruction* (pp. 3–32). Cambridge: Cambridge University Press.

Seeman, T.E. and Crimmins, E. (2001) Social environment effects on health and aging: Integrating epidemiological and demographic approaches and perspectives. In M. Weinstein, A.I. Hermalin and M.A. Stoto (eds) *Population Health and Aging: Strengthening the Dialogue Between Epidemiology and Demography*. Annals of the New York Academy of Sciences No. 954 (pp. 88–117). New York: New York Academy of Sciences.

Yu-lan Fung (1948) *A Short History of Chinese Philosophy*. New York: Free Press.

7 Linguistic Diversity and Early Language Maintenance Efforts in a Recent Migrant Community in Australia: Sudanese Languages, their Speakers and the Challenge of Engagement

Simon Musgrave and John Hajek

Introduction

In recent years, Australia has seen a rapid increase in the settlement of migrants, mainly refugees, originating from Sudan. This phenomenon represents a new phase of migration history in Australia which, apart from an earlier wave of refugees from the Horn of Africa nations (Ethiopia, Eritrea and Somalia), has previously had no experience of a substantial sub-Saharan African population. There is little public awareness of the complexities and needs that characterise this new community in Australia, beyond concerns about socio-economic integration reported in the media (e.g. Oakes, 2012). In this contribution, we aim to provide the first overview of the language issues and maintenance efforts in place relevant to the recently arrived Sudanese population. In so doing, we hope precisely to raise more general (public and official) awareness of some of the issues and challenges concerning language maintenance for new communities, such as the Sudanese, in Australia. We also argue that linguists in Australia could help in addressing the linguistic needs of recently arrived migrant communities such as the Sudanese.

However, current levels of engagement in both directions are disappointingly low, and we will finish by suggesting one possible mechanism – potentially of wider benefit – to increase engagement between such communities, linguists, and other parties who can contribute to solving some of the problems identified and thereby facilitating language support efforts for the communities in question.

Sudan and the newly independent Republic of South Sudan (RSS) are states with great linguistic diversity, especially RSS from where many migrants have come to Australia.[1] This diversity is particularly reflected in the city of Melbourne (4 million inhabitants), where Sudanese refugees arriving in Australia have tended to congregate. As a result, at least 40 Sudanese languages are represented in that metropolitan area alone (see below). It is not surprising then, given these numbers, that language maintenance is a complex issue for this community in Melbourne (as elsewhere in Australia). This is true both for the languages with larger speaker populations, as well as for those with small populations. Thus, although Arabic is also a well-established community language in Australia, issues to do with local (sometimes creolised) varieties, as well as social and religious factors, affect the maintenance possibilities for Sudanese migrants in Australia. The major indigenous language of RSS, Dinka, has several community-based maintenance efforts underway and has also achieved some institutional recognition with state-run classes, but this experience has not been without its problems. For smaller languages, the community-based model is the only currently available possibility; this is exemplified by the Otuho language which has a small education programme offered in Melbourne. The situation as we currently know it is described in more detail for each of these three languages in the section on individual languages and shown to be very different. It also represents the very restricted limits of current language maintenance efforts for the Sudanese in Australia.

Sudanese Migration and Sudanese Languages in Australia

In the last two decades the number of people of African origin in Australia has grown extremely rapidly, from a very small base. Persons resident in Australia and giving a country of birth in Africa rose by 178% between 1990 (111,831 people) and 2010 (311,199 people) as reported in the 2011 census. This compares to a growth in the overall population of 34% between the 1991 census and the 2011 census. The levels of African immigration to the state of Victoria in particular have increased quite significantly in the recent past. Statistics from the 2006 census indicate that of the 248,645 Australians of African descent, 63,391 (or 25.5%) resided in Victoria (Bradshaw *et al.*, 2008; Musgrave *et al.*, 2010). Most African immigrants, especially those from sub-Saharan African countries such as Sudan and RSS, come from multilingual communities, and bring with them a rich repertoire of homeland languages as well as additional ones acquired in transit (Borland & Mphande, 2006, 2009; Musgrave & Hajek, 2010).

Research on Australia's linguistic diversity (e.g. Bradshaw *et al.*, 2008; Clyne, 2003, 2005; Kipp *et al.*, 1995) shows successive waves of immigration bringing new languages and cultures into contact with each other, and with the different varieties of English used by native and non-native speakers in Australia. While there has been extensive research on language issues in more established immigrant communities (cf. Clyne, 2005 for an overview), much of the current research activity with African communities has mainly addressed areas other than language (e.g. Ben-Moshe *et al.*, 2006; Grossman & Sharples, 2010; Pyke & Grossman, 2008; Westoby, 2008). Recently, however, some studies have begun to address linguistic issues – specifically with reference to the Sudanese (Hatoss & Huijser, 2010; Hatoss & Sheely, 2009; Izon, 2005; Musgrave & Hajek, 2010, 2013) or more generally (e.g. Ndhlovu, 2009, 2010, 2011).

If we focus specifically on the Sudanese community in Australia, there is no doubt about the high degree of linguistic diversity we have already referred to, as it merely reflects the situation in Sudan (including RSS). The *Ethnologue* catalogue of the languages of the world lists 133 languages spoken in Sudan[2] (Lewis, 2009). But for Australian census purposes, only 30 African languages, from across the entire African continent, were listed individually in the 2006 census. This increased to 47 in the 2011 census as a result of a greater willingness by the Australian Bureau of Statistics to identify individual languages than in previous census analysis. In both censuses these individual languages are listed alongside two vague categories: 'African languages n(ot) e(lsewhere) c(lassified)' and 'African languages n(ot) f(urther) d(efined)', which are used to capture the rest. The languages listed in 2011 which are primarily spoken in Sudan are: Acholi, Dinka, Luo, Nuer, Shilluk, Anuak, Bari, Madi and Moro. Yet the study by Borland and Mphande (2006) already found at least 50 African languages spoken just in the one state of Victoria, of which Melbourne is the capital. This figure certainly still underreports the actual diversity. Borland and Mphande's work is based on data from social service providers; services are provided only in some languages, typically languages of wider communication for some level of social organisation, and migrants will, as a result, report speaking those languages when they seek to access services. Languages with small speaker communities, either in Africa or in Australia or both, will therefore tend to escape being recorded in statistical or demographic collections.

Within the Sudanese community in Melbourne, it is precisely this situation that can be seen. Borland and Mphande (2006) list 15 languages from Sudan as being present in Victoria, plus various varieties of Arabic. However, more detailed research by Musgrave and Hajek (2010) has found that at least

Table 7.1 Sudanese languages in Melbourne according to two sources, sorted according to *Ethnologue*

Name in: Borland and Mphande (2006)	Musgrave and Hajek (2010)	Ethnologue	ISO639-3 Code[a]
Acholi	Acholi	Acholi	ach
	Afukaya	Avokaya	avu
Anuak	Anyuak	Anuak	anu
	Baka	Baka	bdh
	Buya	Buya	byy
	Mundu	Mündü	muh
	Boeka	Banda-Mbrès	bqk
Bari	Bari	Bari	bfa
	Pajulu	Bari (Pöjulu)	bfa
	Kuku	Bari (Kuku)	bfa
	Yangwara	Bari (Nyangbara)	bfa
	Bashim		
	Didinga	Didinga	did
Dinka	Dinka	Dinka	din
Fur		Fur	fvr
	Gia		
	Heban	Heiban	hbn
	Kādja	Sinyar	sys
Kakwa	Kakuwa	Kakwa	keo
	Koalib	Koalib	kib
	Kurunga	Karanga	kth
	Lango	Lango	lno
	Latuka	Otuho	lot
	Lokoro	Päri	lkr
	Lokoya	Lokoya	lky
Lopit	Lopit	Lopit	lpx
	Lulubo	Olu'bo	lul
Luwo		Luwo	lwo
Ma'di	Madi	Ma'di	mhi
	Masakin Tiwal	Ngile	jle
	Masakin Qusar	Ngile	jle
Morle	Morle	Murle	mur
Moro	Moro	Moro	mor
	Mundari	Mandari	mqu
	Muru	Moru	mgd

Table 7.1 (*Continued*)

Name in: Borland and Mphande (2006)	Musgrave and Hajek (2010)	Ethnologue	ISO639-3 Code[a]
Nuer	Nuer	Nuer	nus
	Nyangatom	Nyangatom	mmj
	Nyimang	Ama	nyi
	Otoro	Otoro	otr
	Shirruk	Shilluk	shk
	Taidjo	Tocho	taz
	Topuasa	Toposa	toq
	Zandi	Zande	zne

Note: [a]ISO639-3 code is an international three-letter identifier for all natural languages.
Source: *Ethnologue* (Lewis, 2009).

40 languages from Sudan are represented in the migrant community in Melbourne in a population reported to be around 7500 in 2006 and known to be growing. Table 7.1 shows the languages identified by the two sources and the correspondences between their lists. It also shows at least two languages, Bashim and Gia, identified by Musgrave and Hajek (2010) as being spoken in Melbourne but for which precise identification in Sudan, according to *Ethnologue* (Lewis, 2009), remains unknown. The table also highlights

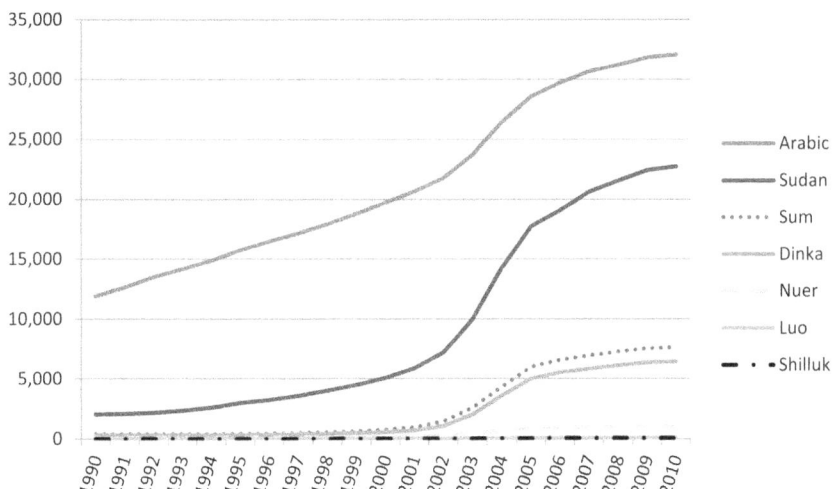

Figure 7.1 Growth in numbers of people in Australia originating from Sudan compared with growth in speaker numbers for major languages from Sudan
Source: ABS data.

how quickly linguistic diversity or, better, superdiversity (Vertovec, 2007) can quickly increase in a relatively small geographical area (Melbourne) – with little or no public and political awareness – over only a short period of time (10–15 years).

Figure 7.1 shows the growth in the Sudanese community in Australia over the last 20 years, as well as cumulative speaker numbers for some of the major languages. The line marked as 'sum' shows the total number of speakers for the five largest languages other than Arabic[3]; most of the difference between this line and the total number of people of Sudanese origin can be assumed to be either speakers of some variety of Arabic or of smaller Sudanese languages that have escaped specific identification in the census instrument. We can also observe that Dinka is far and away the next largest language in this group, having more speakers than the next four identified languages combined. The remaining languages reported by Musgrave and Hajek (2010) have small numbers of speakers, down to single families in some cases.

Overview of Sudanese Language Issues and Maintenance Efforts: Data and Methods

While our overview is intended to have general application to Australia, the data and analysis presented here are focused specifically on the current situation in Victoria, given (a) its marked concentration of Sudanese refugees; (b) our own enhanced ability to gather data first-hand in that state; and (c) difficulties in data collection at a national level, given Australia's large size and its dispersed federal system. The overview is based on a variety of publicly available sources, as well as the researchers' personal contacts with members of the language communities discussed here. In addition to the work of Borland and Mphande (2006, 2009) and the research described in our own publications (Musgrave & Hajek, 2010, 2013), we have also consulted publications and reports from various governmental and quasi-governmental organisations – these are cited in what follows where we present the information derived from them. We have also obtained information from the online presence of several groups conducting language activities around Melbourne. In some cases, members of these groups are known to us and we have additional information from personal contacts. In the case of the information which we present concerning language classes offered by the Victorian School of Languages (VSL), we are grateful to Pandora Petrovska, Assistant Principal (Curriculum) VSL, for her generous assistance.

We also provide in the section that follows some essential background information relevant to the linguistic situation in Sudan. Given that the provision of support services for non-English-speaking members of the Sudanese community has undoubtedly focused on Arabic in some form, it is important, for instance, to understand the place of Arabic in South Sudanese society.

Individual Languages

Arabic

Arabic became the official language of the Sudanese state after independence in 1956 (Idris, 2004), although English was widely used and known throughout the nation, especially in southern parts of Sudan. While Arabic has been the major language of the education system since the 1960s (Yeddi, 2001), in the 1980s and 1990s the Arabic-speaking elite in north Sudan pursued a policy which favoured the use of Arabic in most areas of public life at the expense of English and the many local languages – a policy leading to significant resentment in the south (Kaspir, 1977; Sharkey, 2007). As a result of the 2005 peace agreement between the Arab-dominated national government located in the north and the southern resistance, Sudan no longer had an official language, although Arabic was recognised as a national language and given equal status with English. The newly autonomous South Sudan recognised English as its official language, but allowed for equal use of English and Arabic (Kevlihan, 2007). This compromise decision has now changed with independence for the Republic of South Sudan in 2011: the new constitution of RSS no longer mentions Arabic at all, while English is the nation's sole official working language (Government of South Sudan, 2011). The change in the status of Arabic in RSS, not yet recognised by the Australian authorities, is confirmed by RSS's explicit intention to completely re-orient its population away from Arabic (and from Sudan) towards English- and Swahili-speaking East Africa (Kenya, Tanzania and Uganda), by replacing Arabic with Swahili as a lingua franca of wider regional use (Xinhua, 2011).

Local varieties of Arabic are commonly used in Sudan. Khartoum Arabic is recognised as a distinct variety, albeit still related to major Arabic varieties spoken across north Africa (Dickins, 2007), while the strongly creolised variety known as Juba Arabic (Watson, 1989) is important as a lingua franca in South Sudan, particularly in the southernmost region of Equatoria. It has very few first language speakers (estimated at only 20,000 by *Ethnologue* [Lewis, 2009]). As a result of marked phonological and grammatical simplification, it is not mutually intelligible with other varieties of Arabic, such as Khartoum Arabic, and is most often written in Latin script. It is also used as an identity marker by many South Sudanese when in the Arab-dominated capital, Khartoum, located in Sudan (see Miller, 2000, including texts provided). It is important to note that region (north versus south), religion (Islamic versus Christian) and language use are closely interrelated in Sudan, and refugee/migration paths (either to Arabic-speaking countries or to English-speaking countries) also influence language repertoires. The complexity of the meanings associated with the language 'Arabic' for the Sudanese community in Melbourne can be judged from the following quotation from a community profile:

> It is important, when contracting the services of an Arabic interpreter for a Sudanese person that service providers as[k] for a Sudanese-Arabic interpreter, otherwise the clients may well be unable to understand either the interviewer or their interpreter. (South Eastern Region Migrant Resource Centre, 2007: 43, our correction)

The 'Sudanese-Arabic' referred to here and in other official documents is undoubtedly Juba Arabic. There is also no doubt that linguistic proficiency in any form of Arabic varies significantly among the Southern Sudanese in their homeland as well as in Australia, and is not at all well understood – despite the frequent blanket association by Australian authorities and service providers between 'Arabic' and the Sudanese community.

With respect to language maintenance efforts, there are nevertheless extensive resources available for the teaching and maintenance of Standard Arabic in the state of Victoria and elsewhere in Australia. The website of the Ethnic Schools Association of Victoria (ESAV) reports 21 Arabic schools,[4] and the VSL, an important provider of community languages education outside of normal teaching mode in Victoria, offers after-hours classes at nine locations, as well as by distance education.[5] In view of the complications discussed in the previous paragraph, the availability of these resources does not guarantee a lack of problems for the maintenance of Arabic varieties and competencies. The following quotation from a girl whose family comes from the Nuba region indicates some of the issues faced by young people in the Sudanese community in relation to both mother tongue maintenance and Arabic maintenance:

> I don't speak my family's language. I can understand it a bit but I can't speak it. So when my grandmother phones I can't talk to her ... In Sudan I learnt Arabic and we speak Arabic at home, but I can't read and write it. (South Eastern Region Migrant Resource Centre, 2007: 43)[6]

We have for the moment no information about the extent to which South Sudanese migrants and their families in Australia are involved in efforts, such as after-hours classes, to maintain knowledge of Arabic – in light of the clear downgrading of that language in RSS. We would expect, however, strong alignment on confessional grounds: while the overwhelming majority of South Sudanese in Australia are Christian, the small number of South Sudanese Muslims are always likely to support the learning and retention of Arabic for religious reasons. What is clear is that there are no educational efforts – by official bodies or community led – to organise classes specifically for South Sudanese children or to teach Juba Arabic ('Sudanese-Arabic') to them.

Dinka

Dinka is a Nilotic language from the Nilo-Saharan language family and had the most speakers of any language after Arabic in all of Sudan before RSS independence. It is now the language with the largest number of speakers in RSS. The total speaker population is around 1.35 million (*Ethnologue*, Lewis, 2009) across the five generally recognised dialects distributed over a wide geographical area. As Dinka is a language from the south of Sudan, and a large share of the Sudanese community in Australia comes from that area, it is not surprising that the proportion of Dinka speakers in the Australian population is higher than that in all of Sudan – north and south combined. The Dinka population represented less than 4% of the overall population within the old borders, but Figure 7.1 shows that Dinka speakers make up about one-third of the Australian community. In addition to significant dialect variation, there is no universally accepted orthography for the language (Gilley, 2004), with different practices associated with Protestant and Catholic missionary traditions, and this divergence remains a significant challenge (see below). Earlier research (Izon, 2005) has found that young Dinka people in Australia have positive attitudes to language maintenance. The combination of a substantial population with such attitudes has resulted in a number of language teaching initiatives, but as detailed below, these have not always been very successful.

Dinka in the Victorian School of Languages

The VSL, as previously mentioned, plays a critical role in the provision of distance and after-hours languages teaching in the state of Victoria. As a result of discussions with the Dinka-speaking community, the VSL has taught Dinka since 2008 in after-hours programmes, and has been keen to support and maintain such provision. The Dinka programme has been offered at four metropolitan sites in Melbourne (Sunshine, Westall, Brimbank and Box Hill), although the Box Hill programme was only offered in 2008. Two other sites (Dandenong and Melton) were also considered, but the Dinka programme has since been reduced and is currently offered only at Sunshine and the regional site of Shepparton. The programme at Sunshine has been the most stable. In 2010 courses were offered there at two levels, with 21 students enrolled in the primary (Y1–6) course and 19 in the junior secondary (Y7–10) course.

Various problems, which are shared by many new and emerging language communities, have affected the success of the VSL Dinka programme. First, it has proved hard to recruit and retain suitably qualified teachers. There are stringent requirements for full recognition as a teacher able to work for the VSL, and it is often very difficult for members of migrant communities to meet these requirements, particularly in regard to having any prior teaching qualifications, obtained overseas, recognised in Australia (if indeed they have any).

A second factor which has reduced the effectiveness of the programme is the lack of suitable teaching materials. Courses initially used materials brought from Sudan, but these were felt to be inappropriate – both in content and teaching style – for the Australian context. However, producing new materials in Australia is costly and time consuming. Work to produce materials such as workbooks is proceeding, but not as fast as might be ideal. A further problem with material production follows from the variation in orthography noted above and discussed further below.

Another issue which has negatively affected the success of the VSL Dinka classes has been inconsistent attendance by students. In several cases, a promising start was made at a venue with high initial enrolments but class numbers were not maintained throughout the teaching period. This attrition can be attributed partly to the two factors already mentioned: teaching materials and methods were not appropriate for students who in their normal daytime mainstream Australian schools experienced very different approaches to both of these. But other factors also contributed to the retention problem. Many of the students had also spent time in refugee camps with little or no education, and did not consistently make a successful adjustment to formal schooling. In addition, there are major logistical problems for families in transporting their children to distant community schools in a city as large and dispersed as Melbourne.

It is too early to judge whether the VSL Dinka programme will be successful or not in the longer term. Certainly, there have been problems in the early stages of the programme, but the VSL is aware of the current practical problems we have noted and is working to address them.

Other efforts in favour of Dinka

The programme offered by VSL demonstrates that it is possible for a recent migrant community to attain a degree of official support for language maintenance efforts.[7] In addition, several community groups are undertaking their own maintenance efforts for Dinka. First, the Ethnic Schools Association of Victoria (ESAV) lists a community languages school with four teachers and 51 students.[8] One programme offering language classes has an independent web presence, but it is not clear whether this is the same programme as that listed with ESAV. The Jieng School of Language and Literacy 'aims to preserve the Dinka language and culture in Australia' (Sudanese Luacjang Group of Australia, n.d.). Other objectives listed include:

- teaching children and adults how to read and write the Dinka language;
- teaching any Australian who is interested in learning the Dinka language.

One other group has a current website, the Dinka Language Institute, Australia.[9] The institute originated with Dinka refugees in Egypt in 1995, and has existed in Australia since 2000. Its primary objective is the preservation and maintenance of Dinka language and culture. Its other objectives include:

- promotion of the importance of first language literacy among the Dinka living in Australia;
- development of programmes to address Dinka illiteracy;
- development of language and curriculum resources to support the teaching of the Dinka language;
- development of training programmes to enhance the language skills of Dinka teachers.

The Dinka Language Institute does not offer language classes itself, although one member of the institute has been associated with classes run in Castlemaine, a regional centre in Victoria. Its primary focus is on the preparation of materials for language learning and preservation.

We are aware of the activities of one further group focused on the development of materials. This group, the Centre for Dinka Language Development, formerly had a website which is no longer current. This group has received support to the extent of AU$5000 from the Victorian Multicultural Commission (VMC, 2011)[10] and has been developing a Dinka dictionary and also teaching materials. The Centre for Dinka Language Development states that its aim is the standardisation of Dinka. This aim is being supported by the development of a grammar and a (monolingual) dictionary which will describe the standard, with the possibility of extending the dictionary to bilingual format (Dinka-English) as a later goal.[11]

One aspect of language teaching which is common to these various efforts is the specific focus on literacy in Dinka – for children and adults. We note that this concern is also evident from the perspective of some providers of services such as English language classes and employment assistance, with at least one agency reporting efforts to use Dinka literacy as a bridge to English literacy for adult Dinka-speaking migrants in Australia (ACL, 2009).

Other Sudanese languages

Despite the large number of Sudanese languages spoken in Australia, to the best of our knowledge, the only other community-initiated language maintenance effort originating from the Sudanese community in Melbourne is a language school run by Otuho (Latuka) speakers. This language does not have large speaker populations, with *Ethnologue* in 2009 giving a total number of speakers under 150,000 in Sudan (Lewis, 2009) and Borland and Mphande (2006: 35) estimating that there were fewer than 20 speakers in

Melbourne at the time of their research. The number of speakers in Melbourne appears to have grown since then, enough to allow for the small after-hours community-based Otuho Language School that has operated since 2009 in the suburb of Dandenong. This is a considerable achievement – even attracting some outside participation – but not without many of the same problems reported above for Dinka, as the Otuho community itself notes publicly in its open blog:

> We have 2 weekly sessions with overwhelming numbers attending. Ninety percent being children and adults of Otuho ancestry and ten percent being interested parties. The project has largely been a success reason being it is self initiated and community run. Thanks to all community members who have been dedicated in ensuring continuous attendance and participation. Despite the progress we have experienced significant challenges especially in mobilizing resources in securing a classroom space and supporting teachers with the requirements to meet their teaching obligations.[12]

They also report that the long distances that students travel to the school are a major obstacle (as also for the Dinka programme, see above), serious enough for the Melbourne-based community's main fundraising goal in 2012 to be the purchase of a school bus. This initiative has also been supported by the Victorian Multicultural Commission with small grants of AU$1500 in 2009–2010 and AU$1000 in 2010–2011 (VMC, 2010, 2011).

Comparison with languages from the Horn of Africa

At this point it is worth noting the experience of communities in Melbourne from the Horn of Africa (Ethiopia, Eritrea and Somalia), which neighbours Sudan and RSS. These groups have a similar refugee experience – arriving in large numbers over a relatively short period of time. However, they have been established in Australia for a longer period (since the 1980s), their arrival predating that of the Sudanese by at least 10 years. They have also been more successful, over time, in establishing several well-attended community languages schools. VSL runs only one class in each of two Horn of Africa languages at two suburban sites (Amharic in Footscray and Tigrinya in Dandenong), while ESAV lists classes in four of them, shown in Table 7.2. These cover nine schools and a very substantial total of more than 1300 students.

The high number of teachers reflected in the data in Table 7.2 suggests that the community languages school model, operating within a more flexible framework than the VSL, may indeed be more appropriate for Sudanese groups wishing to teach their languages, much like the Otuho Language School, rather than classes provided in a more formal setting such as the

Table 7.2 Data regarding community languages schools for languages from the Horn of Africa

Language	Schools	Students	Teachers
Harari[a]	2	313	25
Oromo	1	54	10
Somali	5	911	37
Tigrinya	1	32	4
Total	9	1310	76

Note: [a]'Hararian' in the original source.
Source: Data from http://www.esav.org.au/ (accessed 19 July 2012).

VSL, where the requirements such as formally qualified teaching staff are more difficult to satisfy.

A Specific Challenge for Sudanese Language Maintenance Through Literacy: Orthography

There is one issue requiring particular attention that differs somewhat for Sudanese refugees in contrast to most Horn of Africa communities in Australia, whose languages tend to have established written traditions. Given the emphasis, as noted above, by Sudanese groups in Australia on literacy – for children and adults – as a measure and means of language maintenance, one particular long-term challenge for these communities, as well as for linguists and educationalists, in Australia (and elsewhere) is the development and/or choice of writing systems for Sudanese languages. Some of the larger communities face the challenge of competing writing systems that they have brought with them from Sudan. They differ in what they represent orthographically, but also by religious denomination and by major dialect, as already noted for Dinka. It is not surprising, therefore, that there is no general acceptance of a single system for writing Dinka in RSS or in Australia. Indeed, decades of effort by outsiders (missionaries and linguists) to develop an acceptable Dinka orthography continue to this day in RSS (see references in Gilley, 2004; Myhill, 2011, in Ladd, 2012). For other non-Dinka groups, there may be little or no previous experience of a writing system for their language before arriving in Australia. Problems are compounded by the fact that Southern Sudanese languages are extremely complex languages to describe – even for linguists.[13] And there is no doubt that this complexity has an impact on the possible development and choice of writing systems for such languages (see Ladd, 2012 for examples, discussions and some proposals).

Engagement: A More General Problem?

Our earlier introduction of comparative data from other African migrant communities in Melbourne naturally leads to the point that many of the issues that we have discussed in this chapter are not restricted to the Sudanese community. There are an increasing number of groups of migrants originating from various regions of sub-Saharan Africa who have relocated to Australia and in many cases they share similar socio-economic and sociolinguistic characteristics with the Sudanese community. In relation to questions of language maintenance, the two salient characteristics are multilingualism and the small numbers of speakers for some languages, either in Australia or in the homeland or both. Moreover, different varieties within multilingual repertoires may be used for different communicative functions and in different social networks (Musgrave & Hajek, 2013); decisions about which language or languages people try to maintain are not straightforward. Combined with the problem of resourcing language maintenance efforts for small communities, it is clear that there are general problems in providing support for language maintenance in such cases.

In particular, we note in the first instance the lack of official and public awareness of linguistic diversity among the Sudanese community (and other Africans) in Australia. It is frequently assumed, if there is any awareness at all, that since many Sudanese speak Arabic that it is: (a) the same variety of Arabic as is spoken by the large numbers of Lebanese and Iraqis in Australia; and that (b) Arabic is their only or primary language – when in fact it may well be their fourth or fifth and not particularly well mastered. If there is any knowledge of another Sudanese language, Dinka is sometimes identified but more rarely given support (see the examples mentioned above). There is as yet no interest – beyond the very limited work of linguists preparing reports, e.g. Borland and Mphande (2006) and Musgrave and Hajek (2010) – in identifying, let alone supporting other Sudanese language groups in Melbourne and elsewhere in Australia. The small size of most of these groups, while not unproblematic, should not be seen as an automatic barrier to maintenance and promotion efforts. The Otuho language is spoken by one of the smallest Sudanese subgroups in Australia but this community is highly motivated and keen to educate its children in its language. Moreover, a number of small language groups from other parts of the world, e.g. Albanian, Latvian and even Zomi (a recent refugee language from Northern Burma) have successfully overridden significant hurdles to achieve ongoing educational support for language maintenance through the VSL and/or community languages schools.

We believe that linguists have an important contribution to make in addressing all of these problems, including orthography development and other language-related initiatives. However, there is, in our experience, another problem which is prior to any attempt to deal with the issues mentioned above and this is the problem of engagement. For instance, the Research Unit for Multilingualism and Cross-Cultural Communication (RUMACCC)[14] at the University of Melbourne has held an annual seminar on raising children in more than one language for 20 years, but such events attract little or no interest or participation from members of Melbourne's Sudanese and other African migrant communities, despite efforts to publicise the event as widely as possible and to all migrant communities. On the other hand, our own experience in interacting with members of these communities is that there is intense interest in such issues, and this anecdotal evidence is in line with the demographic data and the community initiatives we have discussed. In a related vein, we might also mention the success of the Open Road project of the State Library of Victoria,[15] which has enabled access to electronic resources for several African languages including Dinka, although the long-term impact of the initiative remains unknown.

The issue of engagement also operates in the other direction: there is no tradition of African linguistics in Australia and few linguists in Australia interact directly with the Sudanese communities and their languages. The latter point is perhaps not so surprising given the physical concentration of Sudanese communities in suburban and other areas away from universities in Melbourne and elsewhere in Australia and the lack of any clear mechanism for contact. There is certainly scope for linguists to take a higher profile in interacting with language schools and other maintenance initiatives involving Sudanese (and other African) groups, and to participate in public forums where such issues are discussed – in order to facilitate public and official awareness and support. Efforts towards improved engagement in other relatable situations with refugee communities from Africa have produced impressive results (see, for example, Bigelow, 2010 on one experience in the United States).

One solution to improving bidirectional engagement may be the creation of a forum where interaction around Sudanese languages and African language issues more generally can be facilitated. The initial model for this network (e.g. the Australian African Languages Network) would be an informal meeting place (online and in the real world) for interested parties such as community groups, linguists, other researchers and service providers, in order to raise awareness, collate and exchange information as well as to collaborate. The forum would be directed to providing the opportunity for these different individuals and groups to form new relationships in order to advance their various aims in a mutually beneficial fashion. In this way, the work of the forum and its participants could potentially help address the problems that we have identified in this chapter, encouraging wider community and official participation in early education efforts and improving the longer-term prospects of language maintenance by South Sudanese (and other African) language communities in Australia.

Notes

(1) We continue here to use the term 'Sudanese' – which included until 2011 what is now the newly independent Republic of South Sudan – alongside the more specific term 'South Sudanese'. This is partly because the political division between Sudan and South Sudan remains fiercely contested, with claims that large numbers of South Sudanese and their traditional areas remain involuntarily on the northern side of the new national border. As a result, many so-called South Sudanese in Australia are actually from the north. In any case, the distinction between Sudanese and South Sudanese is still little made in Australia, e.g. Oakes (2012), or in the available linguistic literature.
(2) *Ethnologue* (Lewis, 2009) has not yet been revised to take account of the division into two states, Sudan and RSS.
(3) Luo and Shilluk are mostly indistinguishable in this figure.
(4) See http://www.esav.org.au/ (accessed 16 July 2012).
(5) The VSL provides language education separate from mainstream school programmes that offer language instruction within the curriculum of the school. See http://www.vsl.vic.edu.au/LangInfo.php?LanguageId=59 (accessed 16 July 2012).
(6) One can assume that this girl's family's pathway to Australia was via Khartoum (Sudan's Arabic-speaking capital) and then Egypt, before arriving in Australia. Such a shift to Arabic is not the norm for families that left Sudan via Kenya or Uganda.
(7) The VSL has a brief to provide language classes for groups that can demonstrate the demand, resources and availability of teaching staff.
(8) See http://www.esav.org.au/ (accessed 17 July 2012).
(9) See http://home.vicnet.net.au/~agamlong/dlia/index.en.html (accessed 17 July 2012).
(10) This report also records a grant of AU$2000 to the Dinka Language School (DILAS). We have been unable to identify this organisation as any of the others discussed here.
(11) See http://www.facebook.com/pages/Dinka-Language-Development-Victoria/110113045717525?v=info (accessed 24 July 2012).
(12) See http://otuho.wordpress.com/tag/otuho-language-school/ (accessed 19 July 2012).
(13) This statement is based on our own direct experience, as well as that of other linguists around the world (e.g. Ladd *et al.*, 2009).
(14) See http://rumaccc.unimelb.edu.au/ (accessed 19 July 2012).
(15) See http://www.openroad.net.au/ (accessed 19 July 2012).

References

ACL (Australian Centre for Languages) (2009) *First Language (Dinka) Literacy as a Foundation for English Language, Literacy and Numeracy.* Sydney: ACL. See http://www.deewr.gov.au/Skills/Programs/LitandNum/LiteracyNet/Documents/FirstLanguageDinkaLiteracy.pdf.

Ben-Moshe, D., Babacan, H., Cacciattolo, M., Grossman, M., Sharples, J., Sonn, C. and Zuhair, S. (2006) *Report into the Settlement Experiences of Newly Arrived Humanitarian Entrants: A National Survey.* Canberra: Department of Immigration and Multicultural Affairs.

Bigelow, M. (2010) *Mogadishu on the Mississippi: Language, Racialized Identity, and Education in a New Land.* Chichester and Malden, MA: Wiley-Blackwell.

Borland, H. and Mphande, C. (2006) *The Numbers of Speakers of African Languages Emerging in Victoria: Report to Victorian Office of Multicultural Affairs, Department for Victorian Communities.* Footscray: Victoria University.

Borland, H. and Mphande, C. (2009) Linguistic diversity and language service provision: Emerging African language communities in Victoria. In H. Chen and M. Cruickshank (eds) *Making a Difference: Challenges for Applied Linguistics* (pp. 341–358). Newcastle upon Tyne: Cambridge Scholars Publishing.

Bradshaw, J., Deumert, A. and Burridge, K. (2008) *Victoria's Languages: Gateway to the World*. VITS Language Link. Melbourne: Victorian Interpreting & Translating Service. See http://www.vits.com.au/publications.htm.

Clyne, M. (2003) *Dynamics of Language Contact: English and Immigrant Languages*. Cambridge: Cambridge University Press.

Clyne, M. (2005) *Australia's Language Potential*. Sydney: University of New South Wales Press.

Dickins, J. (2007) Khartoum Arabic. In K. Versteegh, M. Eid, A. Elgibali, M. Woidich and A. Zaborski (eds) *The Encyclopedia of Arabic Language and Linguistics* (Vol. 22) (pp. 559–571). Leiden: Brill.

Gilley, L. (2004) Morphophonemic orthographies in fusional languages: The cases of Dinka and Shilluk. SIL Electronic Working Paper No. 2004-003. See http://www.sil.org/silewp/2004/silewp2004-003.pdf.

Government of South Sudan (2011) *The Transitional Constitution of the Republic of South Sudan, 2011*. Southern Sudan Constitutional Drafting Committee. See http://www.sudantribune.com/IMG/pdf/The_Draft_Transitional_Constitution_of_the_ROSS2-2.pdf (accessed 21 July 2012).

Grossman, M. and Sharples, J. (2010) *Don't Go There: Young People's Perspectives on Community Safety and Policing*. Melbourne: Victoria University (Collaborative Research Project with Victoria Police, Region 2: Westgate).

Hatoss, A. and Huijser, H. (2010) Gendered barriers to educational opportunities: Resettlement of Sudanese refugees in Australia. *Gender and Education* 22 (2), 147–160.

Hatoss, A. and Sheely, T. (2009) Language maintenance and identity among Sudanese-Australian refugee-background youth. *Journal of Multicultural and Multilingual Development* 30 (2), 127–144.

Idris, H.F. (2004) *Modern Developments in the Dinka Language*. Göteborg Africana Informal Series 3. Gothenburg: Göteborg University.

Izon, M. (2005) 'I'm not going to lose my language': A sociolinguistic study of language use and attitudes to language maintenance of multilingual Dinka Sudanese teens. Master's thesis, University of Melbourne, Melbourne.

Kaspir, N. (1977) Southern Sudanese politics since the Addis Ababa Agreement. *African Affairs* 76, 143–166.

Kevlihan, R. (2007) Beyond Creole nationalism? Language policies, education and the challenge of state building in post-conflict Southern Sudan. *Ethnopolitics* 6 (4), 513–543; doi:10.1080/17449050701252791.

Kipp, S., Clyne, M. and Pauwels, A. (1995) *Immigration and Australia's Language Resources*. Canberra: Australian Government Publishing Service.

Ladd, R.D. (2012) *Orthographic Reform in Dinka: Some General Considerations and a Proposal*. Online document. See http://www.lel.ed.ac.uk/~bob/PAPERS/orth.posted.pdf (accessed 21 July 2012).

Ladd, R.D., Remijsen, B. and Manyang, C.A. (2009) On the distinction between regular and irregular inflectional morphology: Evidence from Dinka. *Language* 85 (3), 659–670.

Lewis, M.P. (ed.) (2009) *Ethnologue: Languages of the World* (16th edn). Dallas, TX: SIL International. See http://www.ethnologue.com/16.

Miller, C. (2000) Juba Arabic as a way of expressing a Southern Sudanese identity in Khartoum. In A. Youssi (ed.) *Proceedings of the Fourth International Conference of AÏDA – Association Internationale de Dialectologie Arabe, Marrakesh 1–4 April 2000* (pp. 114–122). Marrakesh: Association Internationale de Dialectologie Arabe.

Musgrave, S. and Hajek, J. (2010) Sudanese languages in Melbourne: Linguistic demography and language maintenance. In Y. Treis and R. de Busser (eds) *Selected Papers from the 2009 Conference of the Australian Linguistic Society*. Melbourne: LaTrobe University. See http://www.als.asn.au/proceedings/als2009/musgravehajek.pdf (accessed 14 July 2012).

Musgrave, S. and Hajek, J. (2013) Minority language speakers as migrants: Some preliminary observations on the Sudanese community in Melbourne. *International Journal of Multilingualism* 10 (4), 394–410.

Musgrave, S., Ndhlovu, F., Bradshaw, J. and Pho, P.D. (2010) *Demography and Language: African Immigration to Australia*. Melbourne: Victoria University.

Ndhlovu, F. (2009) The limitations of language and nationality as prime markers of African Diaspora identities in the State of Victoria. *African Identities* 7 (1), 17–32.

Ndhlovu, F. (2010) Belonging and attitudes towards ethnic languages among African migrants in Australia. *Australian Journal of Linguistics* 30, 299–321.

Ndhlovu, F. (2011) Post-refugee African Australians' perceptions about being and becoming Australian: Language, discourse and participation. *African Identities* 9 (4), 447–465.

Oakes, D. (2012) How the West was lost? *The Age*, 12 July. See http://www.theage.com.au/victoria/how-the-west-was-lost-20120712-21yo1.html.

Pyke, J. and Grossman, M. (2008) *Evaluation of the Refugee Brokerage Program*. Melbourne: Victorian Multicultural Commission.

Sharkey, H.J. (2007) Arab identity and ideology in Sudan: The politics of language, ethnicity, and race. *African Affairs* 107 (426), 21–43. doi:10.1093/afraf/adm068 (accessed 16 July 2012).

South Eastern Region Migrant Resource Centre (2007) *Sudanese in South East Melbourne: Perspectives of a New and Emerging Community*. Melbourne: South Eastern Region Migrant Resource Centre. See http://www.sailprogram.org.au/site/wp-content/uploads/2010/02/2007-Sudanese-Community-Profile-for-MRC-website.pdf (accessed 16 July 2012).

Sudanese Luacjang Group of Australia (n.d.) *Jieng School of Language and Literacy. Language School*. See http://www.ourcommunity.com.au/directories/listing?id=28593 (accessed 18 July 2012).

Vertovec, S. (2007) Super-diversity and its implications. *Ethnic and Racial Studies* 30 (6), 1024–1054.

VMC (Victorian Multicultural Commission) (2010) *Annual Report 2009–10*. Melbourne: Victorian Multicultural Commission. See http://www.multicultural.vic.gov.au/resources/publications/annual-report (accessed 24 July 2012).

VMC (Victorian Multicultural Commission) (2011) *Annual Report 2010–11*. Melbourne: Victorian Multicultural Commission. See http://www.multicultural.vic.gov.au/resources/publications/annual-report (accessed 24 July 2012).

Watson, R.L. (1989) An introduction to Juba Arabic. *Occasional Papers in the Study of Sudanese Language* 6, 95–117.

Westoby, P. (2008) Developing a community-development approach through engaging resettling Southern Sudanese refugees in Australia. *Community Development Journal* 43 (4), 483–495.

Xinhua (2011) South Sudanese still in Kenya despite new state. *Xinhua News Agency*, 6 August.

Yeddi, A.R.M. (2001) Language policy in Sudan. *RELC Journal* 32 (2), 125–130. doi:10.1177/003368820103200208.

8 Language Maintenance and Sociolinguistic Continuity among Two Groups of First-generation Speakers: Macedonians from Aegean Macedonia and the Republic of Macedonia

Jim Hlavac

Introduction

The continued use of a language which, after the migration of its speakers, usually becomes a minority language that is sociopolitically subordinate to the language/s of the new host country, remains a point of interest, not only for 'sociology of language' researchers, but also for those in the fields of sociolinguistics, bi- and multilingualism and translation and interpreting studies. 'Bottom-up' descriptions of individuals' and groups' language use according to features of context or setting (domain-based analysis in the Fishman tradition) exist alongside 'top-down' approaches which focus on demographic features and group members' perceptions of their strength vis-à-vis other groups (cf. ethnolinguistic vitality; Giles *et al.*, 1977). In Australia, qualitative (e.g. Döpke, 1992; Saunders, 1988) and quantitative (e.g. Clyne & Kipp, 1997; Pauwels, 1986) studies in sociolinguistics have employed the framework of 'domains' as a descriptive tool for the analysis of use of language, while ethnolinguistic vitality approaches have also been applied to immigrant language groups vis-à-vis the host society language (Yağmur, 1997) and to the same immigrant language group in Australia versus other diaspora settings (Yağmur, 2004). Further to these approaches, the sociopolitical circumstances of host societies are examined in top-down modelling such as that of Hyltenstam and Stroud (1996), which predicts that different sociopolitical dynamics account for different outcomes in minority language use.

This study adopts a quantitative analysis of language use to present data from certain domains in the lives of first-generation speakers from a migrant language community that demographically records a high level of language maintenance – in this instance the Macedonian community in Australia. It thus seeks to document those settings and contexts that support the continuing use of a minority language. Data are presented not only on first-generation speakers' use of their first language, Macedonian, and English as a code added to most informants' repertoires after migration to Australia, but also on their use of other codes in which they acquired proficiency before migration. These other codes are Greek for some Macedonians from Aegean Macedonia in Greece (hereafter 'Aeg.Mac.'), and Serbian for almost all Macedonians from the independent Republic of Macedonia (hereafter 'Rep. Mac.'), formerly part of Yugoslavia. Proficiency in these codes is a consequence of the vastly different sociopolitical and linguistic settings of the countries of origin of the informants: in Aeg.Mac., Macedonian is a proscribed language (in a linguistic, not legal sense), its use in all educational and public settings strongly discouraged (McDougall, 2009); in the Rep.Mac., it is the official language and the language of instruction at most schools.

This chapter opens with the sociolinguistic background to Macedonian in Greece and the Republic of Macedonia, followed by a description of Macedonian speakers in Australia and a comparison of maintenance patterns in Macedonian and other migrant languages. A group of 50 first-generation speakers, resident in the city of Melbourne (population 4 million) forms the sample of informants whose language use is subjected to a domain-based analysis. This study compares equal numbers of first-generation speakers from both countries of origin to see if different pre-migration experiences of language use result in post-migration differences (or similarities) in language use among two subgroups of the same language community.

Sociolinguistic Features of Macedonian in Aegean Macedonia and the Republic of Macedonia

A detailed description of Macedonian in places where it is spoken as an indigenous language – its status, number of speakers and contexts of use – is beyond the scope of this chapter. In general terms, in Aeg.Mac. in northern Greece, Macedonian suffers the contradictory status of being a language which does not exist and which is, at the same time, discouraged and disparaged (Schmieger, 1998: 126–129). Successive Greek governments have upheld a pan-Hellenist ideology which holds that no non-Hellenic indigenous minority exists in Greece – those Greek citizens who are 'Slavophone' do not speak a language but rather a 'local idiom' that deserves no official status.[1] Greece is not a signatory to the European Charter for Regional and Minority Languages. Although there are estimated to be sizeable numbers of Macedonian speakers (100,000–200,000) in the Greek provinces of west, central and east Macedonia and Thrace, its use is mainly restricted to private and family domains (Schmieger, 1998: 127). Its use in the public domain is strongly discouraged and speakers are discriminated against and harassed (Kramer, 1999: 243–245; McDougall, 2009). These strong disincentives and the officially prescribed use of Greek in all public, educational and transactional settings are leading to a language shift to Greek among Macedonian speakers (Van Boeschoten, 2001: 4–6; Voss, 2003: 180–182). The informants of this study who originate from Aeg.Mac. acquired Macedonian at home and were Macedonian monolinguals or Macedonian-dominant bilinguals at the time of their emigration. For Macedonians in northern Greece today, their linguistic repertoire is triglossic: modern standard Demotic Greek is the H(igh) language, northern Greek dialects and southwest Macedonian dialects are the L(ow) languages (Schmieger, 1998: 140–142).

A contrasting situation exists in Rep.Mac. Although Macedonia is the region in which the first orthography for a Slavic language was devised, modern Macedonian is the 'youngest' codified Slavic language (Friedman, 1985). In Rep.Mac., Macedonian has been the official language since 1944; by the mid-1950s corpus planning and codification had been completed so that the official standard served all educational, cultural-literary and scientific needs (Vidoeski, 1998). Before 1944, Macedonian was the L language – with Serbian the only official language, taught exclusively in all schools. The use of minority languages (e.g. Albanian, Turkish, Vlah) in schooling and the public domain was regulated and until 1991, most citizens, regardless of ethnicity, also had proficiency in Serbian as the ethno-politically dominant language of the Socialist Federal Republic of Yugoslavia (SFRY). Since 2001, Albanian has been elevated to the status of co-official language at the federal level, and at the local level in parts of western Macedonia and the capital Skopje, while Turkish and Romani are co-official languages in a small number of municipalities. For many informants in this study, pre-migration bi- or multilingualism was the norm, and was appropriately recorded, including language use in the post-migration setting.

After migration and arrival in Australia, where English is the sociopolitically dominant language and the lingua franca for most interlingual communication, Macedonian speakers, who in Melbourne number nearly 30,000, find themselves in a city that is host to large numbers of other, Old World languages: 113,000 Greek speakers and 16,000 Serbian speakers (ABS, 2012b). Ethno-political views held in the Old World can be replicated in the New World. In Australia, Macedonians are sometimes subjected to discriminatory views held by some sections of the Greek-Australian community that dispute Macedonians' right to identify themselves and their language as Macedonian. For example, the Australian Hellenic Council (AHC), under the rubric of 'Advocacy Issues', seeks to 'counter claims by the government of the Former Yugoslav Republic of Macedonia (FYROM) and Slavomacedonians to exclusive use of the words "Macedonia" and "Macedonian"' (AHC, 2011, original punctuation). The AHC advocates a view propagated by the Greek Government (Hellenic Republic, 2012) that Macedonians are guilty of 'counterfeiting [of] history and usurpation of Greece's national and historical heritage'. In the 1990s there were arson attacks on Macedonian churches, large public demonstrations by Greeks in Melbourne against the recognition of the Republic of Macedonia, and even a brief period when the state government of Victoria renamed their language 'Macedonian (Slavonic)' (Clyne & Kipp, 2006: 47). Terms such as 'Slavs', 'Bulgarians' or 'Skopians', used in a derogatory way towards Macedonians, still enjoy currency among some Greek Australians, but on the ground and with the passage of time, in many workplaces, neighbourhoods and families, Greeks and Macedonians coexist peacefully.

Relations with Serb Australians are peaceful and harmonious and there are no reports of Serbian organisations in Australia contesting or disputing Macedonian ethnicity or language. In Serbia itself, only peripheral, extreme-right political parties such as the *Serbian Radical Party* view Macedonia as a 'southern province of Serbia', but such views as well as the refusal of the Serbian Orthodox Church to recognise the Macedonian Orthodox Church have little or no influence on the generally good relations between Macedonians and Serbs in Australia, where intermarriage and longstanding personal associations are common.

Language Ecology in Australia and Language Maintenance Data on Languages from Southeastern Europe Spoken in Australia

In Australia, language maintenance at the national level is ascertained through census data that record residents' place of birth and responses to the question: 'Which language do you speak at home?' Data from the 2006 Australian census are drawn on in this study to show language maintenance patterns among first-generation speakers of Macedonian and among first-generation speakers from other, comparable language groups from southeast Europe: Greek, Serbian and Croatian. Language maintenance in Australia for Macedonian (Čašule, 1998; Clyne & Kipp, 2006), Greek (Tamis, 1990), Serbian (Doucet, 1990) and Croatian (Hlavac, 2009) has been investigated and these languages record high (81–100% for Macedonian and Greek) to medium-high (61–80% for Serbian and Croatian) levels of maintenance.[2]

Generally, these languages are well maintained compared to northern European languages (e.g. Dutch, 33.1%), and their level of maintenance is comparable to eastern European language groups (Polish, 70.4%), southern European languages (Italian, 81.4%), Middle Eastern languages (Arabic, 89.4% of Lebanon-born) and southeast Asian languages (Vietnamese, 78%) (Clyne, 2007). Clyne and Kipp (2006: 36–38) include speakers from both Aeg.Mac and Rep.Mac, and identify higher rates of use of Macedonian at home among first- and second-generation speakers from Rep.Mac. compared to Aeg.Mac., which they attribute to the former group's recent migration and their higher proficiency in a variety of registers of Macedonian. At the same time, Clyne and Kipp (2006: 33) identify stronger feelings of allegiance to ethnic heritage among Aeg.Mac. speakers in comparison to those from Rep. Mac. and also a 'commitment to the Macedonian language on account of their negative experiences in the homeland'.

The date of arrival in Australia varies among speakers of languages from southeastern Europe. Large numbers of Greek speakers migrated to Australia from the 1950s to the early 1970s while most Croatian and Serbian speakers migrated to Australia from the 1960s to the early 1980s (Department of Immigration and Citizenship, 2007). The vintages of migration of Macedonian speakers are similar to these three other groups: Aegean Macedonians arrived in the 1950s to the 1970s, while most from Rep.Mac. migrated to Australia from the 1960s to the 1980s. Data from the 2011 census (ABS, 2012a) show that those who report their home language as Macedonian encompass 'older' as well as 'middle-aged' migrants, but also their children (the 'second generation' or 41.6% of the language group = 28,650 speakers) and even their grandchildren (the 'third generation' or 5.3% of the language group = 3650 speakers). Table 8.1 shows selected language and demographic data from 2001 to 2011 for the four language groups.

Table 8.1 shows the number of speakers that report use of Macedonian, Greek, Serbian and Croatian at home. The percentage of speakers born in Australia shows not only the vintage of the language community (older in the case of Greek speakers, and more recent in the case of Serbian speakers) but also the numerical strength of second-generation speakers. A large percentage were born in Australia (i.e. 'second' or 'subsequent' generation speakers) and this along with overall numeric strength are indicators of a high rate of language maintenance. Macedonian shares with Greek a high rate of maintenance; Serbian and Croatian display medium-high rates of maintenance. The 'vitality' of a language group can also be ascertained where it is maintained in exogamous families or families in which one parent is born in Australia, who therefore, regardless of ethnic background, is likely to have high proficiency in English as shown in Table 8.1. Overall maintenance levels in these circumstances are very low for all languages but Macedonian and Greek are maintained slightly more than Serbian or Croatian. The existence of 'third-generation' speakers (speakers whose parents were born in Australia

Table 8.1 National census data on speakers of Macedonian, Greek, Serbian and Croatian as their home language, 2001, 2006 and 2011

		Macedonian	Greek	Serbian	Croatian
2011	No. of speakers	68,848	252,217	55,114	61,547
	% born in Australia	41.6%	54.4%	26.7%	35.3%
	% born elsewhere	49.9% Rep.Mac. 4.3% Greece	34.9% Greece 4.7% Cyprus	28.6% Serbia 15.2% Southeast Europe	50.2% Croatia 7.3% Bosnia-Herzegovina
	Birthplace of parents — Both born overseas	85%	76.1%	91.2%	88.4%
	Only mother born overseas	2.3%	2.5%	1.7%	1.6%
	Only father born overseas	4.7%	6.1%	3.0%	3.2%
	Both parents born in Australia	5.3%	12.6%	1.8%	4.6%
2006	No. of speakers	67,835	252,226	52,534	63,612
	% of those born in 'homeland country who speak that language'	86.3% of those born in Rep. Mac (4.1% speak Albanian)	85.6% of those born in Greece (2.6% speak Macedonian)	77.4% of those born in Serbia (4.6% speak Albanian)	64.7% of those born in Croatia (11.8% speak Serbian)
2001	No. of speakers	71,994	263,718	49,202	69,850
	% change from 1991 to 2001	+11.7%	−7.7%	+102.2%	+10.7%

and grandparents in the country of origin) is also a demonstration of successful transmission: both Macedonian and Greek show modest but respectable percentages, considering that, as an overall group, numbers of those from the third generation are small where immigration to Australia has been comparatively recent.

The 2006 census data in Table 8.1 for Serbian and Croatian show that language maintenance of those born in Serbia is 77% and for Croatia 65%. Although Rep.Mac. is similar culturally and linguistically to both these countries, language maintenance among those born in Rep.Mac. is significantly higher – over 86%.[3] This figure is also higher than the percentage of Greece-born who claim 'Greek' as their home language. The Macedonian language group also includes speakers from Aeg.Mac. in northern Greece. The percentage of Greece-born residents (2006 census) who report their home language as Macedonian is 2.6% or 2860 people. These speakers, together with a high percentage of their children who would also have proficiency in Macedonian, total around 5000 or less than 10% of the total number of Macedonian speakers.

Methodology

The data on first-generation speakers on which this study is based are part of a dataset collected from questionnaires and augmented by videotaped interviews. The data were collected from October 2010 to June 2011, usually at informants' homes by an in-group interviewer, Dr Chris Popov, who was known to around 30 of the informants and who contacted a further 20 informants by way of the 'snowball' effect. Macedonian was the usual code employed in contacting informants and all but one of the questionnaires were completed in Macedonian. The data sample derived from informants' responses to questionnaires is quantitative. The questionnaire was designed by the author, who is not an in-group member, but who is a sociolinguistics researcher with longstanding contacts with Macedonians in Melbourne. This comparative study of language use among two groups of first-generation speakers employs a domain-focused framework, to record how two cohorts of the same language group with differing pre-migration experiences of language use (and maintenance) behave in a post-migration setting.

Profile of Informants

All informants were born in Aeg.Mac. (25) or Rep.Mac. (25) and most came to Australia as young adults: age at arrival in Australia ranged from 12 to 38 with an average age of 21 years. Table 8.2 contains collated information on the two groups.

There are substantial differences in the average and youngest/oldest age ranges of the two groups: Aeg.Mac. informants are, on average, 10 years older than those from Rep.Mac. These differences reflect the differing vintages of migration that each group belongs to. Almost all informants responded that their first language is Macedonian. Most informants grew up in their respective countries and only a small number of Aegean Macedonians also resided in the Republic of Macedonia or other countries (usually evacuation to Soviet-bloc countries during or after the Greek Civil War) before arrival in Australia.[4]

As Table 8.2 shows, the informants in this sample from Aeg.Mac. almost invariably list their first language as Macedonian. Although not presented in this study, data collected from informants also elicited designations of ethnic self-description. All informants selected designations that included the term 'Macedonian', that is, as a monocultural term, or in combination with their adopted nationality, i.e. 'Australian Macedonian' or 'Macedonian Australian'. This sample therefore contains informants from Aeg.Mac. whose ethnic designation is coterminous with their first-acquired linguistic code. There are, on account of the ethno-political discrimination outlined above, many Macedonian-speaking immigrants from northern Greece who choose not to identify ethnically as 'Macedonians', or not to call the language that they have proficiency in 'Macedonian' (cf. Hill, 1989; Radin, 1995). The question of speakers of languages in diaspora settings who disclaim proficiency or use of a language or who practise 'multiple identity and transethnicisation' (Clyne & Kipp, 2006: 49) is not, however, further explored in this chapter.

Table 8.2 Demographic, linguistic and settlement data of informants

		Birthplace: Aeg.Mac.	Birthplace: Rep.Mac.	Total
Average age		71 years	61 years	66 years
Youngest/oldest		57/90 years	37/82 years	37/90 years
Country/ies of childhood	Aeg.Mac.	18	0	18
	Aeg.Mac. and Rep.Mac.	3	0	3
	Aeg.Mac. and elsewhere	4	0	4
	Rep.Mac.	0	25	25
First language: Macedonian		24	25	49
First language: English		1	0	1
Average age at arrival in Australia		19 years	23 years	21 years
Youngest/oldest ages at arrival		12/37 years	12/38 years	12/38 years
Average length of residency in Australia		52 years	38 years	45 years

Data and Discussion

This section opens with data on informants' pre-migration experiences: language(s) learnt and used with parents, relatives, siblings, same-age children in their village, language of instruction at school and acquisition of literacy skills. It then presents data on current language use with spouse and children, social networks including ethnic background of friends and language use with friends, and language use in the work, transactional and neighbourhood domains.

Language(s) of childhood

Most informants were born in villages. Informants from Aeg.Mac. originate from the Lerin (Gr Florina) and Drama (Gr Drama) regions, while those from Rep.Mac. come from villages in the Bitola, Prilep, Ohrid and Kavadarci regions with a small number from the capital, Skopje. All informants reported that the language they spoke with all preceding generations (grandparents, parents, uncles, aunts) and same-age generations (siblings, cousins) was Macedonian. At school, the language of instruction for informants born in Rep.Mac. was Macedonian, with Serbian (then known as 'Serbo-Croatian') as the first foreign language also taught to students in Rep.Mac. In Aeg.Mac., Greek was the only language of instruction. Table 8.3 summarises informants' language use in their early years, including the school domain.

Table 8.3 shows monolingual first language acquisition in Macedonian for all informants, regardless of their country of birth. Two-thirds of those born in Aeg.Mac. report Macedonian as the only code that they used with other same-aged children. A smaller number report the use of Greek (with or without Macedonian) with the children of Pontic Greeks re-settled in Aeg. Mac. after the population exchange between Greece and Turkey in 1923. Table 8.3 shows the diglossic situation in the home towns of the Aeg.Mac. informants where the official H-language, Greek, was employed as the almost exclusive code in teacher–student communication. For almost all Aeg. Mac. informants, school was the only domain in which Greek was acquired and used. In contrast, those from Rep.Mac. benefited from Macedonian as the language of school instruction and this group reports high levels of literacy in Macedonian as well as in Serbian and Croatian, also taught in schools during the time of SFRY. Remarkably, 18 of the 25 Aegean Macedonians report literacy in Macedonian – usually self-taught after arrival in Australia and less often through formal instruction in Macedonian provided to some of the *deca begalci* ('refugee children') evacuated to Soviet-bloc countries such as Hungary and Czechoslovakia after 1946. English was almost invariably acquired in Australia in the workplace and in naturalistic situations, and literacy in English is, for most, self-taught.

Table 8.3 Language use with preceding and same-age generations, language of instruction, and literacy in respective languages

		Birthplace Aeg.Mac.	Birthplace Rep.Mac	Total
Language with parents and preceding generations	Macedonian	25	25	50
Language with siblings	Macedonian	25	25	50
Language with other children in home village/town	Macedonian	17	25	42
	Macedonian and Greek	4	0	4
	Greek	4	0	4
Language with children at school	Macedonian	13	25	38
	Macedonian and Greek	1	0	1
	Greek	7	0	7
	N/A	4	0	4
Language of teacher	Macedonian	3	25	28
	Macedonian and Greek	1	0	1
	Greek	17	0	17
	N/A	4	0	4
Languages in which informants have literacy	Macedonian	18	24	42
	English	17	19	36
	Serbian	3	12	15
	Greek	14	0	14
	Croatian	0	8	8

Language use with spouse and children

As suggested in Table 8.1, children of exogamous relationships are less likely to maintain a minority language where only one parent is a speaker of it. Endogamous relationships are more conducive to language maintenance (Clyne, 2007: 93). Table 8.4 sets out informants' responses with regard to their code choice with spouses. These responses are not unimportant in determining informants' choice of code with their children and their children's choice of code with them.

All informants are married (or widowed) and with almost all spouses, informants speak (or spoke) Macedonian; the rate of endogamy in this sample is 94%. For the Aegean Macedonians of this sample, endogamy is 100% with 84% married to Macedonians from Aeg.Mac. Sixty-four percent of those born in Rep.Mac. are married to someone from the same country. A small number are married to Aegean Macedonians and a further small number are married to Macedonians born in Australia or to Serbs, Croats or non-Macedonians born elsewhere.

Table 8.4 Language choices with spouse and children

		Birthplace Aeg.Mac.	Birthplace Rep.Mac.	Total
Language with spouse	Macedonian	25	22	47
	English	0	3	3
Place of birth of spouse	Aeg.Mac.	21	2	23
	Rep.Mac.	4	16	20
	Elsewhere	0	7	7
Language with children	Macedonian	10	17	27
	Macedonian with some English	4	3	7
	Both Macedonian and English	5	1	6
	English with some Macedonian	5	0	5
	English	1	1	2
Children's language with informant	Macedonian	7	13	20
	Macedonian with some English	4	5	9
	Both Macedonian and English	6	2	8
	English with some Macedonian	5	0	5
	English	3	2	5

All Aeg.Mac. informants have children, while all but three of the Rep. Mac. group have children. Table 8.4 also shows informants' responses about the language(s) that they use in communication with their children and the language(s) that informants report that their children use with them. Elicitations of language use in families are often unable to document variation in language use, even among informants who state that they 'speak only language *x* in their family' as there can be changes in choice of code across settings, contexts, interlocutor and medium of communication, and internal to these as well. The (five) different code choices offered to informants allow only approximate representations of the often varied and nuanced types of speech that can characterise parent–child interactions.

In the first place, use of 'Macedonian' or 'Macedonian with some English' is high in parent>child communication and almost equally high in child>parent communication. Within this context of a Macedonian-dominant variety as the code for parent< >child communication, there is a tendency for informants' children to speak a code which contains some English compared to that of their parents. The phenomenon of receptive bilingualism in parent–child interactions was not investigated (i.e. parent speaks Macedonian; child speaks English) but the general similarity of responses from each generation group suggests that this is not a common occurrence in this sample (cf. Tannenbaum, 2003).

Comparison of language use between Aeg.Mac. and Rep.Mac. informants and their children shows a consistent difference: Aeg.Mac. informants indicate that their own and their children's codes are overall predominantly Macedonian, while a much higher number of Rep.Mac informants respond that the code in parent< >children interactions is monolingual Macedonian. Length of residency in Australia is unlikely to be an explanatory factor for this difference as both groups have, on average, resided for long periods in Australia. Instead, Rep.Mac speakers are more likely to use only Macedonian (including various registers of Macedonian) for a larger number of communicative contexts that they find themselves in with their children, due to having received education in their first language which included acquisition of formal registers and literacy, not available to Aeg.Mac. informants. Aeg.Mac. informants are more likely to transfer items, frequently code-switch or mainly use English when using a register that relates to occupational, educational or 'popular culture' contexts. (Data on self-reported frequency of code-switching as a common phenomenon were elicited and Aeg.Mac. informants report a higher incidence of this, but the data collection did not specify context or register as motivating factors for code-switching.) Nonetheless, both groups display high levels of transmission of Macedonian to the following generation: only two informants report having shifted to English with their children.

The absence of Greek as a code that parents from Aeg.Mac. may pass on to their children is congruent with data on language maintenance of the first language among multilingual parents in an émigré situation. For example, other multilingual groups such as Hungarians from Romania or Slovakia, or ethnic Chinese from southeast Asia usually transmit their L1s but demonstrate little desire to pass on the majority languages of their homelands (e.g. Romanian, Slovak, Vietnamese, Malay, Indonesian) to their children (Ambrosy, 1990; Clyne, 1991). Desired maintenance of a second homeland language in the diaspora is generally unusual. Rare examples where this occurs appear to reflect the desire of parents for their children to acquire a homeland H-language with which they identify in a cultural or religious sense, e.g. many diaspora Cantonese speakers want their children also to learn Mandarin (He, 2006; Li Wei & Zhu Hua, 2010) and some Somali-speaking families also pass on Arabic to their children (Clyne & Kipp, 2006: 75–85).

Social networks and language

Social networks, including friends but also extended family members with whom speakers have regular social contact, can play an important role in language maintenance (cf. Stoessel, 2002). Informants were first asked about the ethnic background of their friends, which is often a guiding indicator for the likelihood of L1 use in the social domain.

Table 8.5 Ethnic background and choice of language with friends and acquaintances

		Birthplace Aeg.Mac.	Birthplace Rep.Mac.	Total
Ethnic background of friends	Mostly Macedonian	22	11	33
	Some Macedonian, some non-Macedonian	3	14	17
	Mostly non-Macedonian	0	0	0
Language used with Macedonian friends	Macedonian	22	21	43
	Both Macedonian and English	3	4	7
	English	0	0	0
Reported use of Macedonian with non-Macedonians who understand it		19	22	41

Table 8.5 shows informants' responses to questions about the ethnicity of their friends and intra-group language choice. Aeg.Mac. informants record a very high rate of intra-ethnic friendships, with 88% of them having 'mostly Macedonian friends'. Informants from Rep.Mac. record roughly equal numbers of responses for the two groups, 'mostly Macedonian' and 'some Macedonian, some non-Macedonian'. All groups are similar in that (monolingual) Macedonian is the most frequently used code with other Macedonian friends – 86%.

These responses indicate close-knit in-group social networks among Aeg. Mac. informants that are likely to be longstanding associations, many going back to the 1950s at the time of their emigration. This indicates that longstanding friendships established after emigration or the replication of pre-migration social networks, through chain migration, are common features of Aegean Macedonians. A similar network of longstanding contacts was found to be conducive to language maintenance among Italians (Bettoni, 1981) and Maltese (Borland, 2006) in Australia and even among some migrants who claim regular use of two immigrant languages (Hlavac, 2013). Length of residence alone need not be a contributing factor to language shift.

Questions about social networks and language use usually presuppose that language maintenance in social networks is enabled chiefly through contact with fellow compatriot, L1 speakers. It is of interest to elicit the role of non-L1, 'out-group' members who may also potentially be Macedonian-speaking interlocutors in social settings among friends and acquaintances. The large number of Serbs and Croats in Melbourne are possible co-interlocutors in receptive bilingual ('lingua receptiva', cf. Verschik, 2013) interactions with Macedonians, with or without accommodation to the other's variety. Eighty-two per cent of informants indicate that they speak Macedonian to 'out-group' members, usually Serbs and Croats, sometimes also to Albanians from former SFRY, and two informants report that they use Macedonian with Pontic Greeks who acquired proficiency in Macedonian before leaving Greece. Although not a major world language, Macedonian has, in Bourdieu's (1991) terms, some 'market-place' value as a code understood by 'other-group' or 'out-group' members.

Workplace, transactional and neighbourhood domains

The last domains to be presented in this chapter are those of non-family, non-social networks – the (former) workplace, shops and neighbours. Table 8.6 presents reported use of Macedonian in these domains.

The responses in Table 8.6 show that over 70% of informants who work(-ed), also use(-d) Macedonian in their workplace, most commonly with workmates. It is also noteworthy that informants list not only oral/aural macro-skills in Macedonian, but also literacy skills (40–50%). There is little difference between Aeg.Mac. and Rep.Mac. informants in the incidence and macro-skill use of Macedonian in the workplace. The high number of informants who use(d) Macedonian with workmates suggests that many informants work(ed) with compatriots. It was a common occurrence for many

Table 8.6 Use of Macedonian in workplace, transactional and neighbourhood domains

		Birthplace Aeg.Mac.	Birthplace Rep.Mac.	Total
Do you/did you use Macedonian in your workplace?	Yes	19	14	33
	No	2	7	9
	No response/never worked	4	4	8
If yes, with whom do you/did you use it?	Employer	2	0	2
	Workmates	9	17	26
	Clients/customers	8	0	8
	No answer	6	8	14
Which macro-skills do you/did you use in Macedonian with employers, workmates and/or clients/customers?	Listening	16	17	33
	Speaking	16	17	33
	Reading	12	12	24
	Writing	5	14	19
Do you ever use Macedonian when shopping or using a service?	Yes	4	11	15
	No	19	13	32
	No answer	3	0	3
Do you have neighbours with whom you speak Macedonian?	Yes	14	6	20
	No	11	19	30

recently arrived migrants to gain or share their workplace with other compatriots, particularly in Melbourne's rapidly expanding manufacturing industries after WWII. Recent models of language ecology (e.g. Karan, 2011) identify occupational advancement as one of the explanatory factors for a temporary or longstanding shift to economically 'powerful' languages such as English (or, in Greece, Greek). The data from this sample show that the languages of workmates, and not only the influence of an 'English as a lingua franca' workplace, can determine language behaviour.

An interesting contrast emerges from the responses on use of Macedonian in transactions and with neighbours. Nearly half of the Rep.Mac. informants report using Macedonian in the transactional domain while few Aeg.Mac. informants report doing this. Conversely, over half of the Aeg.Mac. informants use Macedonian with neighbours while only a small number of Rep. Mac. informants report doing this. Zentella (1997: 56–79) records similarly varied constellations among different vintage Spanish-English bilinguals in New York. Although only one-third of Aeg.Mac. informants live in the two municipalities that contain a high concentration of Macedonian speakers, social networks of L1 speakers in the immediate vicinity are established in a way that does not happen for commercial interactions. Their language choice in the transactional domain is largely English. The younger vintage (Rep. Mac.) group has fewer Macedonian speakers in their immediate vicinity, but avails itself to a greater degree of service providers and retailers who speak Macedonian, through targeted advertising in Macedonian newspapers, which are more commonly read by the Rep.Mac. informants, given their higher levels of literacy in Macedonian.

Conclusion

This study has offered a 'snapshot' presentation of domain-specific responses on language use among two well-established subgroups of the same (minority) language community in Melbourne, an Anglophone New World city. This study sought to examine whether different pre-migration experiences of language use result in post-migration differences (or similarities) in language use. In the first place, responses from both subgroups of first-generation speakers who report high levels of the use of Macedonian – here within informants' families, social networks, workplaces and within the transactional and neighbourhood domains – are in line with census-collected data on Macedonian language maintenance in Australia. For all informants, Macedonian was the first-learnt language, acquired from their parents and siblings and spoken with most same-age children in the (usually) rural places of origin of the informants. Although the sociopolitical status of Macedonian speakers in the two subgroups' countries of origin differs greatly, the pre-migration *local* circumstances of both groups of informants are likely to have been similar: Macedonian was not only historically the L-language but also the undisputed 'in-group' code in both Aeg.Mac. and Rep.Mac. in the areas that the informants originate from. It is this similarity which accounts for the similarly high levels of language maintenance among both subgroups, overriding the contrasts in the sociolinguistic situations at the time of emigration and which still remain today. Post-migration replication of Macedonian language communicative networks, in the first place within informants' families, but also in the work, transactional and neighbourhood domains, is a characteristic of both subgroups which support language maintenance. At the same time, a common L-language in the homelands and 'in-group' status in the diaspora may explain the similarity in maintenance between the two subgroups, but need not account for the overall high level of Macedonian language maintenance. Heightened ethnic-consciousness, due primarily to the refusal of Greece (and Bulgaria) to recognise designations of Macedonian ethnicity, nationhood and linguistic heritage, and due secondly, as previously noted, to lobbying by sections of the Greek diaspora in Australia against Macedonian cultural, ethnic and linguistic identity, appears as an additional explanatory factor for both subgroups' high maintenance rates, especially where each subgroup's sense of endangerment relates not only to its ethno-cultural but also to its *linguistic* identity.

Notes

(1) Minorities in Greece are defined religiously. Thus Muslims constitute an officially recognised minority and, de facto, Turkish is supported in state schools. Turkish speakers are officially 'Muslim Greeks', as are Pomaks and Roms (cf. McDougall, 2009).
(2) Recently released data from the 2011 Australian census that show the overall number of speakers of languages and details on the ancestry of speakers will be drawn on in this study but, at the time of writing, data from the 2011 census cross-tabulating place of birth and home language to show language maintenance patterns were not yet available.
(3) Among those born in Rep.Mac. are 4% who are of Albanian descent and who report Albanian as their home language. When this percentage of Albanian speakers is separated from the total number of those born in Rep.Mac. of Macedonian descent, the percentage of those who report Macedonian as their home language rises to over 90%.
(4) During the Greek Civil War (1945–1949) in northern Greece, Macedonians were highly represented (40–50%; Poulton, 2000: 114) among the Communist Partisans, whose programme included the ethnic and linguistic emancipation of Macedonians in northern Greece. The defeat of the Partisans at the hands of Greek monarchist forces led to the evacuation and expulsion of thousands of Macedonians from northern Greece, the most prominent group of whom were the 28,000 unaccompanied child refugees (MWWNV, 1999).

References

ABS (2012a) *Data Analysis of 2011 Census*. Online database. Canberra: Australian Bureau of Statistics. See http://www.abs.gov.au/websitedbs/censushome.nsf/home/Data.

ABS (2012b) *2011 Census Community Profiles. Greater Melbourne*. Online database. Canberra: Australian Bureau of Statistics. See http://www.censusdata.abs.gov.au/census_services/getproduct/census/2011/communityprofile/2GMEL?opendocument&nav pos = 230.

AHC (2011) *Protection of the Macedonian Heritage*. Online document. Sydney: Australian Hellenic Council. See http://www.helleniccouncil.org.au/index.php?option = com_content&view=article&id=96&Itemid=78.

Ambrosy, A. (1990) *A Survey of the Hungarian Community in Victoria*. Adelaide: Dezsery Ethnic Publications.

Bettoni, C. (1981) *Italian in North Queensland*. Townsville: James Cook University.

Borland, H. (2006) Intergenerational language transmission in an established Australian migrant community: What makes the difference? *International Journal of the Sociology of Language* 18, 23–41.

Bourdieu, P. (1991) *Language and Symbolic Power*. London: Polity Press.

Čašule, I. (1998) The interplay of the Macedonian standard and dialect in a bilingual setting: Macedonian language maintenance in Australia. *International Journal of the Sociology of Language* 131, 105–124.

Clyne, M. (1991) *Community Languages. The Australian Experience*. Cambridge: Cambridge University Press.

Clyne, M. (2007) Sociolinguistic continuity from old to new homeland: Factors in language maintenance and shift seen from the Australian situation. In J. Darquenesse (ed.) *Contact Linguistics and Language Minorities* (pp. 91–102). St Augustin: Asgard.

Clyne, M. and Kipp, S. (1997) Trends and changes in home language use and shift in Australia. *Journal of Multilingual and Multicultural Development* 18, 451–473.

Clyne, M. and Kipp, S. (2006) *Tiles in a Multilingual Mosaic: Macedonian, Somali and Filipino in Melbourne*. Canberra: Pacific Linguistics.

Department of Immigration and Citizenship (2007) *Community Information Summaries*. Online documents. See http://www.immi.gov.au/media/publications/statistics/comm-summ/_pdf/fyr-macedonia.pdf; http://www.immi.gov.au/media/publications/statistics/comm-summ/_pdf/greece.pdf; http://www.immi.gov.au/media/publications/statistics/comm-summ/_pdf/serbia.pdf; http://www.immi.gov.au/media/publications/statistics/comm-summ/_pdf/croatia.pdf.

Döpke, S. (1992) *One Parent One Language – An Interactional Approach*. Amsterdam: John Benjamins.

Doucet, J. (1990) First generation Serbo-Croatian speakers in Queensland: Language maintenance and language shift. In S. Romaine (ed.) *Language in Australia* (pp. 270–284). Cambridge: Cambridge University Press.

Friedman, V. (1985) The sociolinguistics of literary Macedonian. *International Journal of the Sociology of Language* 52, 31–57.

Giles, H., Bourhis, R. and Taylor, D. (1977) Towards a theory of language in ethnic group relations. In H. Giles (ed.) *Language, Ethnicity, and Intergroup Relations* (pp. 307–348). New York: Academic Press.

He, A.W. (2006) Toward an identity theory of the development of Chinese as a heritage language. *Heritage Language Journal* 4 (1), 1–28.

Hellenic Republic (2012) *FYROM Name Issue*. Online document. Athens: Ministry of Foreign Affairs. See http://www.mfa.gr/en/fyrom-name-issue/.

Hill, P. (1989) *The Macedonians in Australia*. Perth: Hesperian Press.

Hlavac, J. (2009) Hrvatski jezik među Australcima hrvatskog podrijetla [The Croatian language amongst second-generation Croatian-Australians]. In J. Granić (ed.) *Jezična politika i jezična stvarnost/Language Policy and Language Reality* (pp. 84–94). Zagreb: Hrvatsko društvo za primjenjenu lingvistiku/Croatian Applied Linguistics Society.

Hlavac, J. (2013) Multilinguals and their sociolinguistic profiles: Observations on language use amongst three vintages of migrants in Melbourne. *International Journal of Multilingualism* 10 (4), 411–440.
Hyltenstam, K. and Stroud, C. (1996) Language maintenance. In H. Goebl, P. Nelde, Z. Stary and W. Wölck (eds) *Contact Linguistics* (pp. 567–578). Berlin: Walter de Gruyter.
Karan, M. (2011) Understanding and forecasting ethnolinguistic vitality. *Journal of Multilingual and Multicultural Development* 32 (2), 137–149.
Kramer, C. (1999) Official language, minority language, no language at all: The history of Macedonian in primary education in the Balkans. *Language Problems and Language Planning* 23 (3), 233–250.
Li Wei and Zhu Hua (2010) Voices from the diaspora: Changing hierarchies and dynamics of Chinese multilingualism. *International Journal of the Sociology of Language* 205, 155–171.
McDougall, G. (2009) *Promotion and Protection of All Human Rights, Civil, Political, Economic, Social and Cultural Rights, Including the Right to Development. Report of the Independent Expert on Minority Issues. Addendum. Mission to Greece, 8–16 September 2008*. Geneva: Human Rights Council, UN General Assembly. Online document. See http://www.scribd.com/doc/13022753/UN-Minorities-Rights-Report-on-Greece-2008.
MWWNV (Macedonian Welfare Workers' Network of Victoria) (1999) *From War to Whittlesea. Oral Histories of Macedonian Child Refugees*. Sydney: Politicon Publications.
Pauwels, A. (1986) *Immigrant Dialects and Language Maintenance in Australia*. Dordrecht: Foris.
Poulton, H. (2000) *Who Are the Macedonians?* (2nd edn). London: Hurst & Company.
Radin, M. (1995) Features of settlement in Australia by Macedonians from the Aegean region. In V. Bivell (ed.) *Macedonian Agenda: Sixteen Essays on the Development of the Macedonian Culture in Australia* (pp. 113–131). Sydney: Politicon Publications.
Saunders, G. (1988) *Bilingual Children: From Birth to Teens*. Clevedon: Multilingual Matters.
Schmieger, R. (1998) The situation of the Macedonian language in Greece: Sociolinguistic analysis. *International Journal of the Sociology of Language* 131, 125–155.
Stoessel, S. (2002) Investigating the role of social networks in language maintenance and shift. *International Journal of the Sociology of Language* 153, 93–131.
Tamis, A. (1990) Language change, language maintenance and ethnic identity: The case of Greek in Australia. *Journal of Multilingual and Multicultural Development* 11 (6), 481–500.
Tannenbaum, M. (2003) The multifaceted aspects of language maintenance: A new measure for its assessment in immigrant families. *International Journal of Bilingual Education and Bilingualism* 6 (5), 374–393.
Van Boeschoten, R. (2001) Usage des langues minoritaires dans les départements de Florina et d'Aridea (Macédonie). *Strates* 10. See http://strates.revues.org/381.
Verschik, A. (2013) Practising receptive multilingualism: Estonian–Finnish communication in Tallinn. *International Journal of Bilingualism* 16 (3), 265–286.
Vidoeski, B. (1998) Five decades since the codification of the Macedonian language. *International Journal of the Sociology of Language* 131, 13–29.
Voss, C. (2003) The situation of the Slavic-speaking minority in Greek Macedonia – ethnic revival, cross-border cohesion or language death? *Jahrbücher für Geschichte und Kultur Südosteuropas* 5, 173–187.
Yağmur, K. (1997) *First Language Attrition Among Turkish Speakers in Sydney*. Tilburg: Tilburg University Press.
Yağmur, K. (2004) Language maintenance patterns of Turkish immigrant communities in Australia and Western Europe: The impact of majority attitudes on ethnolinguistic vitality perceptions. *International Journal of the Sociology of Language* 165, 121–142.
Zentella, A. (1997) *Growing Up Bilingual*. Malden, MA: Blackwell.

9 The Role of Professional Advice in Shaping Language Choice in Migrant-background Families with Deaf Children

Louisa Willoughby

Introduction

Over the last 50 years, Australia has seen, as has much of the English-speaking world, a fundamental shift in the attitudes towards and the advice migrant families receive surrounding language maintenance. In the postwar period, teachers, social workers and other concerned professionals were often insistent in advising migrant parents to speak English only with their children (Ozolins, 1993: 75). However, the research and advocacy of linguists like Michael Clyne (see, for example, 1991, 2005) has shown the many benefits of language maintenance and the problems that can occur if parents feel compelled to shift to English before they are ready. This work has filtered through to many professional training programmes in Australia and it is now reasonably rare for migrant-background families to be advised by teachers or social workers to shift to speaking English only with their children (e.g. Butcher, 1995).

While language maintenance and shift have thus become private matters for most families, the situation changes if a child has a disability – such as deafness – that affects their ability to acquire or use spoken language. In this situation, parents come into contact with a variety of professionals offering advice about communication strategies, which may or may not include a place for the community or heritage language in family communication.

The focus of much professional advice for parents of deaf children is whether to use speech, a sign language, or a combination of both as the primary method of communication. Initially, parents in many countries were advised as to whether to speak or sign with their deaf child on the basis of predictive models that took into account such factors as the degree of hearing loss and the presence of additional disabilities (e.g. Geers & Moog, 1987). However, current best practice recommends a holistic approach that not only looks at the child, but at factors such as family willingness to sign or the availability of spoken/sign language support in the local area. It also stresses that whatever choice is made initially should be monitored and adjusted during the preschool years in response to the deaf child's developing linguistic capacity (Knoors, 2007). While it is still true that the smaller a child's hearing loss, the more likely it is that the parents will choose oral communication as the sole means of communicating with their deaf child (Li *et al.*, 2003), advances in hearing aid and cochlear implant technology mean that some children with severe-profound hearing losses may manage quite well in an oral-only environment (Brown *et al.*, 2006). Conversely, families may choose to use some sign language with a child who has strong oral skills as a means of clarifying difficult concepts or instances of miscommunication (Beazley & Moore, 1995; Gregory *et al.*, 1995).

Complicating matters are sometimes diametrically opposed views about the best way to handle communication with deaf children. At one end of the spectrum there are certain sign language advocates who argue that it is child abuse or genocide to deny deaf children access to a sign language, and thus that all families must sign with their deaf children (Ladd, 2003; Skutnabb-Kangas, 2000). At the other end, service providers advocating the auditory-verbal method (such as the Hear and Say Centre in Sydney, Australia) argue that with technology, all deaf children are capable of learning to speak and hear, but will not realise this potential if they are exposed to any sign language. Unsurprisingly, interviews with parents find that most sit somewhere in the middle between these two views (as do many professionals working in early intervention services, cf. Turner & Lynas, 2000). However, the diversity of views in the sector and the strength with which they are sometimes held means that parents quite frequently complain that the professionals they first encountered were biased towards a particular communication method or did not fully explain all the communication options available (Beazley & Moore, 1995; Meadow-Orlans *et al.*, 2003).

For parents from migrant non-English-speaking backgrounds (NESB), the challenges of establishing successful communication are potentially twofold. The first is in accessing and evaluating information about possible communication methods. Research to date suggests that NESB parents are more dependent on professional advice in understanding and managing their child's hearing loss than English-speaking parents. While the latter group frequently draw on popular books, professional literature, the internet and parents' support groups, NESB parents report only low usage of these and similar resources (Steinberg *et al.*, 2003). In previous work (Willoughby, 2008), I have noted that migrant parents explicitly named English proficiency issues as the major factor limiting their access to information about their child's hearing loss, and as a significant barrier to establishing friendships with and seeking advice from other parents with deaf children. In this matter, it seemed that parents' (lack of) confidence in their ability to speak English was an important limiting factor alongside their actual ability.

Families seeking advice are also hampered by the fact that there has been little research into their specific situation and the needs of migrant-background deaf children, leaving professionals unsure as to which methods or strategies to recommend (Kracht, 2004; Turner & Lynas, 2000). A range of small-scale studies demonstrate both the feasibility and benefits of language maintenance with deaf children from migrant backgrounds (Call, 2005; Thomas *et al.*, 2008; Waltzman *et al.*, 2003). It remains unclear, however, under what circumstances oral or written heritage language maintenance efforts are likely to be successful. Research in deaf education is beginning to tackle the topic of how best to support heritage languages in the classroom (Call, 2005; Gerner de Garcia, 2000), but there appears to be no empirical research evaluating different strategies for promoting language maintenance with deaf children in the home. Families and professionals can also experience dissonance if the family does not have the English proficiency to be able to act on advice the professional firmly believes is in the best interest of the deaf child. This includes advice that the family should use English as the sole method of communication with the deaf child or that the family should learn to sign (which normally requires attending courses taught through written English and mime by deaf adults) and may cause a rupture in the relationship between professionals and the family if a compromise cannot be reached (cf. Ahmad *et al.*, 1998).

Given the potential obstacles migrant-background families face in establishing successful communication with their deaf children, there is a clear need for more research exploring the advice families receive and the communication approaches they end up deciding on. In this chapter, I focus on three related questions:

(1) What language(s) are professionals recommending families use with their deaf children?
(2) To what extent do professionals take families' language ecology into account in making their recommendations?
(3) How do families deal with this advice (e.g. accept, reject, seek alternative opinions)?

Context

This chapter is based on research from a wider study on the situations and needs of deaf people from migrant backgrounds living in the Australian state of Victoria (Willoughby, 2008), which was funded by the Victorian Deaf Society. Victoria is a state with a sizable migrant population: the 2011 Australian census shows 26% of Victorians were born overseas and 23% speak a language other than English at home. Research conducted as part of the wider study shows similar trends are also evident in the state's school-aged deaf population: in 2006, 19% of students attending the state's deaf facilities came from a family that spoke a heritage language at home[1] and 28% had at least one parent born overseas (Willoughby, 2008). Families spoke 44 different heritage languages and, of those languages, Arabic (27 families) was the only one spoken by more than 10 families.

Scholars sometimes use the term 'superdiversity' to describe the increasing heterogeneity seen in migrant populations in terms of origins, migration histories, language repertoires and socio-economic status (Blommaert, 2010; Vertovec, 2007) and this term is apt for describing the situation confronting deafness service providers in Victoria. While providers in less diverse contexts often respond to the needs of large migrant groups by employing bilingual caseworkers or translating written materials (cf. Ahmad et al., 1998), these strategies are not widely used by deafness service providers in Victoria. However, the government does provide limited funding for interpreters to attend meetings with service providers where families have limited English skills. This is the main way in which communication is facilitated among families with very low level English skills, but due to funding limits, families with intermediate skills or higher are often left to muddle through appointments as best they can.

Methodology

Data for this chapter come from interviews with seven migrant-background families with a primary school-aged deaf child. The project hoped to interview a wide variety of parents and deaf adults from migrant backgrounds, as well as service providers. While it was relatively successful in recruiting the last group, only eight parents and three deaf adults responded to calls for participants issued through multiple channels in the six months available for data collection. Of the parents, six had children at one particular primary school with a deaf facility, one had a child in a mainstream school, and the eighth was excluded from this study as her experience as the mother of a deaf child now in his twenties with multiple physical and intellectual disabilities was qualitatively different from those of other participants (interested readers can explore her story in the project report: Willoughby, 2008). The deaf facility that the majority of the participants attended had favoured oral communication in the past but now also supports students who use manual communication methods (including Australian sign language). Since Victorian families are free to choose which deaf facility/school their child attends (with many commuting long distances to attend a school that best matches their communication approach), the high proportion of participants from this particular school likely creates a bias towards families who support an oral approach. It should thus not be seen as representative of all migrant-background families in Victoria.

Despite efforts to advertise the project in multiple languages, all the parents who responded positively to the call for participants did so in English and all declined an interpreter for the interview. Interviews were conducted in participants' homes and typically lasted around an hour. They sought to gather a case history of the family's experiences, including when and how the child's deafness was diagnosed, the communication methods the family has used over the years, how they chose a school for their deaf child, and their frustrations and triumphs in managing their child's deafness. Due to resource constraints on the project and concerns about making participants uncomfortable, the interviews were not recorded. However, extensive notes were taken during and immediately after the interview.

Each family in this study had at least one parent born overseas and all parents were fluent speakers of a language other than English. Parents varied substantially in their English proficiency: Families V, S and I spoke virtually no English before their migration to Australia as adults, while families B, M, N and Z had all had extensive education in English and mothers B and N had worked as English-speaking professionals prior to their migration to Australia. The families also showed quite varied migration histories: in families B, M, N and Z at least one parent was Australian born or migrated as a child/young adult; the parents in families I and S left Eritrea as refugees around the time they started their own families; and families B and V migrated to Australia specifically to access better medical care and support services once their child's hearing loss was diagnosed. Table 9.1 gives more detailed information about the families' backgrounds and the nature of the children's hearing loss.

Results

Families in the sample had different pathways to early intervention services depending on where and when their child's hearing loss was detected. For three families – B, I and Z – the initial diagnosis came through the local children's hospital and resulted in referrals to oralist service providers who advocate the auditory-verbal method discussed in the introduction. Families B and Z were referred to the same provider in Melbourne, while family I was living in Perth at the time and was referred to a local provider. In the cases of B and Z, the hospital also recommended cochlear implantation and both were implanted shortly after diagnosis. In all three cases, parents seem to have received little to no advice that there were other service provider options

Table 9.1 Overview of participants

Family	Ethnic background	Parents' knowledge of English	Child's hearing loss	Amplification device(s) used	Initial language of communication with the deaf child
B	Lao (mother) Australian (father)	Educated in English L1	Congenital; severe-profound; diagnosed at 8 months	Unilateral cochlear implant and hearing aid	English[a]
I	Eritrean	None before migration	Congenital; severe-profound; diagnosed at 8 months	Bilateral hearing aids	English
M	Lebanese	Some schooling in Australia	Congenital; moderate-severe; diagnosed at 6 months	Bilateral hearing aids	Arabic[b]
N	Lebanese	M: Tertiary education in English F: Some schooling in Australia	Congenital; severe-profound; diagnosed at 6 months	Unilateral cochlear implant and hearing aid	English
S	Eritrean	None before migration	Acquired (severe infection at 18 months); moderate-severe; diagnosed at 2 years	Bilateral hearing aids	Arabic
V	Croatian	None before migration	Congenital; profound; diagnosed at 6 months	Unilateral cochlear implant and hearing aid	Croatian[b]
Z	Italian	M: Tertiary education in English F: Some schooling in Australia	Congenital; profound; diagnosed at 2 years	Unilateral cochlear implant and hearing aid	English

Notes: [a]This family has since switched to using a mixture of English and Lao at home, with the mother inspired to introduce Lao after her daughter showed strong progress learning English.
[b]This family has since switched to using a mix of the heritage language and English with their deaf child.

available to them, or that the decision to use speech instead of sign language with a deaf child was in any way controversial. In the case of families B and Z, the parents themselves were strongly committed to using oral language with their deaf child, so the advice they received was a good fit with their own position. It is possible that other options were in fact mentioned briefly but have since been forgotten as they were quickly ruled out at the time.

These families reported that the hospital staff and oralist providers they dealt with gave them strong advice that they must speak only English with their deaf child. Such advice appears common in oralist programmes internationally (Waltzman *et al.*, 2003), and is generally accompanied by the claim that doing otherwise would confuse the deaf child and undermine their chance of acquiring any oral language through the programme. In families B and Z all the parents are bilinguals fluent in English, and thus were able to switch to English without too much difficulty. However, it should be noted that the advice did cause a major disruption to the language ecology of family Z, as up to then the parents and two older children had used Italian as their home language. For family I, however, this advice proved extremely problematic and has had far-reaching consequences. Mrs I arrived in Australia as a refugee with her four-month-old deaf son (who is the eldest child) and was joined by Mr I two years later. The son's hearing loss was diagnosed at eight months of age, at a point where Mrs I had just begun to learn English. She thus found the injunction to speak nothing but English with her deaf son extremely difficult, but believed the professionals had to know best. She did her best to comply, but interpreted the advice as meaning it was more harmful to interact with her son in Arabic than to say nothing at all. Unfortunately, this led to her son receiving limited language input as a small child and may have contributed to his marked language delay by the time of the interview (aged 12).

Once Mr and Mrs I were reunited, they continued speaking Arabic with each other and only used English at home to address their deaf son directly. This pattern of using Arabic for all interactions except those directly involving the deaf son continues with their three younger children and has resulted in a situation where the deaf child is excluded from most family communication. Moreover, as the parents feel weaknesses in their own English ability, this means that the family lacks a common language in which deep and meaningful communication is possible. Of course, many families fluent in English also report that they are not able to communicate well with deaf children they have raised orally (cf. Gregory *et al.*, 1995), and even within the current study family Z reports similar problems despite all speaking English at home. However, the problematic language situation in family I has likely exacerbated these issues and Mrs I views it as the principal cause of her son's language delay. At various points in the interview, Mrs I compared her son to the deaf children of various family friends who continued to speak the heritage language at home, always concluding that her son had a greater language delay than the other children. In telling these stories, she never speculated that different levels/types of hearing loss might be at play, but simply concluded that she had ruined her son's chances by not speaking Arabic with him. This thus adds a complex level of guilt and remorse to an already difficult communicative situation.

In some respects, family M had a similar experience to family I, albeit with a more positive resolution. Unlike the families mentioned above, family M were referred to an early intervention service which advocates the use of Auslan (Australian Sign Language). For a range of reasons (including feelings of shame and a difficulty in accepting her son's deafness), Mrs M reported that she was 'dead against' signing with her deaf son. Devout Muslims, her family see knowledge of Arabic as crucial, and this is the language the parents elected to use with their deaf son and his younger hearing brother. This is a decision that the service provider largely accepted: while Mrs M reported that the early intervention workers would gently point out the advantages of signing with her son, they were also prepared to work with the family on their own terms and provide advice about play learning and other activities to bolster the deaf child's acquisition of Arabic and English and his cognitive development. The compromise has also not been entirely one-sided: Mrs M has developed a much more positive view of sign languages, and while she does not currently sign with her son she works quite proactively to promote this early intervention service to parents with deaf children in the Islamic community.

Only two families, N and S, reported that their referral process introduced them to both signing and oralist early intervention services who worked proactively with the family to find the best fit for their particular needs and circumstances. In both cases, the families were referred after diagnosis to an intermediary service, the Victorian Department of Human Services Parent Advisor for Hearing Impaired Children for their region. At the time, referral to the parent advisor service was only available to families living in designated areas of Melbourne and regional Victoria that are geographically distant from the major early intervention services. As a government employee, the parent advisor is bound to promote all services available, as well as to explain to the parents the different approaches taken by various services. The particular advisor these parents worked with is also bilingual herself and has a strong understanding of the issues and concerns facing families from non-English-speaking backgrounds who are raising deaf children. Through regular visits with these families, she assisted them in deciding on their preferred approach to communication and the best service provider to support their approach. Family N, who decided on English-only and cochlear implantation, were matched with the same provider used by families B and Z, while family S, who decided to keep using oral Arabic after their toddler acquired a post-lingual hearing loss, were matched with the intensive kindergarten/lower primary school run by the provider used by family M for early intervention services. Both families also participated in a

Table 9.2 Deafness service providers

Provider	Services	Families
Oralist	Auditory-verbal therapy, intensive kindergarten	B, Z, N
Oralist	Auditory-verbal therapy, intensive kindergarten	I
Parent advisor	Home visits, intermediary to other services, playgroup	N, S
Signing	Home visits	M
	Intensive kindergarten/junior primary (up to Year 2)	S, V (both stayed to end of first primary year)

small local playgroup for hard of hearing children facilitated by the parent advisor, and built up networks with numerous multilingual families raising deaf children through this service.

Finally, family V followed a different referral process as the deaf son's early childhood was spent in Croatia. When the son's deafness was diagnosed in infancy, his parents began making plans to join the father's parents in Australia under the family reunion scheme in order to access Australia's more developed deafness services. It took some years for this plan to come fruition (due to concerns about the deaf son meeting the health requirement to migrate) and while in Croatia the deaf son received a cochlear implant as a preschooler and attended a kindergarten for deaf children. Since the son already had a cochlear implant, Mrs V's approach on arrival in Australia was to contact Cochlear Inc. and ask them for a referral to the most appropriate service. However, she was anything but passive and took her father-in-law along to appointments with a range of service providers to act as an interpreter and advocate and help her find the right fit. Like Mrs I, Mrs V spoke no English on arrival in Australia, but unlike Mrs I she had family support, a deaf child who had developed some proficiency in the heritage language prior to migration and a healthy dose of self-confidence. She thus dismissed out of hand suggestions that she speak English only with her deaf son and ended up sending her son to the same pre-school to school transition programme as family S.

A summary of the different providers, and the families who use them, is provided in Table 9.2.

Discussion

These seven case studies reveal a number of patterns and issues surrounding language choice in the early years for migrant-background families with deaf children. Most telling is that – at least in the early 2000s when these children were diagnosed – which early intervention services families were referred to was something of a lottery. Referral seemed to have more to do with which agency gave the initial diagnosis or where the family lived rather than all families being made aware of all services from which they might choose. As mentioned in the introduction, this is a particular issue for parents who have more basic English skills and/or are new to Australia, as they will often be the most disadvantaged in trying to investigate for themselves what services are out there or seeking an alternative opinion. Although improving referral pathways for health and social services is a complex area that falls outside the scope of this chapter, the data presented here provide a clear illustration of the challenges facing providers working in superdiverse societies.

The oralist service providers that families in this project had contact with can be characterised as being stuck in the monolingual mindset. Clyne writes that:

> [s]uch a mindset sees everything in terms of monolingualism being the norm ... It views multilingualism as outside the possible experience of 'real Australians' or even in the too hard basket. It is the monolingual mindset that does not understand that developing an individual's language skills in any language benefits their skills in another language. (Clyne, 2005: xi)

The oralist providers appear to be staffed predominantly by monolinguals, and their own experience as monolinguals seems to guide their attitudes and behaviours. Professionals at the signing service, by contrast, all have some experience of bilingualism in Auslan and English (written English only in the case of some deaf staff) and frame their approach in terms of developing bilingualism in written English alongside Auslan (cf. Bartlett & Leane, 2003). This is perhaps the reason why the signing service provider seemed less afflicted with this monolingual mindset and more willing to support families using their heritage language with the deaf child, albeit sometimes with the subtext that they would be better off signing. Families did not give the impression that this provider was an enthusiastic supporter of (oral) multilingualism for deaf children, but nor did the provider show any hostility towards it.

Of the providers, only the parent advisor could be said to have truly transcended the monolingual mindset, and (not coincidentally) she was the only provider who was an oral bilingual herself and took the families' language ecologies into full account in developing communication strategies with the deaf children. The other two providers couched language choice very much in terms of the family doing whatever it took to accommodate to the communicative needs of the deaf child. For the signing service provider, this meant advocating that the family learn and use Auslan: a not unreasonable suggestion, but one that no family took up and that failed to take into account the issues families with low English proficiency (such as S and V) would have in doing so. The oral providers were no less prescriptive in insisting on English only in the home. In cases where the parents were already fluent speakers of English (e.g. B, N, V) this advice was possible, if potentially disruptive. However, family I gives a telling case study of how damaging this thinking can be if they are not.

It is common in the language policy and planning literature to speak of 'unplanned' language planning (Baldauf, 1994) when discussing higher level policy, which fails because it does not consider the language ecology into which it is transplanted. While usually used in reference to government language policy that fails because it does not account for policies or practices that exist at lower levels of organisation (such as in religion, the business world or higher education, cf. Spolsky, 2009), it seems equally applicable in the context of service providers advising families about communication with their deaf children. The need for advice to be tailored to the particular family environment is also a theme taken up in the social services literature, where 'family-centred practice' has been viewed as the benchmark for best practice for many years now (Turner & Lynas, 2000). It should be stressed that family-centred practice is not the same as acquiescing to a family who finds it too much bother to accommodate the needs of their deaf child. Rather it seeks to gain a wide view of the communicative practices in the family, the needs and attitudes of all family members and external factors such as socio-economic position, and to take these factors into account in recommending a course of action. Above all, it recognises that parents will often ignore advice that they find unsuitable, so finding a compromise is likely to lead to better outcomes for the child than insisting on a practice that the parents do not want to commit to.

Family-centred practice is something that providers may achieve to varying degrees. In this study, only Mrs I reported dissatisfaction with the advice she received from her provider. Despite the disruption caused by language shift, family Z were exceedingly enthusiastic about their provider, as were families B, N and S. Families M and V were also keen to stress the many wonderful things about the providers they had interacted with, albeit with the caveat from family M that they got off to a rocky start and from family V that she interviewed a number of providers before settling on the one she found best for her needs.

Conclusion

This short chapter raises a number of issues and challenges for service providers working with an increasingly multilingual population of families with deaf children in Australia, as elsewhere. The case studies presented here reinforce the importance of providers taking the family language ecology into account in making recommendations about communicative practices, but also highlight the gaps in our knowledge and services in following through on this advice. Put simply, there remains a dearth of research or practical strategies for families and providers to refer to if they are interested in maintaining a heritage language with a deaf child, and so it is difficult to know how best to support these families. As mentioned in the literature review, work in this area is emerging, but a more concerted effort is needed if we are serious about meeting the needs of a superdiverse population.

Superdiversity forces deafness service providers to think beyond the monolingual mindset and realise the importance of multiple languages in the deaf child's life. All the parents in this study recognised the benefits of language maintenance in general and in fact only one of the families that started out with English only (family Z) did not attempt to teach the heritage language at some point during the primary school years (see Willoughby, 2012 for more on the families' evolving language practices). International evidence confirms both the feasibility and benefits of language maintenance with deaf children from migrant backgrounds, and particularly the value of developing written proficiency in the heritage language with children who use a sign language rather than speech (Call, 2005; Gerner de Garcia, 2000). While it is clearly important that deaf children living in Australia develop proficiency in written English, this need not be at the expense of proficiency in Auslan or oral or written proficiency in a heritage language. Fundamentally, the challenge for service providers is to assist parents in finding the best language in which they can understand and be understood by their deaf child as – regardless of how widely used that language is in the general population – that will be the most important language for the family and the child's development.

Note

(1) No data are available on how many families use sign language at home.

References

Ahmad, W., Darr, A., Jones, L. and Nisar, G. (1998) *Deafness and Ethnicity: Services Policy and Politics*. Bristol: Policy Press.
Baldauf, R. (1994) 'Unplanned' language policy and planning. In W. Grabe (ed.) *Annual Review of Applied Linguistics*, Vol. 14 (pp. 82–89). Cambridge: Cambridge University Press.
Bartlett, M. and Leane, S. (2003) *Raising Deaf Children Bilingually in Australia*. Melbourne: Research Unit for Multilingualism and Cross-Cultural Communication, University of Melbourne.
Beazley, S. and Moore, M. (1995) *Deaf Children, their Families and Professionals: Dismantling Barriers*. London: David Fulton Publishers.
Blommaert, J. (2010) *The Sociolinguistics Of Globalization*. Cambridge: Cambridge University Press.
Brown, M., Bakra, Z.A., Rickards, F. and Griffin, P. (2006) Family functioning, early intervention support, and spoken language and placement outcomes for children with profound hearing loss. *Deafness and Education International* 8 (4), 207–226.

Butcher, L.S. (1995) *Mother Tongue Literacy Maintenance Among the Children of Recent Chinese Immigrants in Brisbane*. Adelaide: Helios Art & Book Co.
Call, M. (2005) ASL/Spanish/English trilingualism of Hispanic/Latino deaf children in the United States. Unpublished manuscript. See http://www.lifeprint.com/asl101/topics/trilingual.pdf (accessed 24 October 2012).
Clyne, M. (1991) *Community Languages: The Australian Experience*. Cambridge: Cambridge University Press.
Clyne, M. (2005) *Australia's Language Potential*. Sydney: University of New South Wales Press.
Geers, A.E. and Moog, J.S. (1987) Predicting spoken language acquisition in profoundly deaf children. *Journal of Speech and Hearing Disorders* 52, 84–94.
Gerner de Garcia, B. (2000) Meeting the needs of Hispanic/Latino deaf students. In K. Christensen and G. Delgado (eds) *Deaf Plus: A Multicultural Perspective* (pp. 148–198). San Diego: Dawn Sign Press.
Gregory, S., Bishop, J. and Sheldon, L. (1995) *Deaf Young People and their Families: Developing Understanding*. Cambridge: Cambridge University Press.
Knoors, H. (2007) Education responses to varying objectives of parents of deaf children: A Dutch perspective. *Journal of Deaf Studies and Deaf Education* 12 (2), 244–253.
Kracht, A. (2004) Gefährdung und Behinderung mehrsprachiger Entwicklung – Historische und aktuelle Konzeptualisierungen [Threats and obstacles to multilingual development – historical and actual conceptualisations]. In K.-D. Große (ed.) *Hörbehinderte Schülerinnen und Schüler unterschiedlicher nationaler Herkunft: Eine internationale Herausforderung an die Horbehindertenpädagogik [Hearing Impaired Students from Different National Backgrounds: An International Challenge to Deaf Education]* (pp. 55–75). Heidelberg: Universitätsverlag Winter.
Ladd, P. (2003) *Understanding Deaf Culture: In Search of Deafhood*. Clevedon: Multilingual Matters.
Li, Y., Bain, L. and Steinberg, A. (2003) Parental decision making and the choice of communication modality for the child who is deaf. *Archives of Paediatrics and Adolescent Medicine* 157, 162–168.
Meadow-Orlans, K., Mertens, D. and Sass-Lehrer, M. (2003) *Parents and their Deaf Children*. Washington, DC: Gallaudet University Press.
Ozolins, U. (1993) *The Politics of Language in Australia*. Cambridge: Cambridge University Press.
Skutnabb-Kangas, T. (2000) *Linguistic Genocide in Education, or Worldwide Diversity and Human Rights?* Mahwah: Lawrence Erlbaum.
Spolsky, B. (2009) *Language Management*. Cambridge: Cambridge University Press.
Steinberg, A., Delgado, G., Li, Y., Bain, L. and Ruperto, V. (2003) Decisions Hispanic families make after the identification of deafness. *Journal of Deaf Studies and Deaf Education* 8 (3), 291–314.
Thomas, E., El-Kashlan, H. and Zwolan, T. (2008) Children with cochlear implants who live in monolingual and bilingual homes. *Otology and Neurotology* 29, 230–234.
Turner, S. and Lynas, W. (2000) Teachers' perspectives on support for under-fives in families of ethnic minority origin. *Deafness and Education International* 2 (3), 152–164.
Vertovec, S. (2007) Super-diversity and its implications. *Ethnic and Racial Studies* 30 (6), 1024–1054.
Waltzman, S., Robbins, A.M., Green, J. and Cohen, N. (2003) Second oral language capabilities in children with cochlear implants. *Otology and Neurotology* 24, 757–763.
Willoughby, L. (2008) *Catering to a Diverse Community: The Situation and Needs of Deaf People from Migrant Backgrounds Living in Victoria*. Melbourne: Victorian Multicultural Commission and the Victorian Deaf Society.
Willoughby, L. (2012) Language maintenance and the deaf child. *Journal of Multicultural and Multilingual Development* 33 (6), 605–618.

Part 3

Language Policy and Education as Tools for Change in Australia

10 Losing Bilingualism While Promoting Second Language Acquisition in Australian Language Policy

Howard Nicholas

Introduction

Australian language policy development workers, such as Michael Clyne and many others, can be rightly lauded for what they have achieved in the process of shifting Australia from the racist exclusion of diversity that lasted well into the 20th century to a much more inclusive approach that began to be realised in the late 1970s and 1980s. One of the key achievements has been a series of documents that outline diverse and coordinated principles and programmes for language-related action. However, the points of silence and ambiguity in these documents are also instructive. In this chapter I explore one of those areas of silence (or at least an area where various groups have spoken quietly) – the issue of an all-embracing societal multilingualism – one in which the different bilingualisms of individuals and groups are supported to increase the societal capacity to build on and deploy multilingualism. I show how the idea of bilingualism in early versions of the *National Policy on Languages* (Lo Bianco, 1987) was other than it appeared. I argue that it became overwhelmed by fragmentary endeavours to promote second language learning for the presumed monolingual, English-speaking majority at the expense of a more comprehensive approach that would also take advantage of the existing or incipient bilingualism of community members with home or family access to other languages.

Steps in Australia's Recent Language Policy Formation

Australia's language policy framework has had a long history with many players (e.g. Australian Teachers' Federation, 1982; Clyne, 1982, 1991a, 1991b; Commonwealth Department of Education, 1982; Commonwealth Education Portfolio, 1979;[1] Ethnic Communities Council of Queensland, 1982; Federation of Ethnic Communities' Councils of Australia, 1982; Ingram, 1979, 1980; Lo Bianco, 1987; New South Wales Conference on National Language Policy, 1982; Ozolins, 1993). It would not have come about at all if academics, selected politicians and community activists in the early 1980s had not built on work in the 1970s to persuade the, then, conservative coalition Federal Government to support an enquiry into such a policy.[2] The work in the 1970s included consideration of the role of 'migrant' languages in schools (Department of Education (Australia), 1976), more comprehensive support of migrants and views of languages that could be included in the curriculum (Review of Post Arrival Programs and Services to Migrants, 1978; see also the discussions in Lopez, 2000; Jupp, 2002), and supportive social frameworks such as multiculturalism (Australian Ethnic Affairs Council, 1977).

The Senate Enquiry report (Senate Select Committee on Education and the Arts, 1984), which was tabled in 1984 but not released until February 1985, was the result of work that commenced officially in May 1982 in response to a proposal from Senator Baden Teague that the Senate Standing Committee on Education and the Arts conduct an enquiry into the development and implementation of a coordinated language policy for Australia (Australian Senate, 1982a). While the terms of reference were written by Senator Baden Teague, a key shaping influence on the resulting report was the work done by a coalition of academics and community activists. The collaboration between academics and community members – with the extensive and intensive involvement in both directions – was a consistent feature of the way in which Michael Clyne, in particular, worked (Gorter, 2011). The thinking of the academics is recorded in the report of the PLANLangPol Committee (1983) in their publication, *A National Language Policy for Australia*. This committee represented six of the major professional language associations in Australia at the time.[3] In the publication are recorded suggested policy positions on a set of language issues ranging from English, Aboriginal and community languages as both first and second languages to the role of linguistic theory in language policy, translating and interpreting, research and a National Languages Institute.

The contribution of the Ethnic Communities Councils of Australia is not recorded in the PLANLangPol document, but is reflected in the 1984 Senate Enquiry report (Senate Select Committee on Education and the Arts, 1984) and in a series of reports from the various conferences that were held, among them: Ethnic Communities Council of Queensland (1982), New South Wales Conference on National Language Policy (1982), and the Federation of Ethnic Communities' Councils of Australia (1982). The various memberships of the PLANLangPol community and in particular Michael Clyne were, again, a key link in this collaboration. Nevertheless, some key informing ideas were not translated into effective policy and it is instructive to understand the shaping of the various iterations of what is erroneously called Australian language 'policy'.

Distinguishing Policy from Programme

Meehan (1985: 307) defines 'a policy as an action program intended to reify a priority structure'. The priority structure is the set of informing values that the policy attempts to translate into some kind of action. Surprisingly, Meehan's is one of the few attempts to provide a formal academic definition of 'policy' with testable criteria that can be subject to independent analysis. One of Meehan's purposes was to enable people to distinguish between action programmes and policies. In making this distinction, the key term is 'priority structure'. The priority structure is the set of values that frames the text and shapes the nature of the action. In the absence of an explicit and agreed (or in other contexts 'imposed') 'priority structure', all that is left is a vulnerable action programme – not a policy.

Spolsky and Shohamy underline an additional key issue in policy development, that of legitimate authority. They describe language policy as

> an official statement, usually but not necessarily contained in a formal document, about language use. More specifically we will restrict it to cases where the maker of the policy has some form of authority over the person expected to follow it. (Spolsky & Shohamy, 2000: 2)

They distinguish 'policy' from 'practice' (what is habitually done) and 'ideology' (what is believed) (Spolsky & Shohamy, 2000: 2). Spolsky (2012: 8) reshapes this distinction when he uses 'language policy' to encompass the three elements of: (1) a community's language practices; (2) the values assigned to particular language varieties; and (3) management, the attempts by those with authority to achieve change in the language practices of others. This definition coincides with Meehan's notion of 'action program'. It includes some aspects of 'priority structure' when considering 'values', but adds the notion of line of authority. Meehan's definition is particularly useful in that it sets criteria for asking how a particular line of action may be made enduring through establishing agreement on the key values (the priority structure) that inform the plan as a whole. Coupled with Spolsky's point about lines of authority, it becomes easier to see why what was labelled a 'policy' became no more than a series of action plans.

What emerged in Australia in the 1980s is not a 'policy' because the real 'values' that it reflects are not consistent and, no matter how logical and desirable the content of many of the documents, the actual documents that were produced neither enacted a consistent set of values that could unify the various propositions nor reflected a traceable line of 'authority'.[4] The key 'priority structure' that needed to be agreed on was the idea of universal (and varied) bilingualism (see below). The lack of a line of authority reflects Australia's federal structure, where the Commonwealth has control of (among other things) taxation, while states and territories have responsibility for other areas such as education. Thus, the only authority over school education that the Commonwealth had at the time was offering financial incentives for states/territories to adopt particular initiatives. Curriculum content at the time was the exclusive responsibility of states and territories.

Bilingualism and Second Language Learning in Australia's Language Education Programmes

The presentation of a series of action programmes as policy is one of the features of 'language policy' development in Australia. Below I make the case that the required key 'priority structure' of a diverse societal multilingualism based on multiple individual bilingualisms ended up being silenced, perhaps even before it had been fully articulated. The fragile state of consensus surrounding this required priority structure was alluded to in the comments of the then Commonwealth Minister for Education, Senator Peter Baume (Australian Senate, 1982b: 2652): '[t]o the extent that we can help to establish within the national mind the desirability of pursuing a community more competent in languages, we are anxious to do so'. One reason for this fragility is explicitly named in the 1982 submission from the then Commonwealth Department of Education and Youth Affairs (1983: 3) that was published a year later: 'language policy...will not...aim to make Australians bi or multilingual against their will'.

Nevertheless, individual and societal bilingualism was a motivating 'priority structure' for many of the stakeholders who campaigned over many years for the creation of a coordinated language policy. Milne (1982: 4) identified the call for '[t]he opportunity for all Australians to achieve competence in more than one language'. This potential 'priority structure' of individual and societal bilingualism was progressively written out of subsequent documents so that what remained was subject to the variable programme priorities of changing ministers and governments over time (see, for example, Dawkins, 1990).

As a result, it was possible for Hansard (the official record of parliamentary debate in Australia) to record the following exchange:

5th June, 1989 (Australian Senate, 1989b: 3381)
Senator Walsh – On 4 May 1989 (Hansard, page 1797), Senator Jenkins asked me a question without notice concerning the national policy on languages, inter alia:

(a) Is it correct that funding for the implementation of the national language policy is due to run out on June 30 1990?
(b) Can the Minister inform the Senate as to the amount of funds proposed at this stage to be allocated to the implementation of the National Language Policy in the financial year 1989–1990?
(c) What is the intention of the Government with regard to further funding of the implementation of the Policy after 1990? Will funding be maintained, increased, decreased or cut out?
(d) Are funds for the implementation of the national language policy intended to cover the funding of specialist training courses for interpreters and translators?
(e) If National Language Policy implementation funds are allocated for the funding of such courses, can the Minister explain why specialist courses for interpreters and translators conducted by Perth Technical College are not funded from this source but are funded instead from mainstream technical education sources?

The Minister for Employment, Education and Training has provided the following answer to the honourable senator's question:

(a) No.
(b) The amount will be announced in the 1989 budget context.
(c) Funding will continue for 1990–1991. The amount will be announced in the 1990 budget context.
(d) No.
(e) See (d) above.

These responses are much more indicative of a 'programme' frame than a 'policy' frame because of the silences surrounding the values that shape the programme. They reflect a consciousness of the recency of the shift away from the programme of making Australia white that had Alfred Deakin (subsequently Australia's second Prime Minister, who served in the same role a further two times), seeking in his campaign for the first Australian parliament 'a White Australia, in which the absolute mastering and dominating element shall be British' (Jupp, 2002: 11).

In a context only some 10 years after the lifting of race-based immigration restrictions in 1973 that led to the formal ending of the White Australia Policy, it is encouraging that the official submission of the Commonwealth Department of Education and Youth Affairs (1983: S2364) focused on English, first language maintenance, educational opportunity for migrant children and intercultural understanding, specifically:

- for all Australians to have competence in English;
- for all Australians to have the opportunity to have their native language maintained and developed;
- that children whose mother tongue is not English should not be disadvantaged in their overall learning experiences;
- for all Australians to have an appreciation of the cultural and linguistic diversity of Australia.

Given its source, it is perhaps somewhat surprising that this focus was not maintained in subsequent 'policy' documents. In place of the departmental advice (detailed above), the Senate Enquiry acknowledged (Senate Select Committee on Education and the Arts, 1984: 3) the principles included in the submission from the Federation of Ethnic Community Councils in their four pillars:

- competence in English;
- maintenance and development of languages other than English;
- provision of services in languages other than English;
- opportunities for learning second languages.

Placing 'Competence in English' first meant that there was a clear focus on a common means of communication and conformity with the perception of English as the shared language. Referring to 'languages other than English' both reflected the preferred terminology of the Commonwealth Department of Education and Youth Affairs (in contrast to the term suggested in the 1978 Galbally Report on *Migrant Services and Programs* of 'community languages') and also avoided advocating any particular (set of) language(s) to complement English. In using this term, the Federation of Ethnic Communities' Councils intended that Aboriginal and Torres Strait Islander languages were to be embraced, but also made distinctive (Milne, 1982). Nevertheless, Aboriginal and Torres Strait Islander languages were not distinctively identified in the Federation documents (Federation of Ethnic Communities' Councils, 1982). Notable in the separated framing used by the Senate Committee are two things. First, given the origin of the proposal from the Federation of Ethnic Community Councils, the lack of explicit mention of Aboriginal and Torres Strait Islander languages left room for perceptions of exclusion that were reinforced by the actions and words of some participants in the process (see Fesl, 1982).

Second, command of English and command of another language are presented as two distinct achievements. There is no explicit reference in these pillars to a notion of bi- or multilingualism and hence to potential or real relationships between command of one language and command of other languages. This separation can also be found in the PLANLangPol (1983) document, despite the advocacy of bilingual education for all children (PLANLangPol Committee, 1983: 76). This sense of separation is reinforced in the Federation's fourth pillar that focuses only on the development of 'second' languages. The most likely reading of the fourth pillar is the teaching of languages other than English to learners who do not already speak those languages – by default, learners from homes where English is the heritage language. As will be seen below, it is this reading that came to dominate language programme initiatives in Australia. Grosjean (1985) refers to this view of bilingualism as 'fractional' in that it projects a view of bilingualism as made up of two separate languages, each viewed from a monolingual perspective.

The Senate Standing Committee (Senate Select Committee on Education and the Arts, 1984: 4) endorsed word for word the principles originally proposed by the Federation of Ethnic Communities' Councils and, in so doing, perpetuated an implicit division between the learning of specific languages by specific people and any overall goal for those learning activities. It is particularly notable in this context that whereas a goal of 'Competence in English' was mandated, the Committee weakened the driving motivation of both the Federation and PLANLangPol and only mandated 'Opportunities' for second languages – in the context, languages other than English.

In the PLANLangPol document there is no explicit frame such as the Federation's principles. Societal bi- or multilingualism emerges only late in the document. It is first mentioned in relation to Australia being 'in a favourable position to pioneer programmes in bilingual education' (PLANLangPol, 1983: 76), but is later (PLANLangPol, 1983: 115–117) framed as one of a number of 'Controversial issues':

> ... if bilingualism is seen as the exclusive province of children from an ethnic background, ... bilingualism may well be seen as an unfortunate malady of the socially disadvantaged. In this sense, efforts to achieve bilingualism for any group will succeed only to the extent that bilingualism is perceived as desirable for all groups. (PLANLangPol, 1983: 116)

While the position presented is clearly supportive of societal bilingualism, its framing as a controversial issue prevents it from operating as a shaping value for the policy as a whole. The nature and the positioning of framing militates against the very position that both the community and the academic activists sought to have established. Separation of the needs of different groups with different means for addressing the separated needs became a mechanism through which universal societal bilingualism was marginalised. Engagement with more than one language was promoted, but only for some – either what might be termed the particularly 'needy' or the particularly 'able'.

One group of 'needy' learners is those for whom English is a new language. For this group, 'transitional bilingual programs' were endorsed by the Senate Enquiry (Senate Select Committee on Education and the Arts, 1984: 58). But the very framing of this endorsement again marginalises the languages other than English. A transitional programme, by definition, keeps the role of the language other than English temporary. However, for Aboriginal communities, 'maintenance bilingual programs' were recommended (Senate Select Committee on Education and the Arts, 1984: 88). When other languages were involved, the Committee only tentatively endorsed the expansion of bilingual education (Senate Select Committee on Education and the Arts, 1984: 144). That this was a 'choice' can be seen in the various recommendations to the Committee for 'the development of bilingual capacity amongst all Australians' (Australian Teachers' Federation, 1982: 4) that was accompanied by a recommendation for 'the establishment of widespread capacity in community languages'.

Following a change of Federal Government in 1983 and significant lobbying, the subsequent *National Policy on Languages* (Lo Bianco, 1987) was required to bring the issues promoted by the 1984 Senate Report into some form of action. In the 1987 document, the informing principles were identified apparently more strongly as:

- Access to services and information by Australians who do not speak English or who are disabled in ways which involve language ...
- Bilingualism will be promoted as a positive value to individuals and society. ...
- No Australian resident ought to be denied access to ... [services, information or representation] ... because of language disabilities, or lack of adequate, or any, competence in English. (Lo Bianco, 1987: 8)

The wording of the second principle appears to be consistent with universal societal bilingualism, but the focus on 'promoting as a positive value' is eerily reminiscent of the framing of the 1982 Commonwealth Department of Education and Youth Affairs submission to the Senate Enquiry referred to above. The framing is still one of persuasion and the 'policy' lacks the authority to enact what evidence both then and now (Garcia, 2008; Peal & Lambert, 1962) would have clearly identified as a universal good. Lo Bianco's (1987) informing principles were translated into four policy-specific strategies that also appear consistent with societal bilingualism (Lo Bianco, 1987: 70):

- the conservation of Australia's linguistic resources;
- the development and expansion of these resources;

- the integration of Australian language teaching and language use efforts with national economic, social and cultural policies;
- the provision of information and services in languages understood by clients.

The first two of these principles, if tightly and consistently linked, would combine to support the development of societal bilingualism. This seems to be the intention since, in language teaching terms, these principles became 'English for all' (Lo Bianco, 1987: 78ff) and 'A language other than English (LOTE) for all' (Lo Bianco, 1987: 120ff). Both the section on English and the section on LOTE identified both 'first' and 'second' language learning issues – and the need for care in relating them. Relationships between these different programmes and groups of learners were laid out in a table (Lo Bianco, 1987: 143). Nevertheless, and illustrative of the difference between a 'policy' and a 'program' position, the actual budget allocation identified to support this apparent balance was labelled the 'Australian Second Language Learning Program' (ASLLP) (Lo Bianco, 1987: 138). The learning of English was distinguished from the general 'second language learning program' and supported by an 'English Language Learning Project' (ELLP) (Lo Bianco, 1987: 101ff).

The silence that emerges in this way of enacting action is in supporting languages other than English (whether Indigenous or migrant) as first languages.

In all the policy documents, there is a consistent theme of division between English and other languages. There is variation in the role given to the languages of the indigenous Aboriginal and Torres Strait Islander peoples (and in particular in setting up relationships to/differences from non-indigenous languages other than English). The enormous ideological struggle behind the positioning of languages other than English can perhaps be seen in the following exchange recorded in Hansard:

4th December 1986 (Australian Senate, 1986: 3374)

Senator TEAGUE – My question is directed to the Minister for Education. When will the Government respond to the report of the Senate Standing Committee on Education and the Arts entitled 'Towards A National Language Policy', which was completed three years ago and which Ministers have already broadly commended? Why did the Minister fail to respond by May and then by November, as she had promised both in her then urgent interim statement last February and in her statements in August relating to Mr Lo Bianco's appointment as the Government's special consultant to help complete the Government's response? Has Mr Lo Bianco's term of appointment been extended? Finally, does not this failure concerning national language policy further compound the Government's decisions to cut out teaching resources for English as a second language, abolish the multicultural education grants of the Schools Commission, amalgamate the Special Broadcasting Service with the Australian Broadcasting Corporation, abolish the Institute of Multicultural Affairs and restrict government support for ethnic schools?

Senator RYAN – None of those things. Senator Teague is obviously getting himself in shape to do a bit of grandstanding at the Federation of Ethnic Communities Councils of Australia conference. But the answer to most of those questions is no. The reason why the national language policy has been a long time coming is that we have carried out our commitment to have very extensive consultation. Senator Teague probably knows, as he has taken an interest in this matter, that Mr Lo Bianco has travelled widely around Australia, consulting education authorities, ethnic groups, teachers, teacher training institutions and the like, to ensure that the policy, when it emerges, will be as comprehensive as possible.

The complexity of the relationships between hopes and realities can be seen in Lo Bianco (1987: 120) where, following extended elaboration of the complex and multiple roles of languages in the lives of people in Australia:

> [t]his policy explicitly declares that the study of at least one language in addition to English ought to be an expected part of the educational experience of all Australian students, ideally continuously throughout the years of compulsory education. In addition, the policy advocates strongly that all educational planners embrace this objective and aim for students in every Australian school to be offered soundly-based, continuous and serious programs for learning a second language.

The words express desires and hopes rather than values that are being enacted. The further move in this extract from a position advocating the complexity of multiple kinds of bilingualism involving English and another language as variably first or second languages (i.e. bilingualism for all) to a programme that promotes languages other than English as 'second' languages signals the same policy positioning as is evident in the 1984 Senate Committee report. In this context, the programme names exclude particular learners – children from homes where (some variety in relation to) a language other than English is being used. They do not need to learn that language as a 'second' language. The frame of the policy, and the terms we use, reflect the policy values that inform programme design and funding practices.

Being clear and consistent about these terms and values is a task for researchers and academics. Second language acquisition only makes sense in relation to bilingualism, but it is only one half of the emergence of bilingualism. The other half is the development of a first language. It is the second part that became lost.

There are no clear boundaries between bilingualism and second language acquisition. Different investigators have set different criteria (e.g. Bialystok, 2001; Grosjean, 1989; Romaine, 1995).

> The transition from second-language learner to bilingual is likely continuous rather than categorical, but most investigators agree that some description of the relative level of language proficiency is important in interpreting potential effects of bilingualism. (Bialystok *et al.*, 2005: 581)

While Bialystok *et al.* (2005) describe bilingualism as being at the more competent end of deploying two (or more) languages, this definition does not engage with the long history of seeing bilingualism as a much more flexible category commencing with the production of the first meaningful utterance in an additional language (Haugen, 1953: 7), or perhaps even earlier with Diebold's (1961) notion of incipient bilingualism – comprehension without requiring production. These approaches suggest that bilingualism is not so simply to be distinguished from lesser proficiency. Indeed, such a separation would be surprising given the long tradition of exploration of the fragile nature of bilingualism (Chafe, 1962; Fishman, 1966; Weinreich, 1953).

A further confounding issue is the unresolved relationship between bilingualism and multilingualism whereby bilingualism is more readily connected with the behaviour of individuals and multilingualism with features of societies (see Baker, 2011; Clyne, 2005; Grosjean, 2010). This distinction leads to problems since it offers a convenient way for policy makers to promote a country such as Australia as multilingual while overlooking the needs of (emerging) bilingual individuals. Interpreting the distinction between bilingualism and multilingualism as being between individuals and the wider society implies that bilingualism for all is not a value that the action programme is designed to promote. The logic is that if there are lots of languages in the society then the society is already 'multilingual' and therefore action to widen the bilingualism of individuals is not a priority.

A state-based example of the disappearance of bilingualism

Understanding these tensions enables other relevant documents to be understood more clearly in the Australian context. As an example, I will look at language programme innovations in Victoria, the Australian state with the most extensive and sustained commitment to the inclusion of languages and bilingual education in the normal curriculum experience of schools – and in the context of exploring 'policy' – a place where the lines of authority are clear since states have responsibility for education (even if they also need money sourced from Commonwealth Federal taxes to achieve their goals).

From the early 1980s, a series of documents appeared in Victoria that sought to identify a sustainable curriculum position consistent with multilingualism. The Victorian 'Ministerial Paper 6: Curriculum Development and Planning' (Minister for Education (Victoria), 1984) charged each school council to develop programmes that enabled students to:

- Listen and talk appropriately in a variety of situations and to read and write effectively in standard English as it is used in Australia;
- Acquire proficiency in another language used in the Australian community (Minister for Education, 1984: 17).

This view clearly frames an ideology of bilingualism. But the word is not used in these statements of objectives. It is possible that the meaning was meant to come through earlier (Minister for Education, 1984: 16), but there 'bilingual' refers only to students who already speak a language other than English:

> While the main medium of instruction will be English, whenever possible the Education Department will assist schools in developing resources and strategies for bilingual programs to enable students who speak another language to continue using that language for some learning in other subjects.

These conjunctions and slippages indicate that there is not a shared ideology linking 'bilingual', 'first' and 'second' language development and that the distinction between English and other languages compounds the difficulties. This confusion mirrors confusion in the research literature about the relationship between the terms 'second language acquisition' and 'bilingualism'.

It is this space that academics and researchers need to occupy with clear and explicit statements about how the various elements relate to the whole. Despite the dangers of simplifying necessarily complex academic issues, if we don't step in with clear statements, we end up with exactly the policy outcomes that we are seeking to avoid. One example of such an outcome can be seen in the visual representation below of the 2011 statement on the teaching of languages other than English in Victorian schools, *The Victorian Government's Vision for Languages Education*. The image has been generated using Wordle, which creates 'word clouds' out of analysed texts, making more frequently appearing words larger in size. While many of the goals in the document are laudable, the Wordle image at Figure 10.1 reveals that 'bilingual' or 'bilingualism' as terms are infrequent to the point of invisibility in the document.

Figure 10.1 Wordle image of *The Victorian Government's Vision for Languages Education* (DEECD, 2011)

Conclusion

The relationship between attempts to expand the teaching of languages and attempts to promote a view of bilingualism is thought to be a key feature of attempts to develop language policy in Australia, but this representation makes clear that notions of individual or societal bilingualism have been progressively written out of various documents that lay claim to the status of policy. With lack of clarity about values, we will continue to have varied and differently targeted action programmes such as the 'Australia's language' (Department of Employment, Education and Training, 1991) or the 'Asian languages and Australia's economic future' (Rudd, 1994) or the 'Australia in the Asian century' (Australian Government, 2012) programmes, but no policy that develops a coherent and consistent vision of an ultimate goal, even if the documents that are produced to describe the programmes are labelled 'policy' documents.

If societal bilingualism is in fact a desirable goal for Australia, as Clyne (2005) and others argue, language experts, educationists and politicians will need to reach agreement that:

(a) bilingualism for each individual is a shared and desirable long-term goal;
(b) it will be in Australia's interests for different people to be bilingual in different languages;

(c) a necessary step in this direction will be building language education programmes for as many languages as possible among those that are brought to the educational system by learners;
(d) competence in English and competence in another language are complementary skills no matter which languages are involved and for all learners.

The steps outlined above are not easy. Neither are they achievable in the short term. They require the consistent and steady widening of Australia's language base. The work in the 1970s and 1980s occupied a minimum of a decade. Given that even that amount of work did not achieve the consensus that was required, we would anticipate that we will need at least that amount of time to take the next step of building consensus around the required priority structure. Agreement on this priority structure will address the counter-productive competition inherent in attempting to select the few 'best' languages that various programmes have proposed should be taught to all students. This priority structure will provide a basis for Australia's engagement with the world as a whole and for educational provision that will be organised around making the educational experience of all learners a wholistic experience of bilingualism. It will acknowledge as equally important the consistent provision of high-quality first and second language learning experiences – no matter what languages are involved, which is the key feature of making individual bilingualism and societal multilingualism the central informing priority structure of language policy.

Notes

(1) The study group responsible for the discussion paper noted that the major political parties had embraced cultural and linguistic diversity even earlier, the Liberal/National Country Party coalition in 1975 and the Labor Party in 1977, the latter having abolished the White Australia Policy in 1973. Macklin (1987) notes that the Australian Democrats had campaigned for a national language policy in 1977.
(2) The presentation by the then Minister for Immigration and Ethnic Affairs to the October 1982 National Language Policy Conference asking whether there was a greater need for a language policy than for a 'national music policy' (Hodge, 1982: 89) provides some insight into the tensions surrounding the issues.
(3) The Applied Linguistics Association of Australia, the Australian Linguistic Society, the Aboriginal Languages Association, the Australian Association for the Teaching of English, the Australian Federation of Modern Language Teachers' Associations and the Australasian Universities Languages and Literatures Association.
(4) Given the more recent agreement of Australian states and territories to the Commonwealth government's push for a national curriculum (see Ministerial Council on Education, Employment, Training and Youth Affairs, 2008), there is now a traceable line of authority at least for the school domain, but at the time when the majority of the work that I will be referring to took place, each state had control of its own curriculum (although the Australian Capital Territory did have greater Commonwealth involvement).

References

Australian Ethnic Affairs Council (1977) *Australia as a Multicultural Society* (Chair: J. Zubrzycki). Canberra: Australian Government Publishing Services.

Australian Government (2012) *Australia in the Asian Century*. Canberra: Australian Government Publishing Service. See http://pandora.nla.gov.au/pan/133850/20130914-0122/asiancentury.dpmc.gov.au/index.html

Australian Senate (1982a) *Hansard, Thursday 25 March,* 1227. Canberra: Parliament of Australia. See http://www.aph.gov.au/Parliamentary_Business/Hansard/Hanssen 261110.

Australian Senate (1982b) *Hansard, Tuesday 23 November,* 2652. Canberra: Parliament of Australia. See http://www.aph.gov.au/Parliamentary_Business/Hansard/Hanssen 261110.

Australian Senate (1986) *Hansard, Thursday 4 December,* 3374. Canberra: Parliament of Australia. See http://www.aph.gov.au/Parliamentary_Business/Hansard/Hanssen 261110

Australian Senate (1989a) *Hansard, Thursday 4 May,* 1797. Canberra: Parliament of Australia. See http://www.aph.gov.au/Parliamentary_Business/Hansard/Hanssen 261110.

Australian Senate (1989b) *Hansard, Monday 5 June,* 3381. Canberra: Parliament of Australia. See http://www.aph.gov.au/Parliamentary_Business/Hansard/Hanssen 261110.

Australian Teachers' Federation (1982) *The Development and Implementation of a Co-ordinated Language Policy for Australia: Submission to the Standing Committee on Education and the Arts from the Australian Teachers' Federation: The Development and Implementation of a Co-ordinated Language Policy for Australia*. Canberra: Australian Teachers' Federation (mimeo).

Baker, C. (2011) *Foundations of Bilingual Education and Bilingualism* (5th edn). Bristol: Multilingual Matters.

Bialystok, E. (2001) *Bilingualism in Development: Language, Literacy, and Cognition*. New York: Cambridge.

Bialystok, E., McBride-Chang, C. and Luk, G. (2005) Bilingualism, language proficiency, and learning to read in two writing systems. *Journal of Educational Psychology* 97 (4), 580–590.

Chafe, W. (1962) Estimates regarding the present speakers of North American Indian languages. *International Journal of American Linguistics* 28, 162–171.

Clyne, M. (1982) *Multilingual Australia: Resources, Needs, Policies*. Melbourne: River Seine Publications.

Clyne, M. (1991a) *Community Languages: The Australian Experience*. Cambridge: Cambridge University Press.

Clyne, M. (1991b) Australia's language policies: Are we going backwards? *Current Affairs Bulletin* 68 (6), 13–22.

Clyne, M. (2005) *Australia's Language Potential*. Sydney: University of New South Wales Press.

Commonwealth Department of Education (1982) *Towards a National Language Policy*. Canberra: Australian Government Publishing Service.

Commonwealth Department of Education and Youth Affairs (1983) Submission to the Senate Standing Committee on Education and the Arts inquiry into the development and implementation of a co-ordinated language policy for Australia. In Senate Select Committee on Education and the Arts (eds) *Senate Standing Committee on Education and the Arts (Reference: The Development and Implementation of a Co-ordinated Language Policy for Australia): Submissions and Incorporated Documents* (pp. S2361–S2442). Canberra: Commonwealth Government Printer.

Commonwealth Education Portfolio (1979) Education in a multicultural Australia. Reprinted in *Babel* 15 (3), 6–27.
Dawkins, J. (1990) *The Language of Australia: Discussion Paper on an Australian Literacy and Language Policy for the 1990s* (Vol. 1). Canberra: Australian Government Publishing Services.
Department of Education (Australia) (1976) *Report of the Committee on the Teaching of Migrant Languages in Schools*. Canberra: Australian Government Publishing Services.
DEECD (2011) *The Victorian Government's Vision for Languages Education*. Melbourne: Department of Education and Early Childhood Development.
Department of Education, Employment and Training (1991) *Australia's Language: An Australian Language and Literacy Policy*. Canberra: Australian Government Publishing Services.
Diebold, A.R. (1961) Incipient bilingualism. *Language* 37 (1), 97–112.
Ethnic Communities' Council of Queensland (ed.) (1982) *National Language Policy Conference: Papers and Reports*. Brisbane: Ethnic Communities' Council of Queensland (mimeo).
Federation of Ethnic Communities' Councils of Australia (ed.) (1982) *National Language Policy Conference Report*. Sydney: Federation of Ethnic Communities' Councils of Australia (mimeo).
Fesl, E. (1982) Address to Federation of Ethnic Councils' Conference on National Language Policy. *National Language Policy Conference Report* (pp. 141–143). Sydney: Federation of Ethnic Communities' Councils of Australia (mimeo).
Fishman, J.A. (1966) *Language Loyalty in the United States: The Maintenance and Perpetuation of Non-English Mother Tongues by American Ethnic and Religious Groups*. The Hague: Mouton & Co.
Garcia, O. (2008) *Bilingual Education in the 21st Century: A Global Perspective*. Malden, MA: Wiley-Blackwell.
Gorter, D. (2011) Questions for... Michael Clyne. *Language Policy* 10 (1), 59–68.
Grosjean, F. (1985) The bilingual as a competent but specific speaker-hearer. *Journal of Multilingual and Multicultural Development* 6 (6), 467–477.
Grosjean, F. (1989) Neurolinguists, beware! The bilingual is not two monolinguals in one person. *Brain and Language* 36 (1), 3–15.
Grosjean, F. (2010) *Bilingual: Life and Reality*. Cambridge, MA: Harvard University Press.
Haugen, E. (1953) *The Norwegian Language in America: A Study in Bilingual Behavior. Vol. 1: The Bilingual Community; Vol. 2: The American Dialects of Norwegian*. Philadelphia, PA: University of Pennsylvania Press.
Hodge, J. (1982) Opening address to the National Language Policy Conference. *National Language Policy Conference Report* (pp. 83–92). Sydney: Federation of Ethnic Communities' Councils of Australia (mimeo).
Ingram, D. (1979) The case for a national language policy in Australia. *Babel* 15 (1), 3–16.
Ingram, D. (1980) Languages and the core curriculum. *Babel* 16 (3), 4–19.
Jupp, J. (2002) *From White Australia to Woomera*. Cambridge: Cambridge University Press.
Lo Bianco, J. (1987) *National Policy on Languages*. Canberra: Australian Government Publishing Service.
Lopez, M. (2000) *The Origins of Multiculturalism in Australian Politics 1945–1975*. Melbourne: Melbourne University Press.
Macklin, M. (1987) Speech to the Senate. *Hansard, 4th May, 1987*, 2245. Canberra: Parliament of Australia. See http://www.aph.gov.au/Parliamentary_Business/Hansard/Hanssen261110.
Meehan, E. (1985) Policy: Constructing a definition. *Policy Sciences* 18 (4), 291–311.
Milne, F. (1982) Federation of Ethnic Communities' Councils of Australia: Preamble. *National Language Policy Conference Report* (pp. 2–5). Sydney: Federation of Ethnic Communities' Councils of Australia (mimeo).

Minister for Education (Victoria) (1984) *Curriculum Development and Planning in Victoria: Ministerial Paper No. 6.* Melbourne: Minister for Education.

Ministerial Council on Education, Employment, Training and Youth Affairs (2008) *Melbourne Declaration on Educational Goals for Young Australians.* Melbourne: Ministerial Council for Education, Employment, Training and Youth Affairs.

New South Wales Conference on National Language Policy (ed.) (1982) *National Language Policy Conference: N.S.W. Conference Report.* Sydney: Ethnic Communities' Council (mimeo).

Ozolins, U. (1993) *The Politics of Language in Australia.* Cambridge: Cambridge University Press.

Peal, E. and Lambert, W. (1962) The relation of bilingualism to intelligence. *Psychological Monographs: General and Applied* 76 (27), 1–23.

PLANLangPol Committee (1983) *A National Language Policy for Australia.* Kensington: Applied Linguistics Association of Australia and Australian Linguistic Society.

Review of Post Arrival Programs and Services for Migrants (1978) *Migrant Services and Programs (The Galbally Report)* (2 vols). Canberra: AGPS.

Romaine, S. (1995) *Bilingualism* (2nd edn). Oxford: Blackwell.

Rudd, K. (1994) *Asian Languages and Australia's Economic Future: A Report Prepared for the Council of Australian Governments on a Proposed National Asian Languages/Studies Strategy for Australian Schools.* Brisbane: Queensland Government Printer.

Senate Select Committee on Education and the Arts (1983) *Senate Standing Committee on Education and the Arts (Reference: The Development and Implementation of a Co-ordinated Language Policy for Australia): Submissions and Incorporated Documents.* Canberra: Commonwealth Government Printer.

Senate Select Committee on Education and the Arts (1984) *A National Language Policy.* Canberra: Australian Government Publishing Service.

Spolsky, B. (2012) What is language policy? In B. Spolsky (ed.) *The Cambridge Handbook of Language Policy* (pp. 3–15). Cambridge: Cambridge University Press.

Spolsky, B. and Shohamy, E. (2000) Language practice, language ideology and language policy. In R. Lambert and E. Shohamy (eds) *Language Policy and Pedagogy: Essays in Honor of A. Ronald Walton* (pp. 1–42). Amsterdam: John Benjamins.

Weinreich, U. (1953) *Languages in Contact.* New York: Linguistic Circle of New York.

11 Mainstreaming of Italian in Australian Schools: The Paradox of Success?

Yvette Slaughter and John Hajek

Introduction

Although Australia is an English-dominant country, its 2011 national census reveals that 20.4% of Australians predominantly speak a language other than English at home. Hundreds of languages have been identified as spoken in Australia in the 2011 census. The challenge for the Australian education system, for some time now, has been to cultivate the linguistic competence that already exists within Australian society, as well as fostering second language acquisition among all students (Lo Bianco & Slaughter, 2009). With such linguistic diversity, Australia's language communities face the challenge of accessing educational opportunities to help with transmitting and maintaining their languages intergenerationally.

Australia's Italian community, among these groups, has been particularly successful in achieving the widespread mainstreaming of the Italian language as a subject within the nation's primary and secondary education system. One reason for this success has undoubtedly been the sheer demographic weight of Italian migration to Australia in the postwar period. While Australia's migration patterns eventually diversified from their European origins, Italians were the largest single group to migrate and Italians formed the largest non-English-speaking community in Australia for many decades (see also below). It was the vast scale of immigration, mainly from Europe, that helped to transform Australian society. New migrants were initially expected to assimilate into Australian society and leave their languages and cultures behind, but the numerical strength of the migrating communities and a growing recognition of issues of social justice gradually led to substantial changes in attitudes towards the integration of migrants into the Australian community, leading to the emergence of the concept and official policy of 'multiculturalism' in Australia in the 1970s (Herriman, 1996; Ozolins, 1993).

This wave of change also resulted in significant and enduring changes for language education in the Australian education system. Historically, the study of languages predominantly focused on a small range of European languages: in 1964, 75% of language students matriculating from high school were studying French, with German and Latin accounting for the remaining enrolments (Bonyhady, 1965). Italian was taught, but only in a small number of secondary, mainly non-government schools (Wykes & King, 1968). From the 1960s, heated arguments developed around who language study in the education system was for and whose needs were to be addressed (Ozolins, 1993). Up until the 1970s, language study in the education system was 'conceptualized and actualized strictly as "foreign language" teaching' which limited language study mainly to French, and when other languages were taught, care was taken to ensure that they were not taught in schools which contained sizeable communities speaking the language (Clyne *et al.*, 1997: 1). A longstanding division arose between the two supposedly competing goals of second language acquisition by monolingual English speakers and first language development and maintenance for bilingual Australians (Lo Bianco, 2003).[1]

The eventual introduction of the term 'community languages' to replace 'foreign languages', however, due largely to pressure from migrant communities and language teachers, and a push for their inclusion in the education system, led to a political discourse that accepted and then promoted the idea that community languages 'should have *priority*, or at least equality of esteem, with foreign languages' in schools (Lo Bianco, 2007: 22). By the end of the 1970s, also after persistent lobbying by the same community groups and language teachers, an increasing number of European languages gained a more permanent position in the education system of the Australian state of Victoria when they were put in place as matriculation (end of secondary school) subjects. Other Australian states slowly followed suit (Ozolins, 1993). The future of community languages study was further aided by the development of the *National Policy on Languages*, which was eventually endorsed by Australia's federal parliament in 1987 (Lo Bianco, 1987).[2]

Moving Forward

Today, in the 21st century, as a result of these and other developments, over 120 languages are taught in Australia in some kind of educational programme (Lo Bianco & Slaughter, 2009). In the Australian state of Victoria, in 2011, over 60 languages were studied in formal educational contexts, although over 80% of students undertaking language study learnt Italian, Japanese, Indonesian, French or Chinese (Mandarin). This is remarkable progress given that only three languages dominated the education system just a few decades earlier. Arguably, Italian, as the second most studied language in Australia today and the most studied language in Victoria (DEECD, 2012; Lo Bianco & Slaughter, 2009), has benefited most from the responsive change in priorities and rationales for the study of different languages since the 1940s. More fortuitously, in the 1970s and 1980s, Australia's Italian community favoured a shift in focus from Italian as a community language (i.e. for its own community), making a critical decision to push for the greater acceptance of the language as part of the normal curriculum in mainstream schools – no longer to be taught in maintenance form to Italian-background students only but as a beginner language to all students. The purpose of such a stance was to encourage greater social acceptance of Italians and their language[3] and culture, and to facilitate social cohesion and understanding through contact and exposure in Australian schools. With Italian as one of the most studied languages in Australia, and highly positive attitudes to Australia's Italian community and its language, these aspirations appear to have been achieved, as explicitly noted by Rando and Leoni (1992: 174).

Yet despite this success of mainstreaming, there has been surprisingly little interest in investigating and understanding the actual maintenance and long-term provision of Italian in schools, or the degree of student interest in the language across primary and secondary schooling. At the same time, it is also important to understand the potential consequences of the mainstreaming of the language for Italian as a community language. To address this gap, we first explore here the possible impact of the successful mainstreaming of Italian on its community. Utilising the Australian national census, we make comparisons between the Italian- and Greek-speaking communities, which share similar migration histories into Australia, and detail how the positives of the mainstreaming of Italian may be at least partly undermined by longer term negative consequences for language maintenance in the Italian community. Secondly, we present the results of a quantitative comparative analysis of Italian and other languages in a selection of Australian schools in 2011 and patterns and trends over a 10-year period (2002–2011) to show the strengths and weaknesses of Italian study in a challenging educational environment for languages. Our primary attention in the second section of the chapter is on Italian (and comparatively with other languages), specifically in government schools in the Australian state of Victoria, which we use as a case study for the wider Australian context.

Australia's Federal Nature and Victoria as a Case Study

The divided governance of education in Australia has a significant impact on the ability of researchers to investigate and understand language education in Australian schools. Each Australian state and territory is predominantly responsible for its own education system, which is then divided further into three educational jurisdictions – the government (or state), and the smaller and autonomous Catholic and independent schools sectors. In relation to language education, this has resulted in disparate and patchy language education policies across states and territories, as well as jurisdictions. It is also difficult to obtain reliable state and national level data on important variables such as student enrolments, programme types, time spent on language study and teacher qualifications (Liddicoat *et al.*, 2007). Accessibility to data is further complicated by confidentiality concerns across the different jurisdictions.

It is for these reasons that we focus our attention on developments in the state of Victoria, which uniquely and for at least the last decade, has allowed detailed and open quantitative tracking of language provision and teaching in schools – at least in the government sector. Moreover, the state of Victoria has also long been recognised as a leader in language education in Australia – with policies and patterns emerging from this state frequently being reflected in due course elsewhere (see Slaughter & Hajek, 2007). Substantial support has been provided by successive Victorian governments to this day, although they have all *recommended* rather than *mandated* language study from kindergarten to Year 10. As figures presented below indicate, without any change in formal policy, ongoing government goodwill has not maintained language study at a consistent rate in the last decade, leading to an overall pattern of decline, especially evident in the primary sector. However, in 2011 the newly elected state government released a new policy (DEECD, 2011) which includes a commitment that all Victorian government schools would provide a language programme at every year level from Prep (Foundation) to Year 10 by 2025, starting with Prep in 2015.[4]

Italian and Greek as Community Languages

For many involved in the push for an Australian language policy, an underlying hope was the development of societal bilingualism built on individual bilingualism. However, such a consensus was not achieved in the complex negotiations involved in the development of a national policy (see Nicholas, this volume) and to date, bilingualism remains very much an individual achievement in Australia. The success of intergenerational language transmission differs significantly across language groups (see, for example, Clyne & Kipp, 1995), while the provision of community languages in the education system can be seen, we argue, to have positive and negative consequences for the maintenance and development of bilingualism. The differing courses of action taken by the Greek and Italian communities in Australia clearly illustrate the countervailing tensions which help to determine the successful transmission and/or rate of second language acquisition of community languages.

In 1976 Australia's first national census to include a language question[5] recorded 444,672 regular users of Italian and 262,177 regular users of Greek (Clyne, 1991). The challenge for both these communities, as for all migrant groups, has been resisting the pressure to shift from bilingualism (or more) to English-only monolingualism. Language shift is influenced by many variables including the role of the language in that community's cultural value system (Clyne & Kipp, 1995, 2006) and the strong interconnection between language, religion, historical and cultural variables as shapers of those value systems (Smolicz et al., 2001). The differing approaches taken specifically by these two community groups are very instructive about the potential role of education in language maintenance in the Australian setting.

For many decades Italian-speaking Australians represented the largest non-English-speaking group in the country but their numbers have been declining noticeably across Australia. The 444,672 speakers identified in the 1976 census declined to 316,893 in the 2006 census and to 299,834 in the 2011 census when Italian was replaced by Mandarin (336,410 speakers) as the most widely spoken community language in Australia. This equates to a 35.6% decline in Italian speaker numbers between 1976 and 2011. In theory, language speaker numbers will, in the absence of new immigration or local transmission, decline significantly in the next few decades as the population of speakers continues to age. In the 2011 census, 45.2% of Italian speakers were 60 years old or above (135,470 speakers), with the highest number of speakers of Italian recorded in the 70–74-year-old age group. However, while there were only 1600 Australian children (0–14 years old) who were born in Italy, there were 10-fold more children (16,223 children, 0–14 years old) who were predominantly speaking Italian at home. The question remains as to whether or not this is enough to ensure that Italian continues to hold its place as a widely spoken language in the Australian community into the future.

In comparison to Italian Australians, Greek Australians have proven to be better maintainers of their language. Between 1976 and 1991, speakers of the language increased from 262,177 to 285,700 but declined to 252,218 speakers in 2011. This represents a decline of only 3.8% overall between 1976 and 2011 – much less than for Italian. The Greek community is also managing to maintain its language across generations to a greater extent than the Italian community. In the 2011 census, speakers of Greek, 60 years or older, represented 33.5% of the population (84,543 speakers), with the highest number of Greek speakers recorded in the 40–45-year-old age group. Again, as for Italian, the number of Greek-born children was low – 880 Australian children (0–14 years old), but there over 30 times more – 30,386 Australian children (0–14 years old) – who were predominantly speaking Greek at home. This is not to suggest that Greek is not under the same pressures as Italian in relation to language shift or, conversely, that their social and cultural circumstances are entirely the same, but it is clear that, to date, the

Greek community has been more successful in maintaining local intergenerational language transmission.

Catch 22: The Success of Mainstreaming Italian?

All other things being equal, these different language maintenance outcomes for Italian and Greek can, in our view, be at least partly explained by the very different approaches the two communities in question have taken to language education and its role in the community. Initially, the provision of Italian in Australian schools arose in response to the enormous increase in students of an Italian-speaking background entering the education system, and was aimed at language maintenance. In 1975 there were over 76,000 such students in Australian primary and secondary schools (Australian Department of Education, 1976). At first, in addition to after-hours classes run by the community, many Italian lessons were provided through insertion classes where teachers visited schools and specifically taught students with an Italian background. These classes were largely funded by the Italian government and facilitated by the *Comitato Assistenza Italiani* (Co.As.It), an organisation founded in 1967 to provide a range of social services for Italian migrant settlers and their families in Australia. However, as already noted, the Italian community soon came to favour a shift in focus from Italian as a community language, pushing for the language to become a normal part of the curriculum, studied by both background and non-background speakers of the language. In hindsight, the timing of the Italian community's approach was opportune to say the least, with the push for Italian in mainstream schools coinciding with an increase in positive attitudes towards language education (Clyne, 2005).

By 1991, there were 272,070 students around Australia learning Italian in schools, and by 2006 numbers had risen further to 323,023 (23% of languages enrolments nationally) (Di Biase *et al.*, 1994; Lo Bianco & Slaughter, 2009). It is not surprising that since the 1970s, both the composition of the Italian-Australian community and the profile of students of Italian have changed dramatically, as the popularity of Italian in Australia's schools skyrocketed. The vast majority of students of Italian in government schools have not been and are not of an Italian-speaking background. Italian can be studied through mainstream schools (government, Catholic and independent schools), through distance education and through government-run weekend language schools. While Italian can also be studied through community languages schools (CLS) which operate outside school hours and are run by members of the Italian-speaking community, only a relatively small number of students of Italian heritage do so. For example, in 2012 in Victoria, where 36,794 students study a language at a CLS outside school hours, only 905 students attend a CLS for Italian.

At the same time as the Italian community was driving the integration of their language into the school system, most in the Greek community pushed to maintain a strong link specifically between its community and its language. As Hajek and Nicholas note:

> Greek-speaking communities have worked since the 1950s to establish social structures that function to preserve community cohesion, as well as cultural, religious and linguistic transmission across generations. These structures have been created with the assistance of governments at all tiers, as well as through the efforts of the Greek Orthodox Church with which many Greek speakers closely identify. (Hajek & Nicholas, 2004: 197)

For the Greek-speaking community, language education efforts have remained largely within after-hours CLS which target language maintenance and transmission specifically to children of Greek origin. The size and importance of such an effort can be seen by the large numbers attending Greek CLS: 6599 school-aged children in Victoria in 2012. When Greek has been taught in day schools, it has been taught in schools in areas with a high proportion of Greek Australian residents. However, over time, Greek has moved from a geographically concentrated language in Australian urban centres to a more dispersed one, resulting in many such schools being unable to continue with Greek language programmes, given the loss of local demand (Clyne, 2005).

To illustrate the different outcomes in these approaches to language maintenance, Figure 11.1 documents young learners and speakers of Greek and Italian in Victoria. Although there are more than twice as many 0–14-year-olds who speak Greek at home rather than Italian, at the primary level, students are 25 times more likely to study Italian in a government school than they are Greek. When we look at attendance at CLS, there are more than seven times more students in Greek CLS than Italian ones. The Greek community's focus on in-group teaching provision appears to have aided language maintenance – something of particularly high value to Greek identity, as already noted. In addition, anecdotal evidence provided to us by Greek language teachers consistently highlights the reliance second and third generation families of Greek descent make on this in-group teaching for language maintenance purposes (see also Bradshaw & Truckenbrodt, 2003). Conversely, the mainstreaming of Italian has not been matched by the maintenance of large numbers of young speakers, but it has come to be valued by the Italian community as a wider social benefit to all Australians.

There is no doubt that Italian has been successfully transformed from a language studied by Italian-background speakers to a widely accessible language in the Australian education system. Its success provides an important opportunity to develop an understanding of the actual maintenance and

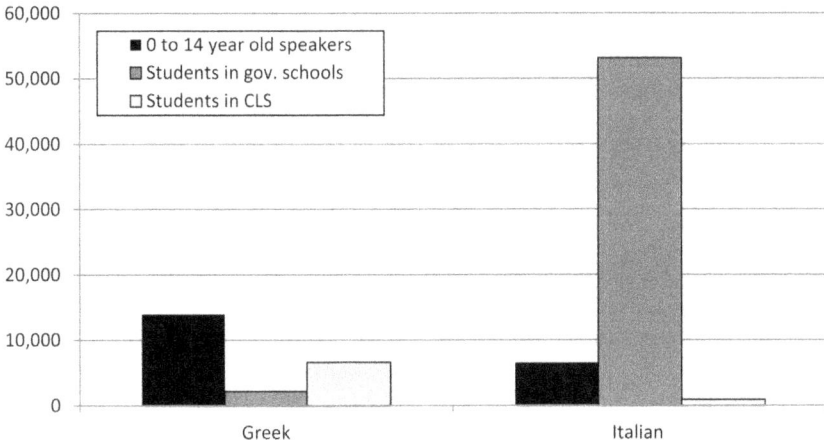

Figure 11.1 Speakers of Italian and Greek (0–14 years) in Victoria, 2011; primary-level study of Italian and Greek in government schools, 2011, and the study of Greek and Italian in community languages schools (all Victoria)
Source: ABS (2012); DEECD (2012).

long-term provision of the language within the education system and variation in enrolments across primary and secondary schooling. To this end, the following section examines the study of Italian in Victorian government schools, with contextualisation provided through a broader comparison with other widely studied languages.

Italian in Victorian Government Schools

In 2011, 48 languages were studied by government school students in Victoria in their schools or through the government-run Victorian School of Languages (VSL) which provides distance and after-hours teaching. Among these languages, Italian was studied by the most students (24.3% of all language enrolments across all government primary and secondary schools) and was offered in more than a quarter of primary and secondary schools with language programmes. The following sections will look at the study of Italian (and other widely taught languages) at the primary level, the secondary level and at final secondary levels (Years 11 and 12), in order to contrast Italian's performance in each of these sectors. What is starkly apparent is the overall decline in language education over the last 10 years, predominantly at the primary level. It is sobering to note that despite this decline Victoria remains a leader in language education in the Australian context. As a result, it is important that any discussion of Italian is situated more broadly within a discussion of languages studied in schools, and that such discussion considers more general variables that might impact on all languages, not only on Italian.

Italian Study at the Primary Level

As Figure 11.2 indicates, the number of Victorian government primary schools offering language programmes has declined by 33.2% over a 10-year period (2002–2011), while language enrolments have decreased by 29.2% (Figure 11.3). There are numerous reasons why language study at the primary level has declined, including a lack of suitably qualified teachers, financial issues within schools, curriculum crowding, the prioritisation of English (only) literacy by federal funding bodies, and changes within the state department of education (Clyne, 2005; DEECD, 2012; Slaughter, 2009). It is within this context that we need to view the changing fortunes of particular languages. The number of schools offering Italian has decreased at a higher than average rate of 39.1% over the 2002–2011 period, resulting in a slightly lower proportion of primary schools with a language programme offering Italian in 2011 than in 2002 (26.3% in 2002 to 24% in 2011).

With respect to student enrolments (Figure 11.3), we can see that numbers for Italian have fallen by almost one-third (31.8%), from 77,893 enrolments in 2002 to 53,114 in 2011. This seems somewhat of an anomaly given that schools providing the language declined by 39.1%. It would seem reasonable to presume that mainly schools with smaller Italian programmes have been closing them and/or that some schools with Italian programmes have been expanding provision to more students within their walls.

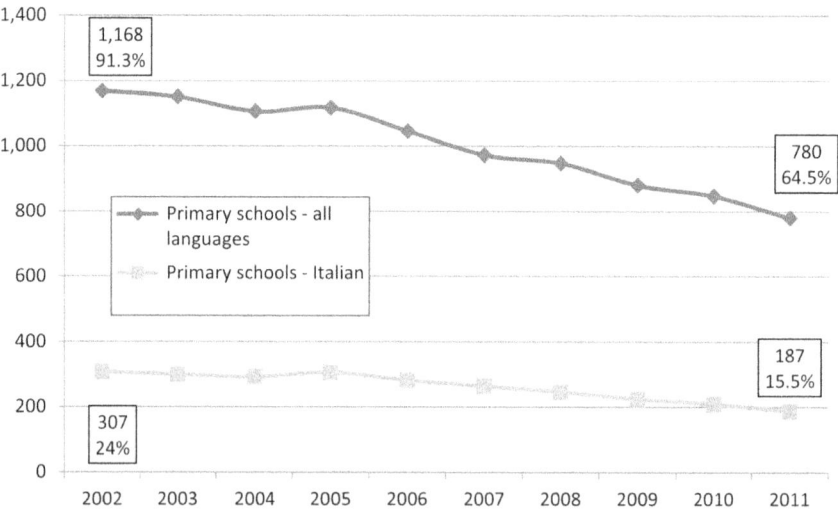

Figure 11.2 Primary schools (no. and %) offering a language programme and offering Italian, 2002–2011 (Victorian government schools)
Source: DEECD (2012).

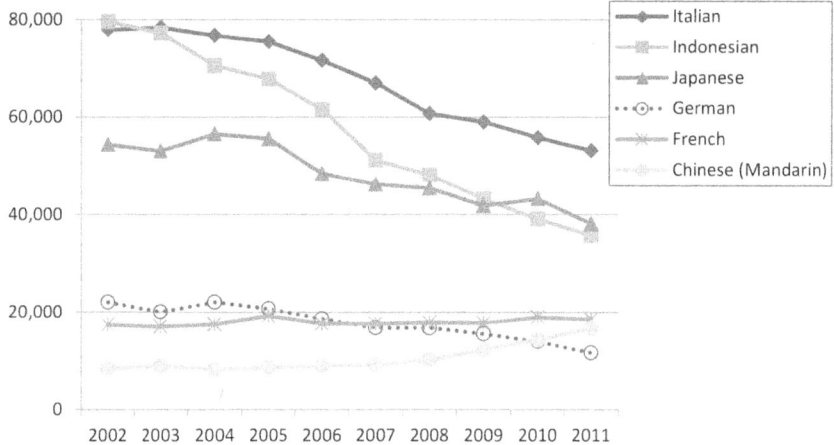

Figure 11.3 Primary-level languages enrolments, six most studied languages, 2002–2011 (Victorian government schools)
Source: DEECD (2012).

With respect to the other widely studied languages (Figure 11.3), the study of Japanese has declined at a similar rate, with enrolments down 29.9% over the same time period. The largest and noticeably steeper decline has been for Indonesian, until recently the most widely taught language in primary schools: enrolments for this language plummeted by 55.1%, influenced by specific social and political events in neighbouring Indonesia (see Slaughter, 2007 for details).

Enrolments in German have also declined almost as dramatically (47.2%), albeit from a smaller base. In contrast, enrolments in Chinese (Mandarin) have almost doubled over this time frame, but again from a small enrolment base. Enrolments in French have instead remained small but steady between 2002 and 2011.

Today Italian appears to have clear leadership as the language with the most primary school enrolments in Victoria. But such an observation needs to be interpreted with care. Its apparent success here is not the result of sustained planning or oversight in favour of Italian, but rather the accidental consequence of Indonesia's much more negative fortunes. Mainstreaming for Italian in Victorian primary schools has indeed occurred, but it shows clear signs of stalling, if not fading.

Italian Study at the Secondary Level

In contrast to the serious fall-off in the study of languages at the primary level, provision at the secondary level in Victorian government schools has remained somewhat stronger over the same 10-year period, with more limited evidence of general decline (Figure 11.4). The number of these schools providing language programmes has fallen by 10.1% between 2002 and 2011, while enrolments have declined by 17.9%. The fate of Italian is opposite to the overall trend in that the number of schools offering the language fell by 17.3% (above average) but enrolments only declined by 8.1%. These figures suggest that secondary schools still offering Italian have been more successful in maintaining student numbers within surviving programmes or have been expanding existing programmes to more year levels than was previously the case. By way of comparison, the numbers of students studying almost all other languages in Figure 11.5 have fallen to a much greater degree: French (−14.3%) and Japanese (−12.3%), but especially German (−33%) and Indonesian (−35.4%). These patterns are somewhat consistent with what was seen at the primary level. Again, Chinese (Mandarin) is the only language to have experienced a consistent increase, with enrolments up 65% between 2002 and 2011.

As a result of these conflicting trends across languages, by 2011, Italian had moved up to become the second most studied language in terms of enrolments – after French – at the secondary level. While this is encouraging news for the study of Italian, a closer examination of retention rates across the secondary school years reveals a significant weakness in the maintenance of student numbers and therefore in the development of higher levels of English/Italian bilingualism among students.

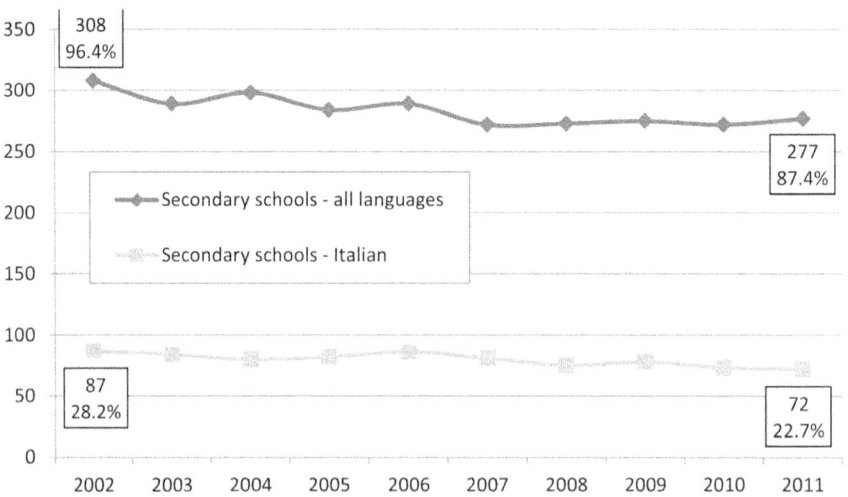

Figure 11.4 Secondary schools offering language programmes and offering Italian, 2002–2011 (Victorian government schools)
Source: DEECD (2012).

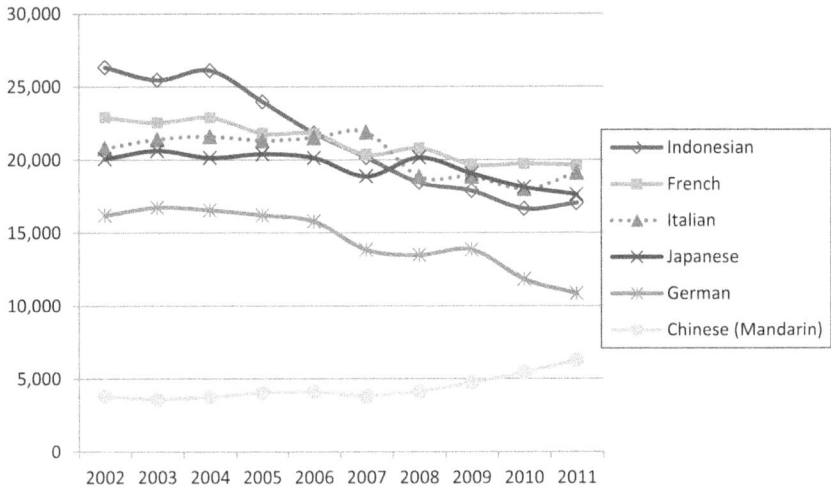

Figure 11.5 Secondary-level languages enrolments, six most studied languages, 2002–2011 (Victorian government schools)
Source: DEECD (2012).

Retention Rates in Secondary Schools (Years 7–12)

Critical to the success of any language programme in the secondary sector is the ability to retain students as they progress through to Year 12. Retention rates across the secondary school years are also recognised to be an important indicator of health for all subject areas, including languages. There are two points to note. First, the single largest contributing factor to the overall decline in language study at the secondary level has been the significant drop in enrolments at the middle-school level at which point, in most schools, language study is no longer compulsory. In 2011, between middle Years 9 and 10, there was a 65% drop in enrolments in languages, noticeably higher than the 50.4% drop seen in 2002. The rate of decline between Years 10 and 11 was a further 50.5% in 2011, albeit lower than the 69.4% decline in 2002. The implications of this are clearer if we look at this situation numerically. In 2002, there were 10,594 Year 10 enrolments in languages, but in 2011 there were only 5728 enrolments. Students are discontinuing language study earlier in 2011 than in 2002.

The second point to note is that the rate of decline across school years is higher for Italian. As can be seen in Table 11.1, at the Year 7 level, French, Indonesian, Italian and Japanese account for 77.5% of enrolments. By the Year 12 level, however, the success in retaining a proportion of enrolments changes quite noticeably. Chinese (Mandarin) is notable for the significant increase in enrolments by Year 12, although this can largely be explained by the significant increase in international students from Chinese-speaking

Table 11.1 Percentage of language enrolments, selected languages, Years 7 and 12, Victorian government schools, 2011

Language	Year 7	Year 12
Chinese (Mandarin)	5.4%	21.6%
French	19.1%	20.6%
German	12%	12.2%
Greek	0.9%	2.3%
Indonesian	19.9%	11.3%
Italian	19%	8.4%
Japanese	19.5%	17.7%
Spanish	1.6%	3%

Source: DEECD (2012).

countries into Years 11 and 12 in Australian schools, in order to facilitate later access into the tertiary education system.

If we look at French, German, Greek, Japanese and Spanish, regardless of the actual number of students studying each language, these language subjects tend to retain their enrolments, proportionately, across the school years and crucially onto the graduating level. However, Indonesian and especially Italian do not manage to do this. As a result, the proportion of language students studying Italian drops dramatically from 19% in Year 7 to only 8.4% in Year 12.

This higher rate of decline can be seen across year levels where enrolments for Italian decline 75.5% between Years 9 and 10 (compared to 65% for all languages) and 70.5% between Years 10 and 11 (compared to 50.5% for all languages). This even more negative pattern for Italian is borne out in Table 11.2, which details the number of students who graduate from a government school having completed a language course. Although Italian is the second most studied language at the secondary level, it is ranked seventh for the number of students who graduate with a language. Additionally, the number of students graduating with Italian contracted 19% between 2008 and 2011. Greek, on the other hand, is ranked eighth for the numbers of graduating students even though the language only has 0.9% of enrolments in Year 7 and 2.3% of enrolments in government schools at the Year 12 level (see also Table 11.1). Although the number of students learning Greek in day schools is low, retention rates are high and well supported by the study of Greek in CLS.

Herein lies the paradox. While the Italian community successfully achieved the widespread integration of Italian study into the education system, this has not been matched by the maintenance of large numbers of young speakers of the language within the Australian Italian community. Furthermore, mainstreaming has had both positive and negative outcomes

Table 11.2 Student enrolments (government colleges) by language, students eligible to graduate from VCE, 2008–2011 (based on VCE unit 4 enrolments)

Language	Number of students			
	2008	2009	2010	2011
Chinese (Mandarin)	1179	1191	1364	1452
French	588	535	549	548
Japanese	539	588	530	526
Vietnamese	284	400	371	422
German	378	360	331	352
Indonesian	470	351	376	325
Italian (7th)	284	220	235	230
Greek	147	134	132	124
Turkish	150	136	129	102
Korean	56	91	90	91
Arabic	88	87	67	80
Other	548	551	559	530
Total	**4711** (17.6%[a])	**4644** (17.5%[a])	**4733** (17.4%[a])	**4782** (17.7%[a])

Notes: [a] As a percentage of all graduating students.
Source: DEECD (2012).

within the education system. Italian is widely studied at the primary and secondary levels but there appears to be a 'fatigue effect' where students become uninterested in continuing either with Italian or possibly with language study altogether. Attrition rates are dramatic from Year 9 onwards and it is important that further research be undertaken to understand why it is seen as so undesirable to complete Italian language study through to Year 12. This reduction in students reaching higher levels of competence in Italian also has a flow-on effect for Italian programmes in the tertiary education system. Despite the apparently large numbers of Australian students learning Italian at some point in primary and secondary schools, Italian enrolments in all Australian universities where the language is taught are concentrated in *ab initio* beginner courses, rather than in intermediate and advanced programmes for those who have done some or have completed Italian language studies in secondary schools, duplicating results seen at the secondary level, with few students reaching higher levels of fluency.

Concluding Remarks

There are, of course, enormous complexities behind the changing patterns of language transmission within different community groups, such as

Italian or Greek communities in Australia, as well as language study within school systems. In this chapter we have utilised simple quantitative measures to highlight some of the intricacies and effects of the relationship between language communities, language maintenance and transmission and the mainstreaming of languages in the school system, specifically in the government school system in Victoria.

In particular, we have looked at the place of Italian as a community language and its transformation into a widely studied language that has become embedded in the education system in Australia – even if some elements of that embedding are now under challenge. While the Italian community has been tremendously successful in increasing Italian study in government schools, the mainstream school system appears to provide little to no opportunity for the maintenance and development of bilingualism among Italian background speakers – a hardly surprising consequence of *ab initio* language teaching only, directed to the much larger school population not of Italian origin.

Concurrently, the transmission of Italian within the Italo-Australian community is little supported by CLS that are able to focus on language maintenance – given the small numbers attending them. While the decline in the number of Italian-speaking students learning Italian has been more than counter-balanced by widespread uptake in the school system, trend figures for the last 10 years show a worrying decline, especially but not exclusively in the primary sector. Italian's apparent success today at the primary (Figure 11.3) and secondary level (Figure 11.5) in government schools is due, in part, to the even more lacklustre performance of other languages, especially Indonesian. Of particular concern for Italian is the poor retention rate of students into the middle years and senior secondary levels – a decline greater than that experienced by most languages. The mainstreaming of Italian, leading to its prevalence at the primary and lower secondary levels in Australian schools, has created a fatigue effect where students are overexposed to the language, and look for a change in language or drop language study altogether. While the widespread provision of Italian to all in Australian schools was successfully achieved by the Italo-Australian community in the 1980s and 1990s, recent trends are in many respects very concerning for the future of Italian both in the school system and in the wider community. These trends, and the reasons for them, need to be carefully considered and addressed for Italian to properly thrive through the school cycle, primary to final secondary, in Australia. In short, mainstreaming requires maintenance and oversight.

Notes

(1) While there has been progress at a societal level around these issues, these tensions are still clearly visible in language education, particularly around the study of Chinese as a first and second language in Australia (Orton, 2008; Slaughter, 2008).

(2) The National Policy on Languages was superseded by the Australian Language and Literacy Policy (Dawkins, 1991), changing the policy focus to English literacy (see Nicholas, this volume).
(3) Although there is significant dialectal variation in Italian, the community was always united around the teaching of standard Italian.
(4) Australian schooling is seven years at the primary level (Foundation and Years 1–6) and six years at the secondary level (Years 7–12).
(5) Note that the language question in the census has changed over time. In the 1976 census Australians were asked if they regularly used a language other than English, but from 2001 the census question asks if the person speaks a language other than English at home. This narrowing of language use to the home domain will have led to an underestimation of multilingualism in Australia, although it is difficult to say by how much.

References

ABS (2012) *Data Analysis of the 2011 Census*. Online database. Canberra: Australian Bureau of Statistics. See http://www.abs.gov.au/websitedbs/censushome.nsf/home/Data.

Australian Department of Education (1976) *Report of the Committee on the Teaching of Languages in Schools*. Canberra: Australian Government Publishing Services.

Bonyhady, A. (1965) Languages taught to matriculation level in Australia. *Babel* 1 (3), 32–33.

Bradshaw, J. and Truckenbrodt, A. (2003) Divergent orientations to Greek and its teaching in an Australian Greek school. *International Journal of Bilingual Education and Bilingualism* 6 (6), 439–457.

Clyne, M. (1991) *Community Languages: The Australian Experience*. Cambridge: Cambridge University Press.

Clyne, M. (2005) *Australia's Language Potential*. Sydney: University of New South Wales Press.

Clyne, M. and Kipp, S. (1995) The extent of community language maintenance in Australia. *People and Place* 3 (4), 4–8.

Clyne, M. and Kipp, S. (2006) Australia's community languages. *International Journal of the Sociology of Language* 180, 7–21.

Clyne, M., Fernandez, S., Chen, I. and Summo-O'Connell, R. (1997) *Background Speakers: Diversity and its Management in LOTE Programs*. Belconnen: Language Australia.

Dawkins, J. (1991) *Australia's Language – The Australian Language and Literacy Policy*. Canberra: Australian Government Publishing Services.

DEECD (2011) *The Victorian Government's Vision for Languages Education*. Melbourne: Department of Education and Early Childhood Development.

DEECD (2012) *Languages Other Than English in Victorian Government Schools, 2011*. Melbourne: Department of Education and Early Childhood Development. See http://www.education.vic.gov.au/studentlearning/teachingresources/lote/research.htm.

Di Biase, B., Andreoni, G., Andreoni, H. and Dyson, B. (1994) *Unlocking Australia's Language Potential: Profiles of 9 key languages in Australia. Vol. 6: Italian*. Deakin: National Languages and Literacy Institute of Australia and Department of Education, Employment and Training.

Hajek, J. and Nicholas, N. (2004) The rise and fall of Modern Greek in Australian universities. *Art and Humanities in Higher Education* 3 (2), 195–209.

Herriman, M. (1996) Language policy in Australia. In M. Herriman and B. Burnaby (eds) *Language Policies in English Dominant Countries* (pp. 35–61). Clevedon: Multilingual Matters.

Liddicoat, A., Scarino, A., Curnow, T., Kohler, M., Scrimgeour, A. and Morgan, A.-M. (2007) *An Investigation of the State and Nature of Languages in Australian Schools*. Canberra: DEEWR.

Lo Bianco, J. (1987) *National Policy on Languages*. Canberra: Australian Government Publishing Service.

Lo Bianco, J. (2003) Making language education policies: A needed response to globalization. *Modern Language Journal* 87, 286–288.

Lo Bianco, J. (2007) Emergent China and Chinese: Language planning categories. *Language Policy* 6, 3–26.

Lo Bianco, J. and Slaughter, Y. (2009) *Second Languages and Australian Schooling*. Melbourne: Australian Council for Educational Research.

Orton, J. (2008) *Chinese Language Education in Australian Schools*. Melbourne: University of Melbourne and Confucius Institute.

Ozolins, U. (1993) *The Politics of Language in Australia*. Cambridge: Cambridge University Press.

Rando, G. and Leoni, F. (1992) The Italian language in Australia: Sociolinguistic aspects. In S. Castles, C. Alcorso, G. Rando and E. Vasta (eds) *Australia's Italians: Culture and Community in a Changing Society* (pp. 169–183). St. Leonard's: Allen & Unwin.

Slaughter, Y. (2007) The rise and fall of Indonesian in Australian schools: Implications for language policy and planning. *Asian Studies Review* 31 (3), 301–322.

Slaughter, Y. (2008) The study of Asian languages in two Australian states: Considerations for language-in-education policy and planning. PhD thesis, University of Melbourne, Melbourne.

Slaughter, Y. (2009) Money and policy make languages go round: Language programs in Australia after NALSAS. *Babel* 43 (2), 4–11.

Slaughter, Y. and Hajek, J. (2007) Community languages and LOTE provision in Victorian primary schools: Mix or match? *Australian Review of Applied Linguistics* 30 (1), 7.1–7.22.

Smolicz, J., Secombe, M. and Hunter, D. (2001) Family collectivism and minority languages as core values of culture among ethnic groups in Australia. *Journal of Multilingual and Multicultural Development* 22, 152–172.

Wykes, O. and King, M.G. (1968) *Teaching of Foreign Languages in Australia*. Melbourne: Australian Council for Educational Research.

12 Understanding the Role of Professional Development and Influences on Teacher Practice: An Australian Case Study of Community Languages Teachers

Margaret Gearon

Introduction

This chapter explores community languages teachers' perceptions of completing certification training for classroom teaching in an Australian setting. The main purpose of the study described here was to elicit and analyse data from these teachers about their own experience of language learning and of the influence of teacher training, in order to contribute to a knowledge-based approach for the provision of professional learning courses directed towards improving community languages teaching.

In an age where multiculturalism and multilingualism have been both challenged and applauded in Australia and elsewhere, the ongoing entry of large numbers of non-English-speaking migrants into major English-speaking nations such as the USA, the UK and Australia continues to change the cultural and linguistic landscape of these countries. Educational support in favour of language maintenance (and thus bilingualism, if not multilingualism) in these migrant communities provides a considerable challenge given the huge diversity of such communities, as well as the limited space for their languages in mainstream education, even if this were a consideration. It is not surprising, therefore, that Australia and other English-speaking countries rely heavily on community (or heritage) languages schools (CLS) and their teachers to provide the desired languages education.

As defined by the Victorian Department of Education and Early Childhood Development (DEECD, 2011: 3):

> [c]ommunity languages schools are community-based, not for profit bodies established by community groups and individuals to provide language classes to school age students out of school hours. In [the Australian state of] Victoria, such after hours providers conduct classes for more than 30,000 students in over 50 languages, many of which are not available in any of the mainstream day schools. In some of these community languages, qualified teachers are not available to conduct the classes.

The reliance by communities and education authorities in Victoria and elsewhere in Australia on such schools, and particularly on unqualified native-speaker teachers, should not be understated. This is the case for the languages of communities more recently established in Australia such as Thai, Korean, Sinhalese and Tamil. However, even in more established communities such as Russian, Ukrainian, Greek, Chinese and Vietnamese, community members teaching in the after-hours schools frequently do not have an Australian teaching qualification. Even if they have a teaching qualification from their own country, this is rarely recognised as having an Australian equivalent and, usually, would not have provided them with the knowledge and skills to teach second language learners in an Australian context.

Despite the obvious problems of teacher training and quality, there is no doubt about the important educational and cultural role that CLS play in Australia, as similar schools do in other English-speaking countries. In the wider Australian context, they allow for over 70 languages across the nation to be offered as part of a recognised, and government supported, after-hours complementary system. They are a large and influential sector, represented by important key bodies, the Ethnic Schools[1] Associations and the Federations of Community Languages Schools, all of which operate under the national leadership of Community Languages Australia. Their vision is to promote active bilingualism and biculturalism for the children who attend the schools, to assist in the maintenance of multiculturalism and to encourage harmony and tolerance in Australian society (Community Languages Australia, 2007: 2). Many migrant communities in Australia are very, if not entirely, dependent on such schools for the formal teaching of their languages and cultures.

Australian education authorities formally recognise the important role of CLS and indeed these schools must be registered and accredited in the state or territory where they operate in order to be eligible for government funding. For example, in 2012 in the state of Victoria, schools which are registered received an annual allowance of AU$190.00 per student. This funding enables the community or individual that operates the school to fund the hire of facilities and contribute to the payment of teacher stipends. Victoria, among all the Australian states and territories, has led the way in the development of professional learning programmes since 1993, and most recently, since 2009, in the preparation of a vocational training programme for instructors and teachers – the Certificate IV in Community Languages Teaching, which is accredited by the Victorian Registration and Qualifications Framework and linked to the Australian Qualifications Framework.[2] The certificate is a vocational training qualification which can be offered by registered training organisations, not universities. It consists of a number of units of competency, some of which contain the same content as the 30-hour professional learning courses for CLS teachers offered by three universities in Victoria (see below). These competency units develop the knowledge and skills required for teaching and/or training in particular settings, such as a CLS. However, to date, despite good intentions, the Certificate IV has not been offered because no Registered Training Organisation has been willing to deliver it.

A study by the Centre for Information on Language Teaching and Research (CILTR) in the UK has shown that, as in Australia, 'few community languages teachers have specific training in language learning and teaching' (McPake et al., 2007: 103). The authors note that these teachers are concerned that there are not enough opportunities for continuous professional development, particularly in areas such as effective classroom management and catering for mixed-ability levels using differentiated teaching and learning strategies (McPake et al., 2007: 104). Similar concerns are also shared by teachers in CLS in Victoria. The main difference between teachers in Victoria and those in the UK is the relative ease of access for the former to professional development workshops and courses, especially in Melbourne, where the overwhelming majority of Victorians, including migrants and refugees, reside and where most CLS operate.

In response to the frequent lack of formal pedagogical training experienced by community languages teachers, since 1993 a number of universities in Victoria have been conducting limited professional learning courses ranging between 15 and 30 hours.[3] Our focus here is on the participants on targeted training courses provided by one of these universities over a recent four-year period (2007–2010).

Language Teacher Training and the Community Languages Teacher

Learning to become a second language teacher through formal training, which includes theoretical principles and practical application, is considered essential for those wanting to teach in regular government and non-government day schools. Such an expectation is not generally the case for teachers in CLS in Australia. CLS teachers with varying levels of bilingual competence in their first language and English are currently able to access only a 30-hour professional learning course, offered by three Victorian universities twice a year and focused on the teaching of language and culture in their particular context and not within the remit of Certificate IV. Records show that only a small number (10%) actually attend these training courses, and another 26% attend professional learning seminars. This training, albeit somewhat limited in contact hours, is to ensure that they have a basic understanding of second language and bilingual teaching and learning principles and practices, as well as the Victorian state government's curriculum framework for teaching and assessing languages. For the present study, a number of community languages teachers involved in training provided by Monash University completed an open-ended questionnaire to seek their views on the way/s in which their language learning experiences influence how they teach, their beliefs about best pedagogical practices in CLS, and how the professional development course at Monash University may have assisted them, in their view, to become better CLS teachers.

In many countries, the preparation of mainstream, i.e. normal day school, teachers of languages usually follows the same process-product approach as that of teachers in general. This is certainly the case in Australia, with the most common pathways for those who wish to qualify as teachers of languages: a four-year, double degree (Bachelor of Arts/Bachelor of Education) as an undergraduate pathway, or a one-year, full-time Graduate Diploma of Education or two-year Bachelor/Master of Education, both of which are postgraduate in nature and assume a completed undergraduate degree and thus focus solely on the theoretical and practical aspects of becoming a teacher. For teachers working in CLS contexts, the current pathways available to mainstream languages teachers are, however, not readily available or feasible, given that they are generally required to work full-time in another sector to support themselves and their families – giving them neither the time nor the resources to support extensive full-time teacher training. The teacher education route proposed by Freeman and Johnson (1998: 399) whereby 'learning to teach [is] viewed as learning about teaching in one context (the teacher education programme), observing and practising teaching in another (the practicum), and eventually developing effective teaching behaviours in yet a third context (usually in the first years of teaching)' is simply not viable, as these three contexts are not easily accessible for community languages teachers. Those working in the CLS sector, voluntarily or for a stipend, typically learn to teach 'on the job' and often develop their own methods, usually based on the best means of surviving in an after-hours language classroom with students who may or may not desire to be part of the class.

Freeman and Johnson (1998: 405) also suggest that 'the knowledge-base of language teacher education responds to a deceptively simple question: Who teaches what to whom, where?' This statement would seem to be a very good starting point for the development of teacher training courses for community languages teachers in Australia, given the conditions of their employment. Indeed, focusing on the personal and social context of these teachers (frequently called 'instructors' as many have no previous experience of pedagogical or second language teaching and learning studies) in such a particular language teaching and learning situation would enable teacher education institutions to better respond to their needs while developing a recognised formal pathway for certification for them, and contribute to the proper professionalisation of this large body of language teachers. Given the particular nature of teaching in a CLS, and the results of research involving mainstream teachers which showed that 'the notion of work context has been recognised as central in shaping teachers' conceptions of their profession' (Freeman & Johnson, 1998: 400), it was felt imperative to investigate here the participants' reactions and attitudes towards the professional learning courses in which they had engaged in order to discover the extent to which their classroom practices and their beliefs about language teaching were influenced by a theoretical framework and pedagogical knowledge.

The following statements also by Freeman and Johnson (1998: 402) appear very applicable to community languages teachers: 'learning to teach is affected by the sum of a person's experiences, ... and ... it requires the acquisition and interaction of knowledge and beliefs about oneself as a teacher, of the content to be taught, of one's students, and of classroom life', and 'learning to teach is a long-term, complex, developmental process that operates through participation in the social practices and contexts associated with learning and teaching'. These social practices and contexts are particular to each community, and teachers of a community language are influenced by the community's language and culture, as experienced both in their country of origin and in the Australian context. This study therefore aims to answer the following:

(1) To what extent do community languages teachers believe their prior language learning experiences influence their classroom practices?
(2) According to these teachers, to what extent does participation in a 30-hour language teaching professional learning course modify their classroom practices?

Understanding Community Languages Teachers and their Needs

The need for a concerted effort to address training for community languages teachers was highlighted in a special issue of the *International Journal of Bilingual Education and Bilingualism* (2005). It focuses on heritage/community languages in the USA and Australia and on discussions held at a series of meetings, seminars and conferences in both countries between 1998 and 2002. Their purpose was to determine ways to advance heritage/community languages education through research priorities. The 2001 Melbourne seminar led to a number of recommendations, one set of which emanated from the Policy and Teacher Education Group. Hornberger (2005: 105) recommended that 'a combined ethnographic and quantitative investigation of US and Australian practices of teacher education in community and heritage language programmes be undertaken' and that a key outcome of the research would be 'the documentation of exemplar programmes based on a range of different models and settings addressing teacher professional development ... and certification (formal and non-formal)'. The present study is a step towards documenting the effects of one model of professional learning for community languages teachers, in order to develop an understanding of what CLS teachers build on in their training and how, through self-reflection, they raise their awareness of how to best utilise their knowledge in the classroom.

Kramsch, for example, emphasises the need to expand the base of teacher education for language teachers in general. She argues that 'beyond the traditional knowledge of cultural facts, an intercultural approach aims at gaining an understanding of the way these facts are related, i.e. how as a pattern they form the cultural fabric of society' (Kramsch, 1996: 6). This is very pertinent to teachers in the CLS sector because of the nature of the student population and the backgrounds of the teachers. These schools provide ideal contexts where learners can develop knowledge about both of their cultures, and come to understand themselves in relation to these, thus developing their intercultural understandings (Scarino & Liddicoat, 2009: 21). Furthermore, Scarino and Liddicoat (2009: 21–22) claim that 'learning to be intercultural ... involves learning to understand how one's own culture shapes perceptions of oneself, of the world, and of our relationship with others'. In the community languages classroom, a bilingual and bicultural context, there are two languages and two cultures at play for the students, although *one* of these languages/cultures may be dominant. For the teachers, particularly those who have recently migrated to Australia, it may be the target language and culture which are dominant (their first language and culture). This creates a dynamic in which the development of the students' communication skills in the target language is shaped by the intersection of their cultural understandings and practices as second language learners, and those of their teachers who are transmitting a language and culture which are considered as their first or 'native' ones. Since teachers in CLS play such an important role in the development of the students' multilingual and multicultural identities, it is critical that they undertake teacher training and/or professional development so that their classroom practices reflect current second language pedagogical approaches and the development of bilingual and intercultural competence.

Furthermore, in recent years, there has been growing interest in Australia, the UK and the USA in community languages classes and in their relationship to mainstream or regular schools (e.g. Baldauf, 2005; Creese & Martin, 2006; Liu, 2008). As Creese and Martin (2006: 2) comment, although some aspects of CLS have been studied (e.g. Li Wei, 1993; Mirza & Reay, 2000), there is still a dearth of literature about them and their role. They also note that such schools 'remain unexamined for the interaction, learning and identity formation processes which are probably at the heart of sustaining community languages and developing their identities through socialisation practices' (Creese & Martin, 2006: 2).

Context of the Study

The data for this study were collected in Australia between 2007 and 2010 with volunteer teachers from CLS who were participating in beginner languages methodology courses and the trialling of some new units as part of these in the Faculty of Education at Monash University, in the Victorian capital city of Melbourne. Each year, the Ethnic Schools Association of Victoria (ESAV) advertises 30-hour methodology courses (three hours per week over 10 weeks, in the evenings) at two levels for people who teach in after-hours CLS. The two levels enable teachers to complete up to 60 hours of training. This is the amount of language methodology required for mainstream language teachers undertaking this training as part of a recognised teacher training programme. Participants in these CLS-directed courses are often novice teachers, who have little or no pedagogical background and frequently limited English language proficiency, but who are committed to the maintenance of their first language, culture and traditions in Australia. The range of languages taught by participant teachers is wide and includes both traditionally taught languages such as Russian, Chinese and Greek and more recently offered languages such as Tamil, Thai and Korean.

Data Collection

As part of their community languages basic methodology course, participants were asked to volunteer to complete a questionnaire where they responded to the following questions:

(1) Does the way in which you were taught your language influence how you teach? Give two or three examples.
(2) What do you believe is the best way to teach your language to the students in the Ethnic School where you work?
(3) What kinds of things do you think help you to become a better teacher each year? Give TWO reasons for your answer.

(4) Give THREE examples of how a LOTE [Language Other Than English] methodology or professional development workshop has prepared you to teach in your Ethnic School.
(5) In the chart below, list the major influences both positive and negative, on your particular Ethnic School language teaching practices.

The questions were formulated in light of Vélez-Rendón (2002, 2006) who provides a useful overview of the issues facing language teachers in general and in the context of CLS teachers specifically.

In all, 118 participants in six community languages methodology courses were surveyed and their written responses to each question were collected and recorded verbatim. The open-ended questionnaire is used as the primary data source here because this allowed the participants to take their time to reflect on their responses. The other main data source was the participants' six reflective journal entries during the 10 weeks in the course. These entries have been analysed and reported on elsewhere by a course tutor and will not be mentioned further here (see Morgan, 2009).

Analysis of the Data

Given space limitations, only the responses of the participants to Questions 1, 2 and 4 are analysed and reported on in this chapter, since these were the questions with the most responses. All of the participants have English as an additional language, and some do not have a high level of proficiency in writing. Where English spelling or grammatical errors occurred in their written responses, these have been recorded as such. Three participants responded in their first language (Thai), and these written comments were later translated into English. To maintain survey anonymity, language background was not specifically asked for, but some respondents volunteered this information. Where the language background of the respondent was specifically noted, this information has been included when discussing individual responses.

The effect of prior experience and beliefs about good teaching

Vélez-Rendón (2002: 463) presents as one component of her proposed knowledge base for language teachers 'a critical evaluation of prior experiences as language learners and beliefs, assumptions, attitudes'. This forms the basis of Questions 1 and 2 of the questionnaire.

With respect to Question 1 (Does the way you were taught your language influence how you teach?), 55% of the participants specifically acknowledged the influence of their prior language learning experiences, although they differed in how these affected their current classroom teaching style; 13% responded negatively, 27% misunderstood the question and provided irrelevant responses, while the remaining participants did not respond at all.

One Thai teacher in Semester 2, 2009 wrote:

> I use the way of learning reading & writing form I was taught in primary school in Thailand. I also use dictation/spelling vocab in the prep class.

Teacher Y from Semester 1, 2008 wrote:

> My primary school teacher will stay always a role model for me in her manners as well as her way of teaching. I still prefer the old way of spelling and connecting letters to make a word and making sense of what we are reading.

Some participants noted that their previous experiences ensured that they would not teach young children in the same way as they had been treated. For example, one participant from Semester 2, 2007 stated:

> I was taught in a monotone-constant repetition approach. In my class I have gone the opposite and try to give my students the hands-on experience to learning.

Another from the same group wrote:

> When I was at school, my first teacher at grade 1 was very strict and hardly never gave us compliment. So I always try to make children happy and comfortable with lots of compliments.

One German teacher (2010) commented:

> I learned through strict structure. So it is hard for me to accept New Methods of teaching these days. e.g. Vocabs needed to be learned by heart. Grammar was done over and over again. There weren't any modern tools in my days.

Others, such as a participant from Semester 2, 2009, referred to their own language learning as being their first language, whereas the children they are teaching in Australia are learning the language and culture as their second one.

Question 2 asked the participants to comment on what they believed is the best way to teach their language to the students in the CLS, i.e. whether their beliefs influence the conduct of their lessons and determine their practice (Vélez-Rendón, 2002, 2006). Many of the answers reflected the lecturers' emphasis on concrete and experiential learning activities and the importance of lesson planning (see also below). This response is seen in comments such as 'through a lot of fun and interesting activities that are well planned and according to well-known practices' (Teacher 5, Semester 1, 2009); 'I believe activity like as games, singing is the best way to teach my language' (Thai teacher, Semester 2, 2009).

Other teachers also commented on the need to make lessons fun and interesting in order to engage students who give up their Saturdays to attend language classes. Teacher 1, Semester 2, 2007 commented: 'I believe children need to feel safe and comfortable while learning a new language. It has to be interesting and fun so children become engaged and want to learn.' Teacher 8 from Semester 2, 2009 stated: 'Try every method which can attract student's interest. Games, music, DVD, learning while playing' and one of the Greek teachers from Semester 2, 2007 wrote: 'I believe the best way of teaching is a combination of teaching and playing together. For a Saturday school teaching must be fun (not too fun).'

In 2010, some of the comments differed from previous years, with more participants making reference to the need to motivate students attending CLS. One Chinese teacher wrote, 'Let students love Chinese class, enjoy learning. Not too academic', and a Vietnamese participant listed three best ways for teaching: 'Motivate students. Listen to students in need. Help students learn in their own way.' These comments indicate a shift from a highly teacher-centred approach to one where the students' needs are influencing the teaching, closer to approaches in regular day schools.

Factors Influencing Learning How to Teach a Community Language

Another purpose of the survey was to determine the extent to which the community languages teachers who undertook the courses were influenced by what was presented to them as to how they approached their teaching after the course. In their responses to Question 4 (Give THREE examples of how a LOTE methodology or professional development workshop has prepared you to teach in your Ethnic School), 20% of respondents mentioned the lecturers' focus on the need for planning and writing lesson plans, the latter being part of the major assignment.

One Thai teacher wrote:

> I think my lesson plan help me to become a better teacher each year because my lesson plan can show me that I success in teaching by follow the plan or not. If not I can improve my lesson plan for the next semester and next year.

A Tamil participant expressed even stronger support for the lesson plan, writing:

Every day we are writing the lesson plan. Each students like our teaching methods.

Reason: because we write the lesson plan. We plan it before so that's easy way to teaching.

Another key element of the courses was the emphasis on Gardner's Multiple Intelligences, which formed the basis of one of the assessment tasks, yet only 9% of the responses referred to the importance of including these in lessons. For example, one of the Tamil teachers (2010) wrote: 'From Gardner Multiple Intelligence theory, I got idea to teach every topic.' Student needs were again the focus of a 2010 participant who wrote 'I am more aware of student needs. I know and understand more now about the mainstream culture' (referring to how language teachers in regular day schools plan).

Discussion and Conclusion

The majority of the community languages teachers surveyed had positive responses to the 30-hour course in which they had enrolled. Many recorded a strong belief that the course had introduced them to new classroom teaching strategies and to the importance of being prepared prior to walking into their own language classes. For example, they cited writing lesson plans, preparing materials and resources, linking their teaching to current government language curriculum documents and approaches to teaching primary school students as aspects of the course which benefited them most.

Johnson (1996: 766–767) notes that 'what teachers know about teaching is not simply an extended body of facts and theories, but is instead largely experiential and socially constructed out of the experiences and classrooms from which [they] have come'. This comment certainly reflects the responses from the teachers who responded to the questionnaire. They are largely responsible for constructing a language pedagogy themselves, and rely on what they have experienced, what they believe is suitable for the children at the school, and on attendance at professional learning courses during which they share experiences, as exemplified in comments from some of them:

Teachers need to attend class like we do now. It gives us new ideas and motivation to make a better class. (Teacher 4, Semester 2, 2007)

Teacher 9 from the same group referred to the importance of experience in the following comment:

[I need] to experience more learners and to know what kind of ways and activities are more valuable to learners.

In seeking to understand the impact of community languages teachers' beliefs about language teaching and learning, and the potential influence of a 30-hour language methodology course on their classroom practices, we have reported here on a sample of the comments which they provided to the surveys between 2007 and 2010. Of note is that the varying level of English language proficiency of the participants led to them misinterpreting some questions on the initial survey. For example, Question 1 (Does the way in which you were taught your language influence how you teach?) was frequently interpreted as asking for the influence of the language teacher training programme, rather than their beliefs about the influence of their own language learning experiences on how they teach. Similarly, Question 4 (Give THREE examples of how a LOTE methodology or professional development workshop has prepared you to teach in your Ethnic School) elicited a number of responses which could be seen as providing the lecturer/researcher with the correct/required answer. One participant noted the following points in almost rote fashion:

> From classroom activity, I have planned to do more games ideas; from Gardner Multiple Intelligence theory, I got idea to teach every topic; from journal entry, I understood that how I can approach every skills to improve students' interest.

With regard to the first research question, the majority of respondents agreed that their own language learning experiences as children did have an influence on their own teaching practice – some reacted positively to them and maintained practices they had undertaken as learners, while others were careful to avoid them as negative and not to be used with their own students.

As for the second research question, it is not possible to provide a comprehensive answer as the responses only addressed how teachers felt the course had helped them or modified their classroom practices. Although they reported implementing strategies they had learned, their responses did not reveal any clear examples of differences in their beliefs about appropriate pedagogical approaches. A comprehensive investigation of this question requires classroom observation together with teacher reflections on recorded instances of their teaching, in order to determine the relationship between their beliefs and actual as opposed to reported classroom practices. This step would be in line with the approach suggested by Hornberger (2005) as cited above.

In terms of the knowledge base for language teacher education for teachers in a CLS, a combination of Freeman and Johnson's framework (1998: 406) and Vélez-Rendón's (2002) approach may be the most applicable. However, the particular nature of such complementary education needs to be re-framed by this combined model as the process of schooling is very different from regular or mainstream contexts. These community languages teachers are indeed learners of their craft, which involves developing their own bilingual and intercultural knowledge as suggested by Kramsch (1996) and Scarino and Liddicoat (2009), as well as developing competence in their own language and culture among their first-, second- and third-generation students. These teachers belong to a particular 'community of practice', one which they recognise when they meet other teachers on courses such as those referred to in this chapter.

The late Michael Clyne was a key advocate of CLS, as they embodied his view that Australia should develop its multilingual and multicultural resources and provide every young Australian, no matter what their background, with the opportunities to become multilingual (Clyne, 2005). It is to be hoped that this goal will come to fruition through the promotion and expansion of training for teachers in these after-hours schools, together with the identification and development of an adequate and fully recognised framework for the knowledge and skills base required for teaching in them. A first step in this direction has been the development of the Certificate IV in Community Languages Teaching which was accredited in late 2011, but which, disappointingly, is yet to proceed. As previously noted, the challenges faced by CLS teachers in Australia are matched by those in other English-speaking countries. What can be understood and applied here can therefore be of value elsewhere.

Notes

(1) The term 'ethnic school' is widely used and accepted in Australia for community languages schools (AQF, 2007; AQTF, 2007).
(2) The Australian Qualifications Framework provides for a national system of post-compulsory education and training qualifications articulated according to the particular education sector (e.g. university, vocational). Within the vocational education and training sector, these qualifications range from Certificates I–IV, followed by Diploma, Advanced Diploma, Vocational Graduate Certificate and Vocational Graduate Diploma levels.
(3) In contrast, a full-time Graduate Diploma of Education student could expect 15 hours per week over 24 weeks.

References

AQF (2007) *Australian Qualifications Framework, Implementation Handbook* (4th edn). Carlton: Australian Qualifications Framework Advisory Board.
AQTF (2007) *Australian Qualifications and Training Framework, Standards for Accredited Courses.* Canberra: Commonwealth of Australia. See http://www.nssc.natese.gov.au/_data/assets/pdf_file/0005/69341/AQTF_2007_Standards_for_Accredited_Courses.pdf.
Baldauf, R. (2005) Coordinating government and community support for community languages teaching in Australia: Overview with special attention to New South Wales. *International Journal of Bilingual Education and Bilingualism* 8 (2), 132–144.

Clyne, M. (2005) *Australia's Language Potential.* Sydney: University of New South Wales Press.
Community Languages Australia (2007) *Community Languages Schools: Contributing to Quality Languages Education in Australia.* Canberra: Commonwealth of Australia. See http://www.communitylanguagesaustralia.org.au.
Creese, A. and Martin, P.W. (eds) (2006) Interaction in complementary school contexts. Developing identities of choice: An introduction. *Language and Education* 20 (1), 1–4.
DEECD (2011) *The Victorian Government's Vision for Languages Education.* Melbourne: Department of Education and Early Childhood Development.
Freeman, D. and Johnson, K. (1998) Reconceptualising the knowledge-base of language teacher education. *TESOL Quarterly* 32 (3), 397–417.
Hornberger, N. (2005) Heritage/community language education: US and Australian perspectives. *International Journal of Bilingual Education and Bilingualism* 8 (2), 101–108.
Johnson, K. (1996) The role of theory in L2 teacher education. *TESOL Quarterly* 30 (4), 765–771.
Kramsch, C. (1996) The cultural component of language teaching. *Zeitschrift für Interkulturellen Fremdsprachenunterricht* 1 (2). See http://zif.spz.tu-darmstadt.de/projekt_ejournal/jg-01-2/beitrag/kramsch2.htm. Originally published in *Language, Culture and Curriculum* 8 (2), 83–92.
Liu, P. (2008) Community-based Chinese schools in Southern California: A survey of teachers. *Language, Culture and Curriculum* 19 (2), 237–247.
Li Wei (1993) Mother tongue maintenance in a Chinese community school in Newcastle upon Tyne: Developing a social network perspective. *Language and Education* 7 (3), 199–215.
McPake, J., Tinsley, T. and James, C. (2007) Making provision for community languages: Issues for teacher education in the UK. *Language Learning Journal* 35 (1), 99–112.
Mirza, H.S. and Reay, D. (2000) Spaces and places of black educational desire: Rethinking black supplementary schools as a New Social Movement. *Sociology* 34 (3), 521–544.
Morgan, M. (2009) Analysis of reflections of teachers in community languages schools' methodology programmes. Paper delivered at *International Conference on Bilingualism and Bilingual Education: Fostering Multiliteracies through Education: a Middle Eastern Perspective*, American University of Sharjah, UAE.
Scarino, A. and Liddicoat, A. (2009) *Teaching and Learning Languages: A Guide.* Carlton South: Curriculum Corporation.
Vélez-Rendón, G. (2002) Second language teacher education: A review of the literature. *Foreign Language Annals* 35 (4), 457–467.
Vélez-Rendón, G. (2006) From student to teacher: A successful transition. *Foreign Language Annals* 39 (2), 320–334.

13 'A Somewhat Disconcerting Truth': The Perils of Monolingualism as Seen Through the Early Years of the RAAF School of Languages

Colin Nettelbeck

Introduction

Ongoing debates about the weak position in Australian schools and universities of the teaching and learning of languages other than English (e.g. Group of Eight, 2007; Liddicoat *et al.*, 2007; Lo Bianco & Slaughter, 2009; White & Baldauf, 2006) have almost completely ignored what the nation does about languages at the foremost edge of its interactions with the rest of the world, namely in the diplomatic corps and armed forces. This study aims to begin to redress that situation by analysing aspects of the work of the Royal Australian Air Force (RAAF) School of Languages which, for those who have been engaged in the struggle against Australia's culture of monolingualism (e.g. Clyne, 2005), has been a consistent if largely invisible ally. Renamed in 1993 as the Australian Defence Forces School of Languages, and again in 2008 as the Defence Forces School of Languages, it had in fact served all the services almost from its inception. Very little has been written to date about the School, almost all of it by insiders or former insiders (e.g. Funch, 2003; Garrick, 1967; Turner, 1983). There are, however, abundant archival materials now available in the Australian National Archives.[1] Because of space constraints, the present analysis cannot seek to cover the full history of the School and of the broader political contexts in which it has operated (see, for example, Beaumont, 2003). However, through a focus on the period under the governance of Flight Lieutenant, then Wing Commander Toby Garrick (1950–1968), it will be possible to give both an account of the dynamic development of the School, and due credit to the commitment, shrewdness and innovative spirit of Garrick himself, as well as to the philosophy of teaching and learning that underpinned his approach. I shall argue that a fuller knowledge and understanding of the experience and work of the RAAF School provides valuable lessons for everyone engaged in the promotion of languages.

Prehistory

A comprehensive, thoroughly documented history of the circumstances leading to the founding of the RAAF School of Languages in 1944 can be found in Colin Funch's (2003) *Linguists in Uniform: The Japanese Experience*. In the preface to this book, Major General Gordon Maitland optimistically opined that with the hindsight of the wartime experience, there might henceforth be better understanding of the need for languages. However, in his introductory comments, David Walker provides a less rosy view, arguing that, rather than any pre-war planning, it was luck, improvisation and hard work that helped Australia meet its needs. He pointedly notes that, despite growing signs of possible conflict with Japan through the 1930s, the small Japanese language programme conducted at the Royal Military College, Duntroon (in Australia's capital, Canberra), was closed down by the Department of Defence at the end of 1937, Japanese being deemed to be a language of 'no great cultural value' and, given that it was so hard to learn, a waste of time as well (Funch, 2003: 1). When the need for linguists in the conduct of the Pacific war became evident – for signals interception, decoding and interpreting documents, interrogating prisoners of war, as well as other intelligence and propaganda activities – it was initially a happenstance group of about 50 'ready-made' linguists (Funch, 2003: 5–6, 282–283) who had to be called upon. These were people who had learned Japanese for personal reasons. Some had training in the relatively established University of Sydney programme (see Akami, 1996), or in the more fragile one at the University of Melbourne (see Torney-Parlicki, 2005: 31ff). Some had lived for long periods in Japan; others had worked up their skills through private study.

One such 'ready-made' linguist was the Russian immigrant to Adelaide, Max Wiadrowski, who would go on to become the first Commanding Officer and Chief Instructor of the RAAF Language School in Sydney. Funch's account of the setting up of the School shows that, even when the need for linguists was urgent and patent, there was little commitment or leadership from the top. Indeed, some at ATIS (the Allied Translator and

Interpreter Service – the joint Australian-American WWII intelligence agency dealing with Japanese operations in the Pacific), even as they relied more and more heavily on American linguists, expressed the belief that 'the Australian character was not really suited to the discipline of language study' (Funch, 2003: 51ff; for ATIS, see also Gilmore, 2003).

The USA had set up its own school (the Military Intelligence Service Language School) in Minnesota not long before Pearl Harbour (in November 1941), but in Australia, it took the fall of Singapore (February 1942) and the bombing of Darwin (February and March 1942) to bring any real action. Jack Bleakley (1992), in *The Eavesdroppers*, documents the extreme difficulties under which the RAAF intelligence operations had to be carried out, especially in the early part of the war against Japan. Funch (2003: 52) stresses the importance of RAAF pressure in the eventual decision to begin training, and Bleakley (1992: 7) explains that RAAF prominence in the political lobbying derived from its special responsibilities in radio interception, instituted in mid-1941. Formal classes opened in July 1944. Despite RAAF doubts about the practical effectiveness of academic language programmes, Flying Officer Wiadrowski worked in collaboration with Arthur Sadler's Department of Oriental Studies at the University of Sydney. Teaching was shared by academic and military staff, with classes taking place both at the university and at the Coogee Bay Hotel, where the students were billeted. The learning was intensive: 10 hours per day, six days per week. The course, one year in duration, contained some history and culture of Japan, but also military terminology and material from captured Japanese documents. Testing took place weekly, with the pass level set at 90% (Funch, 2003: 56–57). The positive outcomes were numerous. Graduates of the programme were involved in a broad range of critical work, including the translation of thousands of captured documents, the interrogation of prisoners and production of reports, and the collection, collation and dissemination of information (Funch, 2003: 106–107). One graduate, Ray Trebilco, testifies colourfully:

> We interpreted at courts-martial, went on military police patrols, checked schools for banned literature, boarded fishing boats at sea for illegal immigrants or illegal activities, searched for hidden arms or ammunition, liaised with Japanese police and detectives, covered the first democratic elections in 1947, at which women were given the vote for the first time, checked brothels to ensure that women there were not being held under duress, and in general were available at all times for all forms of interpreting/translating assistance. (ADF SOL, 1993)

Funch signals that Wiadrowski, in a 1945 report on the completion of the first Japanese course, discerned a longer term benefit: 'The men trained at this school are one of Australia's most powerful arguments in claiming a share of post-war administration in the Pacific' (Funch, 2003: 68).

In mid-1945, it was decided to move the School to Melbourne, where it was at first located with the No 1 Engineering School at the Flemington racecourse, then at the Showgrounds in Ascot Vale, before eventually being set up within the RAAF complex at Point Cook in March 1946 (Funch, 2003: 69–74). It continued to teach Japanese until October 1948, when it was temporarily closed, opening again in May 1950.[2] Further investigation of this period of hiatus is needed, but it is reasonable to hypothesise that once the immediate needs caused by the war had disappeared, there was insufficient pressure to continue the teaching or the financial outlay it entailed. The reopening of the School, for Chinese and Russian, occurred in the lead-up to war in Korea, in a political context that included the belief of the Menzies government that a new war was imminent (Lowe, 1999: 43ff; 2010: 123–141).

What general points can we derive from this initial period? First, we should note that the decision to create a language school was reactive, and not, despite the strenuous but isolated efforts of E.L. Piesse in the Australian Prime Minister's Pacific Branch (see Meany, 1996), the result of strategic planning. Secondly, there seems to have been no thought that language instruction should be ongoing: introduced only as a result of direct military conflict, it appears to have been considered as useful only in that context of extreme necessity – witness the series of temporary accommodation solutions, in hotels and at racetracks, and the prompt closure. This reluctance to institutionalise the School would be one of the main targets of the Commanding Officer when the School was reopened. Thirdly, the collaboration between the military and academic worlds worked reasonably well, and the model of mixing military and civilian teachers would, as we shall see, be called upon in the post-1950 School. Fourthly, the programme would not have succeeded without the extraordinary enthusiasm of the teaching staff and the dedication and resilience of the students. That resilience was not a given. Funch (2003: 246) reports that in 1946 the Personnel Branch of the RAAF expressed its concern about the impact of the rigours of intensive language training on trainees: over the life of the programme 13% had been removed because of health problems, and there had even been suicides. The testimony we have cited provides compelling evidence that the service provided by the linguists was crucial to defending and safeguarding the nation; in acknowledging that service, we can see just how potentially harmful to national interest were the ignorance and blindness of the higher authorities.

The 1950 RAAF School of Languages: A Founding Document

In the months leading up to the reopening of the School in 1950, RAAF Headquarters sought, and received, detailed information about similar operations both in Britain and in the USA.[3] Focused on Russian and Chinese, this information was very comprehensive, covering the aims and structures of the training, the standards applied, issues about the selection of students, success rates, teaching methods and materials, and so on. We do not know to what degree the incoming director had input into the request for information. Garrick himself, who was working in military intelligence in Japan until his appointment, suggests that his involvement was considerable:

> I was recalled to Canberra, where I was told, more or less: 'We want to start a language institution to teach various languages and we've selected you to run it, so get cracking'. I had about three months to wander around and organise a location. Finally I settled for Point Cook in Victoria. (Baker, 1991: 6)

What is clear is that the accumulation of data was informed by an impressive knowledge of language training issues, and of organisational matters. These were qualities that Garrick possessed abundantly.

Who was Alex John ('Toby') Garrick? He was in fact Alexei Ivanovich Gavriloff, born in Vladivostock in 1919, raised and educated in China, migrating to Australia in early 1940.[4] An outstanding graduate of the first 1944 RAAF Japanese course in Sydney, he was selected by Wiadrowski to assist with the interrogation of Japanese POWs in Queensland, and later acted as an interpreter in the former Dutch East Indies and elsewhere during surrender operations. He was then posted to Japan with the occupation forces. After his 18-year stint at Point Cook, he became the foundation director of the Institute of Languages of the University of NSW, remaining in that position until his retirement in 1981. He died in 1995.

Garrick's suitability for the enormous responsibilities involved in commanding the revived School of Languages can be appreciated from a number of viewpoints. Whether or not he was directly responsible for the gathering of information from Britain and the US, his determination from the start that his School would be a good one, and respected by his superiors, can be seen in a number of documents that predate the beginning of actual classes. One of these, dated 15 June 1950[5] (training was supposed to have begun on 15 May!), states that courses in Russian and Chinese should begin 'sometime in August 1950', but adds: 'Indication of an actual commencement date cannot be laid down at this juncture, as the date will be governed by a number of factors beyond control of the staff of the School.' These factors included building refurbishment (not yet started), availability of textbooks, furniture and other equipment (all of which had been ordered but had not arrived), and availability of instructors (for whom requirements had been submitted, without any action having been taken). While it is signed by his superior, other archival documents leave no doubt that the letter was drafted by Garrick himself, and he stuck to his guns, refusing to let instruction begin until the physical setting, teaching materials and staffing arrangements were to his satisfaction. This meant that Russian instruction did not begin until 31 October 1950, and Chinese until 2 February 1951.[6] Throughout his entire tenure at Point Cook, Garrick would demonstrate similar firmness of purpose and stubbornness in his dealings with the often unresponsive guardians of the system within which he worked.

During these early months, Garrick penned another document entitled 'A Service Approach to the Study of European and Oriental Languages'.[7] This is a kind of manifesto that summarises Garrick's philosophy about languages and his plans for the RAAF School. As a founding text, it is not an entirely polished one – there are awkwardnesses and overstatements – and not every aspect of it would elicit complete approval from language teachers today. Nevertheless, much of it is visionary, evidence of a pioneering spirit that, when translated into the achievements that Garrick was able to make from it, deserves considerable respect.

The opening two paragraphs are worthy of being quoted in full, both for their content and for the pugnacious style:

> A knowledge of one or more foreign languages must today be regarded as an essential part of the education of everybody who does not wish to be excluded from a reasonably full life. There has never been a time when a knowledge of language was more necessary than this time in which we live. But, a somewhat disconcerting truth must be faced; neither the teaching or learning of languages can be considered as satisfactory or even seriously regarded here in Australia or in Britain and U.S.A. (*sic*) It does not take one long to discover that both teaching and learning are half suffocated by the obstinate employment of old-fashioned methods, old ideas, old prejudices – and old vested interests in going slow.
>
> When one considers the amount of time and energy spent by both teachers and learners in this highly important branch of education the only conclusion is that the results are far below what they might be if full advantage were taken of what is now known about this subject. A great speeding up and a great improvement is possible and essential. A revolutionary outlook in approaching the subject of language teaching and language learning is necessary, especially in service language training. (Garrick, 1950: 1)

Garrick's opening three sentences are as potently true today as they were when he wrote them, well in advance of Marshall McCluhan's articulation of the idea of the 'global village' in the early 1960s, and there can be no doubt that Garrick would have been even more 'disconcerted' by today's widespread and erroneous conviction that a full life can be led in the global village if one is a monolingual English speaker (see, for example, Price, 2011). The document goes on to express the belief that anyone can learn another language, and that notwithstanding slower absorption rates at later ages, barriers associated with age can largely be overcome through motivation and hard work.

That belief was not, however, applied to the potential students at Point Cook, who had to face a rigorous selection process based on age, previous educational achievements, an IQ test and a language aptitude test. Much of the rest of the document is concerned with stating and explaining the intensive nature of the planned training, and the methodology. Students were to be quartered together, with 10 hours of learning per day, Monday to Friday, over 50 weeks, and would be expected to 'use the language on every occasion during the working day'. Even 'physical exercise and sport and other aspects of service life are to be carried out in the language wherever practical' (Garrick, 1950: 3).

The ambitions for outcomes were demanding. With a staff:student ratio not exceeding 1:5, a 'good linguist' on completion of the course should not only be able to read, write, understand and speak the language well enough to 'put the natives completely at their ease', but he should also have strong 'background knowledge of the country, its geography, history, economics, culture, literature and so on' (Garrick, 1950: 8). Primacy was given to accurate pronunciation:

> A good pronunciation stands first before all other considerations. Without at least a passable pronunciation, speech – the soul of a language – must be either imperfect, clumsy or agonizing for the listener, or ineffective for its purpose, or, as sometimes happens, just so much meaningless noise. (Garrick, 1950: 6)

The emphasis is resolutely on the *practical*: indeed, the teaching of grammar, phonetics or any other theory is scathingly rejected:

> It is the school's contention that a language is best acquired by oral imitation and constant reading and study IN the language rather than by talking or hearing about the language in English. Of course this is sometimes unavoidable, but it is limited as much as practicable. (Garrick, 1950: 4)

While conceding that the learning of 'grammar in action' could be useful, Garrick was the committed disciple of a 'direct' methodology almost two decades before such ideas received any attention in Australian universities. As part of this method, he argued strongly for the use of every available technology to assist the learning process: sound recordings, radio, and visual aids including slides and films. Later, in 1961, again ahead of the university sector, his School would be the first in Australia to introduce a fully equipped language laboratory.

Perhaps the most controversial aspect of the document is its assertion that 'instructors need not be experienced teachers in the language', and that 'a well planned and coordinated syllabus will neutralize any inexperience in teaching' (Garrick, 1950: 7). For Garrick at this point, the best possible teacher was a native speaker with no knowledge of English. Fortunately, in this respect, he does not appear to have practised entirely what he preached. If there were undoubtedly instructors (both military and civilian) engaged during Garrick's tenure who had little or no teaching experience, many, like Waclav A. (Bin) Binental (ADF SOL, 1994: 11–13), gained long experience on the job. But also among the first appointments to the Russian programme was Stefan Stawicki, a Kiev-educated Pole with 'extensive teaching experience' (ADF SOL, 1994: 19). One sustained pattern is noticeable in the recruitment of teaching staff across the years of the School, and that is the tendency to use the best former students as teachers; in this way, learning a language intensively became a kind of apprenticeship for teaching.

A final element in this policy document was its emphasis on the importance of physical comfort for the learners. We have seen the resistance to beginning classes in 1950 before the buildings had been refurbished. In 'A Service Approach', Garrick (1950: 6) explains:

> ... a good cheerful and comfortable building with every facility for instructing and private study would reduce factors such as study fatigue, language neurosis, and other similar conditions that are ultimately met in the intensive day after day study of languages, especially oriental.

In a language learning environment dependent on learners' 'urge and incentive' (Garrick, 1950: 7), Garrick's sensitivity to external conditions was certainly informed by his wartime experience. The focus on adequate and congenial learning spaces would be another constant in Garrick's administration as the School began its rapid growth. That his correspondence to his superiors should have referred with great regularity to accommodation matters is not surprising in the light of Turner's (1983: 18) description of the 'outhouses' in which the School had to operate:

> The outhouses are pre-war weatherboard buildings on the foreshore of RAAF Base Point Cook. The smell, nauseating in summer but thankfully absent in winter, comes from seaweed that lies racked over sand exposed at low tide on either side of a decaying jetty. The scrub along the foreshore is thick with tiger snakes in summer. Winter days can be long and depressing and when a dank sea mist closes in, the atmosphere is undiluted Gulag.

The outhouses were hardly Garrick's ideal of the congenial learning space. Above all, once again, this description reinforces the sense that the authorities accorded languages no sense of permanency.

Growth 1950–1968: Achievements and Problems

As we have seen, the RAAF School of Languages in 1950 began with two courses, Russian and Chinese. By 1968, it was providing instruction in 11 languages – Vietnamese, Indonesian, Thai, Chinese, French, Burmese, Cambodian, Laotian, Russian, Italian and Malay – with three different delivery modes: the full-time year-long course; so-called 'ad hoc' intensive courses; and refresher courses for previous graduates of the long courses. As with Russian and Chinese, the adoption of other languages followed the development of Australia's strategic relations with the rest of the world. Thus, Indonesian was introduced in 1956 in the context of the ambiguous mix of mutual distrust and the need to establish better relations that characterised the so-called Sukarno-Menzies era. Vietnamese came in just before direct Australian engagement in the Vietnam war, French with the decision to purchase military aircraft (Mirage, Mystère), and so on. The School did not chart its own development, or directly determine its own expansion – it was always an instrument of government policy – and in a general way, we can see that its take-up of new languages is a reflection of Australia's increasing sense of the importance of regional factors, particularly southeast Asia.

This lack of autonomy was at times a source of aggravation for Garrick. The process for getting increases in staffing, accommodation and equipment was ponderous and bureaucratic, and Garrick's frequent, detailed and carefully argued requests were met with responses that were always sluggish and often negative. A document entitled 'Functions of the RAAF School of Languages' that he put together in the mid-1960s[8] offers a useful snapshot of how the School's responsibilities had grown. It lists six points:

(1) To plan and prepare up-to-date syllabuses of courses for all Defence and Commonwealth Departments in the undermentioned languages and to conduct these courses accordingly; either on a full time, ad hoc, or refresher basis: Chinese National, Indonesian, Malay, Vietnamese, Thai, French, Japanese, Italian, Cambodian, Burmese, Russian.
(2) To plan, prepare and conduct other language courses as required to meet changing defence needs for all Defence and Commonwealth Departments.
(3) To conduct examinations for all Defence and Commonwealth Departments to determine eligibility for payment of Language Bounties in accordance with Treasury Regulations.
(4) To process and select applicants for language training from the Defence and Commonwealth Departments.
(5) To carry out translations of miscellaneous language material and to provide language personnel for language duties as may be necessary by (sic) all Defence Departments.

(6) To maintain a specialised reference library and other facilities to carry out these above functions and perform research into language training material and methods as applicable to the intensive training system used at the School.

A number of these points need elucidation. The 'ad hoc' courses provided by the School to satisfy various demands lasted anything from a few weeks to some months. They could occur in any language: thus, for example, in French in 1965, the Department of External Affairs required training (all at different times) for its Counsellor to the Embassy in Saigon, its High Commissioner to Ghana and a Counsellor to the Delegation in Geneva, while the Department of Supply, the Department of Air and the Government Aircraft Company all required training (once again at different times) for people involved in the Mirage Project. During the same period, there were similar demands in Malay, Russian and Japanese. Anyone with administrative experience will readily understand the headaches that such a situation can cause when rigid establishment rules bring resistance to any notion of flexible hiring of part-time or temporary staff. And those with experience of defending the special demands of language teaching will undoubtedly sympathise with Garrick's frustrations, and the very considerable efforts he had to put into providing his superiors with facts, figures, diagrams, tables and so forth, about every aspect of the workings of his School.

The 'refresher' courses were related to the Language Bounties mentioned in Point 3. The idea of using cash incentives for language trainees, as Garrick documents in a September 1957 review,[9] had been discussed since the late 1940s, based on a successful existing UK model. It was introduced on a joint services basis by the Defence Ministry in early 1956, for linguists qualified in Chinese (both Mandarin and Cantonese), Indonesian, Malay and Russian. Intended not as a reward for achievement, but as an incentive for keeping the language up to standard, the scheme paid £50 to eligible graduates, and a further £50 per annum thereafter, provided that the candidates passed a yearly test at the appropriate level. This appears to be the first time that Australian authorities actually placed a monetary value on the maintenance of a pool of linguistic competence – a de facto recognition, at least, of the value of languages in the national economy. More relevant here, however, is the scheme's impact on the activity and workload of the School of Languages, which became responsible for testing, issuing certificates, providing refresher courses for candidates in advance of the tests, and general troubleshooting.

The selection processes mentioned in Point 4 were another distinguishing feature of the School's operations. We saw earlier that Garrick believed that any motivated person could learn a language, but he also knew that some were more likely to succeed (and less likely to drop out) than others. In the early days, selection was based on what was at the time quite limited research: both British and American advice was relatively vague, referring to factors such as previous educational achievement, age, adaptability, verbal fluency in English, and motivation.[10] Garrick kept a close eye on developments in this area, however, and was quick to take up the Harvard-based Modern Language Aptitude Test when it was released in 1959. It continues to be widely used today, a longevity that Sasaki (2012) ascribes to the test's fundamental robustness. Its rapid adoption in the RAAF School is evidence of Garrick's good judgement and alertness to innovation.

Point 6 refers to the library, and to 'other facilities', which include the language laboratory, another example of Garrick's innovative approach. We have already mentioned that this laboratory, created in 1961, was the first of its kind in Australia. In the following several years, Point Cook became a veritable pilgrimage site for university language departments as they sought to cope with the paradigm shift occurring in the content and methodologies of their fields.

In addition, the School regularly responded to requests from universities to provide copies of the tapes used in its programmes, especially in Asian languages. A letter from Garrick to the University of Queensland's Institute of Modern Languages shows an exemplary collaborative spirit:

> Thank you very much for your letter requesting our aid in the supply of language training material. We are at all times pleased to be able to assist other language training institutes in whatever manner we can.[11]

The growth in the number of languages at the School, and that of the numbers of students and staff, led to concomitant growth in print resources and technical equipment, all of which required maintenance and management. Between 1964 and 1967, laboratory equipment doubled in volume; in 1968, the library held almost 7000 books, 2500 additional miscellaneous publications, and subscribed to over 100 magazines and newspapers in nine foreign languages and English.[12] Whatever pride Garrick may rightly have felt in the vitality of his institution, it must surely have been tempered by the unceasing battles he was obliged to wage with his superiors in order to ensure that the School had enough space and manpower to fulfil its mandate. A 1967 letter from Air Commodore C.F. Read of RAAF Headquarters Support Command would have worried Garrick by its ambiguities:

> It is not possible for me at this level to determine with certainty, whether or not all the present training is absolutely essential. We are accepting students from non-service departments and from overseas, and we are also providing thirteen to fifteen Refresher Courses per annum for linguists to maintain their proficiency and to retain their bounty payment. Not all these latter people are subsequently posted immediately to day to day language duties. It is possible that some training could be diverted into other language training organisations.[13]

Conclusion: A Permanent Quest for Excellence

Squadron Leader Barry Turner, a director of studies at Point Cook, quotes a visitor as describing the School of Languages (SOL) as 'an institute of world standing' (Turner, 1983: 18), and credits Garrick with laying the foundations for that level of excellence (Turner, 1983: 23). All evidence indeed points to Garrick's unwavering concern for the quality of his operation throughout his years of leadership. This can be seen at every level, from the meticulous tracking of the progress of every individual student, through the permanent scrutiny of the processes and methodologies of teaching and learning (including the quality of teaching spaces), to the willingness to be subject to frequent detailed reviews, and the desire to 'benchmark' Point Cook against comparable institutions in Britain and the US. We have noted the rapidity with which Garrick introduced the American aptitude testing and American-inspired language laboratory techniques; he was also able to use knowledge of overseas systems to argue for the maintenance of favourable staff:students ratios.

Never afraid to point out the achievements of his School, Garrick was not, however, a man to rest on his laurels. In 1966, in one of the innumerable requests he made to his superiors for more resources, he stressed the need for continuous innovation:

> The RAAF School of Languages has now developed to such a size, and grown to such a place of leadership in the field of practical language teaching, that constant research and development of new ideas is imperative, if it is to maintain this lead and continue to produce high grade language personnel.[14]

Not many Australian university languages departments of that era could have boasted such enthusiasm and drive, especially in relation to the Asian languages that dominated the SOL curriculum. Garrick's leadership qualities remain an admirable model today, as do the clarity with which he articulated his objectives and his determination in developing, evaluating and adapting the most effective methods for attaining those goals. His patience and courage in repeatedly explaining, to those decision-makers above him, what was special and different about languages, also remains exemplary.

University colleagues can learn from all those qualities. But the history of the RAAF School of Languages offers an even more potent instrument in the struggle against Anglo-centred monolingualism in Australia and elsewhere. From its very early days in wartime and in postwar Japan, it was producing linguists who reached levels of understanding more wide reaching than simply breaking codes or intercepting enemy transmissions. They learned that speaking quietly in another person's language could be more effective than shouting loudly in English. In prisoners of war, they discovered people rather than stereotypes, and possibilities of communication and cooperation where many of their superiors saw only conflict. As Garrick put it:

> We wondered: how do you behave with them? Do you slap them on the face when you're asking them questions or do you do something else? With the Japanese (...), if you took the rough road and tried to get tough, you got nowhere, whereas if you understood their feelings and slowly got around them, they would tell you everything. In many respects, I felt that acquiring this kind of knowledge was an essential upbringing in terms of linguistics, language and speech. (Baker, 1991: 3–4)

As we have seen, the development of those intercultural spaces to which only high levels of language proficiency can give access was the goal that Wiadrowski and Garrick fostered in their students, too often against those whom Turner (1983: 23) dubs 'the unwilling or unwitting authorities'. It is a goal that university languages and culture programmes, particularly, can admire and share: it is a worthy and humane one, and its realisation can enrich and strengthen individuals and communities as they confront today's momentous global shifts.

Notes

(1) While individual folders are generally well classified, documents within those folders are not always dated or numbered. We have attempted to make our references as unambiguous as possible.
(2) Australian National Archives B5832 3.1AIR ONE (Formation and Organisation RAAF School of Languages) document 1A, Southern Area Administrative Instruction No. 1/50, 11 April 1950.
(3) Information was received from the British Air Force, and from the naval and army schools in the USA. See, for British involvement, Australian National Archives B5832/1.1/47AIR, and for US involvement B5832/1.1/3AIR.
(4) Details of Garrick's life are compiled from Dillon (1995), Baker (1991), ADF SOL (1994) and Funch (2003). Funch does not reveal any awareness that Garrick and Gavriloff were the same person.
(5) Australian National Archives B5832 3/2AIR 5A.
(6) Australian National Archives B5832 1.4/1AIR.
(7) Australian National Archives B5832 57 2AIR 1.
(8) Australian National Archives B6853AIR 4.1.2/3. The document is not dated, but its position in the folder makes it likely that it is from 1964 or 1965.
(9) Australian National Archives B5832 57/20AIR 1 (Bounties).
(10) B5832/1.1/47AIR and B5832/1.1/3AIR. In the early stages of the school, candidates were obliged to submit to psychological testing.
(11) B5853 57/2/AIR. Letter dated 18 April 1961.
(12) B5853AIR 4.1.2/3.
(13) B5853AIR 4.1.2/3. Letter dated 17 March 1967.
(14) B5853AIR 4.1.2/3. Document dated 11 February 1966.

References

ADF SOL (Australian Defence Force School of Languages) (1994) Special anniversary issue. *Festina Lente* 2 (3).

Akami, T. (1996) The liberal dilemma. PhD thesis, Australian National University, Canberra.

Baker, V. (ed.) (1991) Interview with Alex John (Toby) Garrick by Laurie Dillon, November 1981. In *The University Oral History Project*. Sydney: University of New South Wales Archives.

Beaumont, J. (2003) Creating an elite? The Diplomatic Cadet Scheme, 1943–1956. In J. Beaumont, C. Waters, D. Lowe and G. Woodward (eds) *Ministers, Mandarins and Diplomats: Australia's Foreign Policy Making 1941–1969* (pp. 19–44). Melbourne: Melbourne University Press.

Bleakley, J. (1992) *The Eavesdroppers*. Canberra: Australian Government Publishing Office.

Clyne, M. (2005) *Australia's Language Potential*. Sydney: University of New South Wales Press.

Dillon, L. (1995) Campaigner for Asian languages. *The Australian* 19 May, p. 18.

Funch, C. (2003) *Linguists in Uniform: The Japanese Experience*, Melbourne: The Japanese Studies Centre, Monash University.

Garrick, A.J. (1950) *A Service Approach to the Study of European and Oriental Languages*. B5832 57 2AIR 1 (pp. 1–8). Canberra: Australian National Archives.

Garrick, A.J. (1967) Authentic materials for integrated language laboratory courses. *Babel* 3 (3), 20–21.

Gilmore, A. (2003) The allied translator and interpreter section: The critical role of allied linguists in the process of propaganda creation, 1943–1944. In P. Dennis and J. Grey (eds) *The Foundations of Victory: The Pacific War 1943–1944: The 2003 Chief of Army's Military History Conference* (pp. 149–167). Canberra: Army History Unit, Department of Defence.

Group of Eight (2007) *Languages in Crisis: A Rescue Plan for Australia*. Canberra: Group of Eight Universities. See https://go8.edu.au/sites/default/files/agreements/go8-languages-in-crisis-discussion-paper.pdf.

Liddicoat, A.J., Scarino, A., Curnow, T.J., Kohler, M., Scrimgeour, A. and Morgan, A.-M. (2007) *An Investigation of the State and Nature of Languages in Australian Schools*. Canberra: Department of Education, Employment and Workplace Relations.

Lo Bianco, J. and Slaughter, Y. (2009) *Second Languages and Australian Schooling*. Melbourne: Australian Council for Educational Research.

Lowe, D. (1999) *Menzies and the 'Great World Struggle': Australia's Cold War 1948–1954*. Sydney: University of New South Wales Press.

Lowe, D. (2010) *Australian Between Empires: The Life of Percy Spender*. London: Pickering and Chatto.

Meaney, N. (1996) *Fears and Phobias: E.L. Piesse and the Problem of Japan 1909–39*. Canberra: National Library of Australia.

Price, S. (2011) Let's ditch the study of languages. *Herald Sun*, 2 February. See http://www.heraldsun.com.au/opinion/lets-ditch-the-study-of-languages/story-e6frfhqf-1225999139631.

Sasaki, M. (2012) The Modern Language Aptitude Test (paper-and-pencil version). *Language Testing* 29, 315–332.

Torney-Parlicki, P. (2005) *Behind the News: A Biography of Peter Russo*. Crawley: University of Western Australia Press.

Turner, B. (1983) Outhouses of excellence: The development of the RAAF School of Languages. *Defence Force Journal* 38, January/February, 18–24.

White, P. and Baldauf, R. (2006) *Re-Examining Australia's Tertiary Language Programs: A Five Year Retrospective on Teaching and Collaboration*. St Lucia: University of Queensland.

14 'Die Erfüllung eines Traums': Challenging the Monolingual Mindset Through the Establishment of an Early Immersion Language Programme

Averil Grieve

This chapter focuses on the establishment of early immersion bilingual schools in an English majority language setting. It provides in-depth discussion of overcoming the monolingual mindset and establishing bilingual models that cater for a wide range of language abilities and interests. Using case study data from a German-English early immersion independent school in Australia, the chapter explores the adaptation of early immersion models, curriculum development and the complexity of issues that need to be taken into account when establishing a new bilingual programme. These include the interests of potential parents and pupils, governmental registration hurdles and funding. Such discussions are essential due to long-standing resistance to total immersion language programmes in Australia. By challenging this resistance, the late Michael Clyne's (2005) vision for an Australian society in which multilingualism is accepted and celebrated may eventually be realised.

The chapter begins with a brief overview of early total immersion schooling in the Australian context, current two-way early immersion models and simultaneous versus sequential literacy. The chapter then focuses on the establishment of the Deutsche Schule Melbourne (DSM), including an overview of the school, considerations informing bilingual programme design and adaptation of the two-way immersion model. It concludes with a discussion of the challenges and advantages of the current DSM model.

Early Total Immersion in Australia

Similar to the situations in other English-dominant countries such as England and the USA, in the Australian context 'bilingualism, becoming bilingual, and the encouragement of innovative language education programs within the core or basic curriculum of public education are so often viewed as *problematic, difficult* or *undesirable*' (Tucker & Dubiner, 2008: 267). Unfortunately, in Australia we tend to celebrate multiculturalism but denigrate multilingualism. It is a multicultural society with a monolingual mindset in which individuals (including policy makers) remain oblivious to the social, economic, political, medical, academic and personal advantages of more than one language (Clyne, 2005).

A prime example is recent governmental attitudes to bilingual education programmes in Australia's Northern Territory, in which the languages of instruction were an indigenous language and English. In 2008, after over 30 years of existence, these bilingual programmes were effectively dismantled due to a mandate that the first four hours of each school day were to be taught exclusively in English (see Northern Territory Government, 2008). This was a knee-jerk reaction to the results of National Assessment Program – Literacy and Numeracy (NAPLAN) tests in May 2008, which indicated that Indigenous children in remote communities had the lowest test scores across Australia. While bilingual programmes were immediately problematised, low test scores were more likely due to the content of the tests themselves, which was inappropriate for children living in remote Indigenous communities. Test content relied on cultural knowledge that Indigenous children cannot be expected to have, which placed them in a disadvantaged position compared to children living in urban areas whose first language was Australian English (Wigglesworth *et al.*, 2011). The tests were also exclusively in English, so did not take children's mathematical and literacy abilities in languages other than English into account.

The introduction of nationwide literacy and numeracy testing (NAPLAN) in 2008 increased the prioritisation of English literacy over and above literacy in any other language (Molyneux, 2009). NAPLAN is conducted in English only and, in the Australian school context, language proficiency has become synonymous with mastering reading, writing, speaking and listening skills *in English*. Teachers feel increasingly pressured to ensure that students speedily reach English proficiency benchmarks in Years 3, 5, 7 and 9 and no account is made for the literacy skills of children in any language other than English. Contrary to both national and state-level policy statements (see Douglas, 2012; Molyneux, 2009), the importance of languages other than English and the needs of English as a second language (ESL) students have been marginalised by insisting that all Australian school children pass literacy tests that are prepared according to the expected development of mainstream groups of English-speaking Australian children (McKay, 2001; Wigglesworth *et al.*, 2011).

While bilingual school programmes exist in Australia, immersion programmes are rare. Immersion programmes are those in which the language of instruction is in two languages for equal amounts of school time or a non-dominant language is the medium of instruction for more than 50% of the school day (Molyneux, 2009). If immersion programmes are established and supported in the Australian context, they are typically only partial immersion where the majority of subjects are taught in English (Truckenbrodt & De Courcy, 2002), and are often seen to be of relevance to community speakers only. Indeed, for multilingualism to become the norm in Australia, the aim of school curricula 'should be to make languages a compulsory, unproblematic and celebrated part of the education of all Australian children' (Lo Bianco & Slaughter, 2009b: 62).

As pointed out by Molyneux (2009), in the state of Victoria, which is the main focus of both his and this study, there are 1600 government schools. In 2012, only 12 schools offered bilingual education in which at least two curriculum areas are taught in a language other than English and face-to-face teaching in the non-English language occurs for at least 7.5 hours per week. This poor representation of immersion programmes in the state of Victoria may partly be due to the fact that until 2005, the Victorian Education Act (1958) explicitly stated that the language of instruction in all Victorian schools must be English unless otherwise decided by the Minister of Education. It was only through the ongoing concerted efforts of citizens of Victoria, especially those of Michael Clyne, that the Act was amended in the Spring session of Victoria's State Parliament in 2005. The Education Act 1958 (as at 5 April 2005) and the 2006 Victorian Education and Training Reform Act now make no restrictions as to the language of instruction.

It was in this climate of hesitation and problematising of bilingual programmes in both Australia and the state of Victoria that the Deutsche Schule Melbourne (DSM) was established. The school's bilingual programme is an adaptation of a two-way early total immersion model.

Two-way Early Total Immersion

Two-way early total immersion programmes were originally designed for (monolingual) speakers of either the majority or minority language (Baker, 2006). They aim to have approximately equal representation of speakers of each language in the classroom. Students are integrated for most if not all instruction, and academic subjects and literacy skills are taught through both languages. The model strives for both oral and written proficiency in the minority and majority tongues (Baker, 2006; Lindholm-Leary & Howard, 2008).

Time allocated to each language of instruction varies somewhat in two-way early immersion programmes, but typically they can be divided into two main models: 90/10 or 50/50. In the 90/10 model, 90% of teaching is initially conducted in the minority language in the first one or two years of schooling (i.e. in the state of Victoria 'Foundation'[1] and 'Grade 1'). Hours of instruction in the majority language are gradually increased until 50% of the instruction is in each language (see Figure 14.1). In the 90/10 model, children are first introduced to literacy in the minority language before the introduction of formal majority language reading in the third year of schooling (sequential literacy) (Genesee, 2008; Lindholm-Leary & Howard, 2008).

In the 50/50 model, students receive half of their instruction in the majority language and the other half in the partner language throughout primary school. At some schools, students learn to read first in their primary language and second language literacy is introduced in Grade 2 or 3. In other schools students learn to read and write in both languages simultaneously.

In schools where simultaneous literacy acquisition is practised, children learn to read and write in both languages at the same time and, in doing so, they seek out connections between different writing systems. Sequential literacy is when children learn to read and write in the minority language first and then the majority language. These children show a high level of transfer of literacy skills from one language to another (e.g. decoding and reading strategies). Children learning literacy simultaneously tend to have an initial advantage over children who learn to read in two languages sequentially (Bialystok, 2001), but there is no conclusive evidence as to which approach to bilingual literacy is better (Verhoeven, 1987). Results do, however, indicate that 'there is no reason not to teach literacy simultaneously' (Clyne, personal communication).

When two-way immersion programmes are implemented, they tend to be highly successful on a range of levels. After 4–7 years, two-way

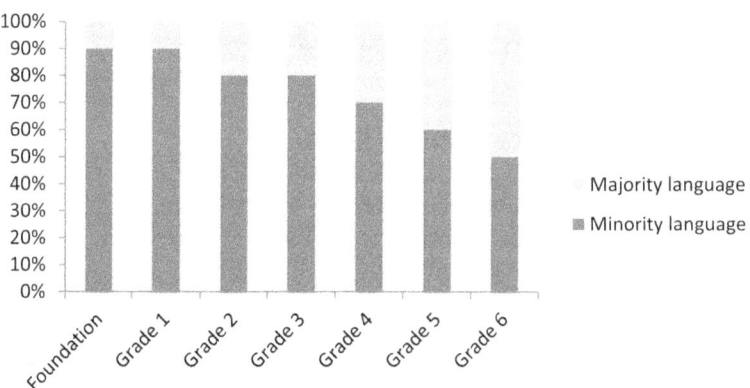

Figure 14.1 90/10 two-way early immersion model

immersion students equal or outperform monolingually educated English speakers in a range of subjects (e.g. Garcia, 2003; Lindholm-Leary & Borsato, 2006) and all students in two-way immersion demonstrate high levels of majority language proficiency (Christian *et al.*, 2004). Differences are found among students from a minority or majority speaker background, whereby native speakers of the minority language tend to be more balanced in oral proficiency than native speakers of the majority language (Howard & Christian, 1997). Comparing 90/10 and 50/50 two-way immersion outcomes, students in 90/10 programmes tend to develop higher levels of bilingual proficiency than those in 50/50 programmes (Lindholm-Leary, 2001). On a non-academic note, two-way immersion also enhances inter-group communicative competence and cultural awareness. Children educated in two-way immersion programmes are more likely to be tolerant, sensitive and equalised in status than those who are educated monolingually (Genesee & Gándara, 1999). Bilingual programmes empower students by stimulating and expanding their self-worth, intellect, imagination and experience of the world (Garcia, 2009). Indeed, research consistently shows that 'immersion methodology is a valid, effective and durable mode for second language learning as well as for imparting the general curriculum to young learners, while supporting their English development' (Lo Bianco & Slaughter, 2009a: 29).

Deutsche Schule Melbourne

The Deutsche Schule Melbourne (DSM) represents the first German-English early immersion bilingual programme in the state of Victoria, Australia. As described in detail by Douglas (2012), the formation of the DSM was sparked by a talk given by the then Principal of the German International School Sydney, Klaus Steinmetz, in the city of Melbourne in 2004. Together with the Consul General of the Federal Republic of Germany in Melbourne, Steinmetz organised a tour across Australian capital cities to talk about the Sydney school and plant the seed for similar schools to be established around Australia. From 2004 to 2008 interested individuals worked towards establishing a bilingual German-English school in Melbourne and the school opened in February 2008 with:

- 14 pupils from Foundation–Year 2;
- 13 families;
- 1 full-time teacher;
- 3 part-time teachers.

The 14 students were in one composite class with one German-speaking and one English-speaking teacher. As discussed below, four of these pupils spoke German only or German and another language at home, five spoke

English and German and five spoke English only or English and another language in the home environment. The DSM model insists that all teachers are bilingual in German and English and instruct in their strongest mother tongue. Bilingual education follows a 90/10 two-way early total immersion model with adaptations, which are discussed in detail below. The curriculum fulfils the requirements of two curricula: the Victorian Essential Learning Standards (VELS) and the Thuringia state curriculum of Germany. When, or if, a national Australian curriculum is introduced, the school will retain the Thuringian curriculum and incorporate the Australian national standards. Enrolments have steadily increased from 14 in 2008 to 45 in 2012 and a full roll-out of all primary school levels (Foundation–Grade 6) in 2014 with 73 pupils.

To create the school, a number of critical activities were undertaken, such as gauging the level of interest, attracting support and finding key drivers and developing the 'machinery' (Douglas, 2012). This included finding a building, writing curricula and policy documents, and establishing an appropriate bilingual model. When developing the DSM bilingual model, a range of considerations needed to be taken into account. As shown in Figure 14.2, the interests of four primary parties needed to be included: potential school parents, the Victorian Registration and Qualifications Authority (VRQA),[2] funding bodies and the DSM board.

A survey of potential school parents clearly indicated an interest in creating not only a bilingual but also a bicultural and biliterate educational model. A running theme in all feedback was the fear of creating a *deutsche Insel* or an enclave of German-speaking families that had little connection to the Australian schooling system or way of life. This meant that the school

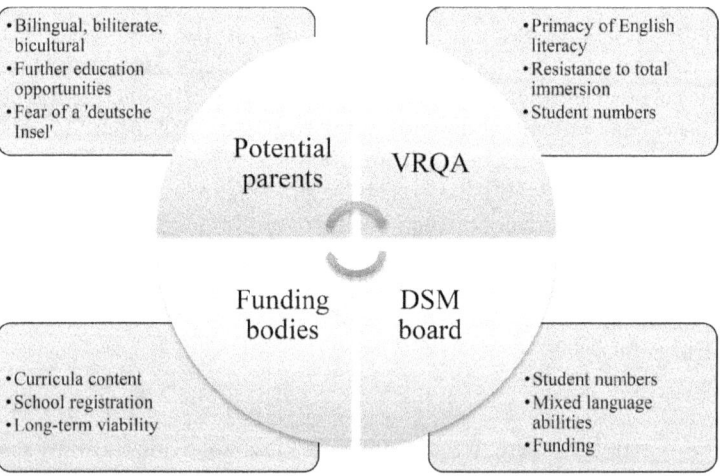

Figure 14.2 Considerations informing development of DSM model

needed to cater not only for non-Australian short-stay families, but for all families intending to stay in Australia for the long term, including those with little or no connection to German-speaking countries. Potential families were also interested in a school that provided children with the opportunity to seamlessly continue their education in either Australia or German-speaking countries, e.g. university education without having to sit additional entry exams, or entering or re-entering German primary or secondary education without having to repeat any year levels.

The VRQA sets clear guidelines as to what a school must have for registration. In order to operate in the state of Victoria, a school is required to fulfil all mandatory requirements set by the VRQA. These are listed in a guide for new schools and include minimum standards in the areas of school governance, enrolment, curriculum and student learning, monitoring and reporting on students' performances, student welfare, discipline, attendance, staff employment, school infrastructure and educational facilities. While these state-wide regulations are currently based on the Education and Training Reform Act 2006 and the Education and Training Reform Regulations 2007, at the time of preparing documents for the registration of the DSM, the restrictive Victorian Education Act 1958 was still in force. This meant that all schools at the time had to have English as the language of instruction, unless otherwise decided by the Minister of Education. This legal requirement caused issues in preparing documents for the registration of the DSM: the VRQA clearly indicated hesitation in supporting a full early immersion bilingual school, making it clear that gaining registration for such schools was rare and difficult. As pointed out by Joanne Sweeney, a former DSM board member:

> ... there it was, bold as brass, written in the Education Act that you couldn't teach in any other language besides English. I think in years gone by it had been trotted out as a reason that it was always going to be difficult to start a school that taught in a language that wasn't English. (Douglas, 2012: 42)

The key party involved in establishing the school was the DSM board. The 10–12 board members were democratically elected at a meeting of 50–80 interested individuals at Trinity Lutheran Church Hall, Melbourne in 2004 (Douglas, 2012). While board membership has changed considerably since inception, foundation members included a minister of the Lutheran German Church of Melbourne, an applied linguist, a management consultant, a speech therapist, a psychologist, two lawyers and language teachers. A representative of the Consulate General of the Federal Republic of Germany was an invited non-elected guest to all board meetings.

One important issue faced by the board was that of funding. Start-up funds of AU$200,000 were provided by the Lutheran German Church and the Catholic German Church, which immediately introduced the interests of two new stakeholders. Funds from the Australian government would be available as of registration and the German government would begin providing funds after two years of successful operation. Student numbers were of critical importance to the board, not only in terms of VRQA registration requirements, but also in relation to financial viability. Numbers were inextricably related to finding a viable location for the school. The location itself had to be an affordable property that was centrally located, with good transport access and able to pass all relevant zoning, building and VRQA regulations (VRQA, 2011), e.g. a permit to operate an educational centre, compliance with local planning regulations and the Building Code of Australia, and age-appropriate and adequate facilities for the effective delivery of primary school programmes.

The mixed language abilities of potential pupils were also a key factor in board decision-making processes. Even if many potential pupils had been introduced to German in the home environment, there were large variations in proficiency levels. For example, some spoke German exclusively in the home; others spoke German to one parent only and the degree of input depended very much on the hours the parent spent with the child and his/her consistency in speaking only German. While many of those students who spoke German in the home environment were balanced bilinguals (e.g. English was learnt via friendships with Australian children or kindergarten), others had only recently arrived in Australia and spoke little English. Some children of interested families did not speak German in the immediate home environment, but had German-speaking grandparents. This mix of language abilities had to be taken into account in curriculum and bilingual model design as well as in marketing programmes to attract families from non-German-speaking backgrounds.

The interests of all primary parties were inextricably connected and, at times, conflicting. For example, the board and potential school parents wanted children to gain literacy skills in both languages, but the VRQA insisted on an emphasis in gaining literacy in English and was sceptical this could be achieved by simultaneous literacy. While much of the preparatory work of the DSM board involved making concessions to fulfil the needs of interested parties, full early immersion was never considered negotiable. It is to a brief discussion of the development of the early total immersion model that we now turn.

Adaptation of two-way 90/10 early total immersion

Given the perceived greater benefit of a 90/10 over a 50/50 model (see above), especially in terms of the highly divergent proficiencies of potential students, a two-way 90/10 early total immersion model was selected. However, it was then adapted to meet the demands of interested parties.

Firstly, as discussed above, 90/10 early total immersion typically focuses on monolingual speakers of either the majority or minority languages and requires an equal split of language representation. This was adapted in the DSM model, which necessarily caters for a wide range of student language backgrounds (including monolingual speakers of the majority or minority languages, bilingual speakers of both languages, as well as bilingual speakers of languages other than German or English). The DSM model also tends to promote higher numbers of minority language speakers (i.e. German) than majority language speakers (i.e. Australian English). These adaptations were made to ensure the rapid acquisition of both English and/or German and, at the same time, to avoid the creation of an exclusive *deutsche Insel* in the Melbourne Australian context. Additionally, by opening the doors to children of all language and cultural backgrounds, potential student numbers were increased.

Analysis of student home language backgrounds shows large fluctuations from 2008 to 2014. Although the dataset is too small to indicate any clear trends, the school's decision not to insist on an equal representation of language abilities has proven advantageous in terms of ensuring an increase in student numbers and a mix of linguistic and cultural backgrounds. As shown in Table 14.1, start-up pupils were typically from a bilingual background (71.4%). Fifty percent of these were families with one Australian and one German-speaking parent, while other families spoke German exclusively in the home environment or spoke English and another language (e.g. Spanish). As mentioned above, typically children who spoke German only at home and had lived in Australia for an extended period were highly proficient in both English and German.

Proficiency levels of German varied greatly in those families where both German and English were spoken. Clearly, in the start-up year, parents who had already actively promoted bilingualism in the home environment were those who were most likely to send their children to a bilingual school. This was also the case after two years of operation (78.3%), but in 2012, pupils

Table 14.1 Language backgrounds of students (2008, 2010, 2012 and 2014)

Language background	2008	2010	2012	2014
Bilingual				
• German-English[a]				
• German-Other	71.4%	78.3%	54.3%	61.6%
• English-Other				
Monolingual				
• English non-German heritage	28.6%	21.7%	45.7%	38.4%
• English German heritage				

Note: [a]Includes children who speak German and English in the home and those who speak German only at home but have learnt English through living in an English majority language environment.

from a pre-existing bilingual background decreased to just over half (54.3%) of the student cohort. Comparatively, the percentage of children from a monolingual English background increased from 28.6% in 2008 to 45.7% in 2012. In 2014 61% were from bilingual backgrounds, meaning the monolingual English background pupils decreased slightly to 38%. While fluctuations can be seen in the English-monolingual cohort (i.e. decrease to 21.7% in 2010 and 38% in 2014), an analysis of English German heritage versus English non-German heritage speakers indicates that the number of pupils from English German heritage families has consistently increased from 2008 to 2014 (e.g. two pupils in 2008, four in 2010 and 14 in 2014). English German heritage pupils are those who have German grandparents on one or both sides of the family, but the German language is not spoken at home as it was not passed on to the children's own parents. It has essentially skipped a generation. English non-German heritage pupils increased from one in 2010 to nine in 2012 to 14 in 2014. The 2012 figure was mostly due to an influx of non-German speakers from another local school that had made large changes to its teaching philosophy and classroom structure. While the data sample is too small to draw any firm conclusions, it may indicate a change in commitment to bilingual education. Initially, mostly those already open to bilingualism enrolled their children in the school. After six years of the school's existence, monolingual English-speaking families seem to be increasingly interested in bilingualism. In the school setting, the drivers of this group are monolingual families with a heritage link to the German language and culture.

The second significant adaptation of the 90/10 model was in the area of literacy. Sequential literacy (e.g. German then English) in a 90/10 model was changed to simultaneous literacy (e.g. German and English from Foundation) in the DSM bilingual programme. This ensured a seamless transition between the German and Australian school systems and increased both the likelihood of registration by the VRQA and the interest of German-speaking and non-German-speaking families in the school. Additionally, differences in approaches to literacy in German and English were seen to be complementary and advantageous for student learning. Using *Lesen durch Schreiben*, a relatively new concept in teaching German literacy in German primary schools, German writing is learnt before reading. This method was developed in Germany due to large differences in the language abilities of pupils in German primary schools and was, therefore, highly suitable to the DSM language proficiency context. Similar to Victorian primary school public education, a range of different materials and phonic approaches are used to teach literacy in English. The initial focus in English literacy is on reading and phonics, although writing is also introduced in Foundation (e.g. recounts, class letterbox).

Due to the recent establishment and relatively small number of students at the school, no reliable data have yet been collected for the analysis of success in literacy and mathematics. However, informal interviews with the head teacher in 2009–2010, individual school reports written by class teachers and discussions with parents of children at the school indicate that this approach to biliteracy is working for all language abilities. It seems that students with no German or English are not necessarily slower to complete the materials and three non-German-speaking students in the 2009 intake developed literacy and maths at highly varied rates. Teachers indicated that academic achievement was not necessarily tied to initial proficiency in German and that English and German literacy is age appropriate or higher both for children who started school as balanced bilinguals and for most monolingual speakers. It also appears that English monolingual Foundation students struggle more with vocabulary than literacy skills, e.g. they can read the same text as more balanced bilinguals but have lower levels of comprehension due to lower levels of vocabulary. To rapidly increase their knowledge of essential vocabulary, monolingual Foundation students usually require one-to-one immersion teaching assistance in Terms 1 and 2. In 2011, additional support lessons for monolingual children were introduced, which focus on increasing vocabulary, grammar and speaking in English or German. Teachers at the school believe that all students' abilities in English literacy will be comparable to monolingual English children by Grade 5. While such reports from teachers, parents and students are positive, an in-depth understanding of academic success in both English and German will require longitudinal research in the near future. At this stage, NAPLAN results cannot be used for analysing the literacy and numeracy of children in English due to the very low numbers of DSM children who have taken the test so far, and the fact that the test may discriminate against children in bilingual educational settings (Wigglesworth *et al.*, 2011).

Finally, while not directly related to the adaptation of the 90/10 early immersion model, a key decision made by the DSM founding board members was to use a mixed Australian and German curriculum. As already noted, the primary school curriculum at DSM is a combination of the German Thuringa state curriculum and the Victorian Essential Learning Standards (VELS). This reduced the risk of creating a *deutsche Insel* and, similar to factors driving the decision to introduce simultaneous literacy, the combined curriculum allowed for the transfer of pupils within the Australian or to the German primary school systems, enabled funding from both Germany and Australia and increased the likelihood of registration by VRQA. By combining two curricula, the school's ability to use existing high-quality resource material from both countries was also increased.

Challenges and advantages of the DSM early immersion model

While the 90/10 early immersion model seems to be functioning well, the DSM continues to face a number of challenges related to early immersion education. The school's model and mission focus on including children and families from all language backgrounds. Despite a shift towards more local

English German heritage and English non-heritage speaker enrolments, only a very small number of monolingual Australian families send their children to the school (e.g. those in the local catchment). Related to this are benchmarking systems that are entirely in English (e.g. NAPLAN) and fail to take children's abilities in languages other than English into account. Prospective parents may not realise that the tests unfairly discriminate against bilingual programmes and pupils. Financial issues may also play a part when deciding to enrol a child at the DSM. While there are no annual fees for attending a local government school, families sending their children to a private school such as the DSM are required to pay annual school fees.

On a more practical level, the school continually needs to recruit administrative staff and teachers with highly specialised abilities and backgrounds. Administrative staff must be bilingual and biliterate in German and English. All teachers need to be bilingual, highly trained and able to differentiate content according to both academic and linguistic abilities. A key skill of teachers (as well as parents of children attending the school) is being able to clearly separate language issues from other developmental issues. As pointed out by the DSM's head teacher in an informal interview, the ultimate success of children in the DSM immersion programme is heavily reliant on non-German-speaking parents' openness to both bilingualism and the German language.

The advantages of the DSM immersion model clearly outweigh the significance of such challenges. By opening the doors of the school to a wide range of language abilities, children at the DSM experience a need to speak both languages in a bilingual and bicultural environment on a daily basis. Monolingual German families arriving in Melbourne for short-term stays (0–3 years) are showing increased interest in the school. This means the school community is characterised by a core group of families and a continuous flow of short-term families (e.g. those here on university sabbaticals). This undoubtedly prepares them for life in a global village (Tucker & Dubiner, 2008) by providing first-hand experience of acceptance of difference and a continuous need to help integrate children from a range of cultural and linguistic backgrounds (e.g. Germany, Austria, Switzerland, South Africa, Argentina). Children at the school are constantly negotiating and adapting their use of languages to the changing linguistic abilities of their peers. As already noted, this means the children develop a range of valuable interpersonal skills in addition to the benefits of bilingualism, e.g. language negotiation and assistance (Genesee & Gándara, 1999).

By introducing literacy in English and German simultaneously, there is promotion of literacy and academic development in both languages via content, as well as a focus on form and function (Tucker & Dubiner, 2008). Simultaneous literacy and the combined VELS and Thuringa curriculum also allows the use of quality (mainstream) printed resources from both Germany and Australia, which in turn promotes a seamless transfer to and from other

Australian and German schools. Perhaps of primary importance in the Australian context, by broadening the traditional base of those to be included in immersion programmes (Lo Bianco & Slaughter, 2009b; Tucker & Dubiner, 2008), schools such as the DSM clearly show that all children in an English-dominant country have the potential to become bilingual.

Conclusion

The establishment of an immersion programme involves high levels of stamina and an unwavering commitment to bilingualism. It must take the interests and needs of a range of interested parties into account. Despite conflicting interests, the DSM model has shown that solutions can be found that do not entail compromising full early immersion models. The DSM model also clearly shows that immersion schooling need not be only for community speakers. Indeed, large differences in language abilities and degrees of bilingualism can be used as a resource in two-way early immersion models by careful teaching and selection of teaching materials. The DSM model also indicates that it is possible to teach literacy simultaneously in 90/10 early immersion languages, although this may be dependent on the languages being taught. Further investigation of the academic success of children in simultaneous immersion literacy programmes is undoubtedly high on the research agenda for both the DSM and bilingual schooling in general. Considering the Australian government's focus on English literacy, successful simultaneous literacy in 90/10 immersion in a range of language combinations may pave the way for the establishment of more immersion primary schools in Australia (or, at the very least, in Victoria). Such proliferation of immersion programmes was undoubtedly one of Michael Clyne's (2005) visions for Australian society and the DSM was *'die Erfüllung eines Traums'* [the fulfilment of a dream] (Clyne, personal communication).

Notes

(1) Previously called 'prep' in the state of Victoria.
(2) Up until the Education and Training Reform Act in 2006, the Victorian schools registration body was called the Registered Schools Board (RCB).

References

Baker, C. (2006) *Foundations of Bilingual Education and Bilingualism* (4th edn). Clevedon: Multilingual Matters.
Bialystok, E. (2001) Literacy: The extension of languages through other means. In R.L. Cooper, E. Shohamy and J. Walkers (eds) *New Perspectives and Issues in Educational Language Policy: A Festschrift for Bernard Dov Spolsky* (pp. 19–33). Amsterdam: John Benjamins.

Christian, D., Genesee, F., Lindholm-Leary, K. and Howard, E.R. (2004) *Final Progress Report: CAL/CREDE Study of Two-Way Immersion Education*. Alexandria, VA: Center for Applied Linguistics. See http://www.cal.org/twi/CREDEfinal.doc.

Clyne, M. (2005) *Australia's Language Potential*. Sydney: University of New South Wales Press.

Douglas, E.L. (2012) A community-led bilingual school in action: The Deutsche Schule Melbourne (DSM). Unpublished Masters thesis, University of Melbourne, Melbourne.

Garcia, Y. (2003) Korean/English two-way immersion at Cahuenga Elementary School. *NABE News* 26, 8–11, 25.

Garcia, Y. (2009) *Bilingual Education in the 21st Century: A Global Perspective*. Chichester: Wiley-Blackwell.

Genesee, F. (2008) Dual language in the global village. In T. Williams Fortune and D.J. Tedick (eds) *Pathways to Multilingualism: Evolving Perspectives on Immersion Education* (pp. 22–48). Clevedon: Multilingual Matters.

Genesee, F. and Gándara, P. (1999) Bilingual education programs: A cross national perspective. *Journal of Social Issues* 55 (4), 665–685.

Howard, E.R. and Christian, D. (1997) The development of bilingualism and biliteracy in two-way immersion students. Paper presented at the *Annual Meeting of the American Educational Research Association, Chicago, IL* (ERIC Document Reproduction Service No. ED 405741).

Lindholm-Leary, K. (2001) *Dual Language Education*. Clevedon: Multilingual Matters.

Lindholm-Leary, K. and Borsato, G. (2006) Academic achievement. In F. Genesee, K. Lindholm-Leary, W. Saunders and D. Christian (eds) *Educating English Language Learners* (pp. 176–222). New York: Cambridge University Press.

Lindholm-Leary, K. and Howard, E.R. (2008) Language development and academic achievement in two-way immersion programs. In T. Williams Fortune and D.J. Tedick (eds) *Pathways to Multilingualism: Evolving Perspectives on Immersion Education* (pp. 177–200). Clevedon: Multilingual Matters.

Lo Bianco, J. and Slaughter, Y. (2009a) Language teaching and learning: Choice, pedagogy, rationale and goals. *Babel* 44 (1), 24–35.

Lo Bianco, J. and Slaughter, Y. (2009b) *Second Languages and Australian Schooling*. Melbourne: Australian Council for Educational Research.

McKay, P. (2001) National literacy benchmarks and the outstreaming of ESL learners. In J. Lo Bianco and R. Wickert (eds) *Australian Policy Activism in Language and Literacy* (pp. 221–237). Melbourne: Language Australia.

Molyneux, P. (2009) Education for biliteracy: Maximising the linguistic potential of diverse learners in Australia's primary schools. *Australian Journal of Language and Literacy* 32, 97–117.

Northern Territory Government (2008) *Media Release: Education Restructure Includes Greater Emphasis on English*. Darwin: Northern Territory Government Newsroom. See http://newsroom.nt.gov.au/index.cfm?fuseaction=viewRelease&id=4599&d=5.

Truckenbrodt, A. and De Courcy, M. (2002) *Implementing a Bilingual Program*. Melbourne: Association of Independent Schools of Victoria.

Tucker, G. and Dubiner, D. (2008) Concluding thoughts: Does the immersion pathway lead to multilingualism? In T. Williams Fortune and D.J. Tedick (eds) *Pathways to Multilingualism: Evolving Perspectives on Immersion Education* (pp. 267–277). Clevedon: Multilingual Matters.

Verhoeven, L. (1987) *Ethnic Minority Children Acquiring Literacy*. Dordrecht: Foris Publications.

VRQA (2011) *Guide for a Registered School: Minimum Standards and Requirements for School Registration*. Melbourne: Victorian Registration and Qualifications Authority.

Wigglesworth, G., Simpson, J. and Loakes, D. (2011) NAPLAN language assessments for Indigenous children in remote communities: Issues and problems. *Australian Review of Applied Linguistics* 34 (3), 320–343.

Index

Aboriginal languages (*see*: Indigenous languages)
ABS (Australian Bureau of Statistics) 97, 115, 133, 135, 189
academic communication 23, 78–79, 92–93
academics, public engagement of 113, 126–127, 166, 171, 174, 176–178
access to language information and services 150–151, 170, 172
accreditation of bilingual programmes 227, 232–233
Achebe, C. 51
ACL (Australian Centre for Languages) 123
address 63–77, 78–94 (*see also*: pronominal address; nominal address)
  and age 81, 88–90, 91, 93
  and cultural background 64, 68, 75, 81, 83–87, 93
  and language background 81, 83–87, 89–91
  and pluricentricity 63–65, 74–75, 91–92
  and social distance 79–82, 84–86, 88–90
  and status 90–92
  formality 65–72, 74, 84–86, 87–91
  in Austria 64, 67–69, 71, 91–92
  in German 63–77, 91–92
  in Germany 63–64, 66–69, 71, 74, 91–92
  in service encounters 68, 74
  in Switzerland 63–77
  in workplaces 66–68, 74
  intercultural 64, 75, 78–79, 87, 93
  nominal 63, 70–71, 73, 78–94
  non–reciprocal 66, 82–83
  pronominal 63–72, 74, 111 fn
  title use 64, 70–71, 74, 78–93

ADF SOL (Australian Defence Forces School of Languages) 215, 225 fn (*see also*: RAAF School of Languages
Aebi, M. 68
Aegean Macedonia (Greece) 131–132, 135, 137–146 (*see also*: Republic of Macedonia)
age 99, 102, 108 (*see also*: intergenerational communication)
  variable in address 81, 88–90, 91, 93
AHC (Australian Hellenic Council) 134
Ahmad, W. 151–152
Akami, T. 214
Albanian 133, 146 fn
Altwegg, J. 66
Ambrosy, A. 142
Angel, J. 97
Angel, R. 97
AQF (Australian Qualifications Framework) 211 fn
Arabic 114–115, 118–121, 126, 128 fn, 154–156 (*see also*: Juba Arabic, Khartoum Arabic)
attitudes (*see also*: language attitudes)
  to bilingual education 159, 228
  to English 19–21, 29
  to other languages 21, 184, 187
attrition rates (*see*: retention rates)
Auslan 152, 156, 158, 160
Australian Bureau of Statistics (*see*: ABS)
Australian Centre for Languages (*see*: ACL)
Australian Defence Forces School of Languages (*see*: RAAF School of Languages)
Australian Department of Education 187
Australian Ethnic Affairs Council 166
Australian Hellenic Council (*see*: AHC)
Australian National Archives 213, 225 fn

Australian Qualifications Framework
  (see: AQF)
Australian Senate 166, 168–169, 173
Australian Sign Language (see: Auslan)
Australian Teachers' Federation 166, 172
Austria, address in 64, 67–69, 71, 91–92

Bahasa Melayu (see: Malay)
Baker, C. 175, 229
Baker, V. 217, 225, 225 fn
Baldauf, R. 159, 205, 213
Bandura, A. 102
Bartlett, M. 158
Beaumont, J. 214
Beazley, S. 150
Beligan, A. 45 fn
Ben Moshe, D. 115
Ben-Rafael, E. 18
Besch, W. 66
Bettoni, C. 143
Bhatt, R.M. 57
Bialystok, E. 175, 230
Bigelow, M. 127
bilingual education 171, 227–232 (see also: immersion)
bilingual literacy (see: biliteracy)
bilingual programme design 227–239
bilingualism 165, 168, 171–173, 175, 177–178, 185, 199–200 (see also: multilingualism)
  as a result of community language maintenance 143, 168–175, 183 196
  with Auslan 158
  with English 21, 26, 30, 33, 36, 42–45, 49–51, 174
biliteracy
  simultaneous 227, 230, 234, 236–239
  sequential 227, 230
Bleakley, J. 215
Blogwiese 70, 72–74
Blommaert, J. 7, 152
Bokhorst-Heng, W. 34, 43
Bolton, K. 56
Bonnet, G. 19
Bonyhady, A. 183
Borland, H. 115–118, 123, 126, 143
Borsato, G. 231
Bourdieu, P. 144
Boyd, S. 24, 29
Bradshaw, J. 114–115, 188
Brown, M. 150
Brown, P. 79

Bruckner, W. 71
Brummel, S. 97
Brutt-Griffler, J. 58
Bucholtz, M. 101
Bundesamt für Migration 64
Butcher, L.S. 149
Byram, M. 58

Cabau, B. 22–23, 25
Caleon, I.S. 43
Call, M. 151, 160
Canagarajah, S. 58
Carnevale, N.C.A. 38
Cavallaro, F. 38–39, 41–43
Čašule, I. 134
census data
  Australia 6–7, 114–115, 118, 134–136, 145, 146 fn, 184, 186, 197 fn
  Singapore 33–34, 37, 39, 41, 44
Certificate IV in Community Languages Teaching 201, 211
Chafe, W. 175
Chinese
  as a community language 100, 106–108, 196 fn
  Mandarin 35–39, 42, 44, 99–100, 107, 183, 191–195
  teaching of 183, 191–195, 216–218, 221
  varieties 33–39, 42, 44
Chinese-speaking older migrants 100, 106–108
Christ, H. 2
Christen, H. 64, 71–72
Christian, D. 231
Clyne, M. 1–4, 6–7, 30, 38, 49, 54, 57, 60, 79–80, 83, 90–92, 97–98, 101, 110, 115, 131, 134–135, 138, 140, 142, 149, 158, 165–167, 175, 177, 183, 185–188, 190, 211, 213, 227–229, 239
Co.As.It (Comitato Assistenza Italiani) 187
Cochlear implantation 150, 153–154, 156–157
code-switching 17–18, 20, 29, 142
Commonwealth Department of Education and Youth Affairs 166, 168, 170
Commonwealth Education Portfolio 166
communication with deaf children (spoken vs sign language) 149–161
communicative style 68, 74
community activists 113, 126–127, 166, 171, 174, 176–178

community languages 149, 154–155, 158–160, 166, 170, 172–173, 176, 183
Community Languages Australia 200
community languages schools 40, 122–125, 174, 187–188, 196, 200–202
community languages teachers 121, 124, 199–211
community–based language teaching 114, 120–123, 126–127, 199–100, 204
conference (setting) 78–93 (see also: academic communication)
Confucianism 106, 108
contextualisation cues 98, 101
Cordella, M. 100, 110
Correa–Zoli, Y. 38
Creese, A. 205
Crimmins, E. 97
Crittenden, K.S. 97
Croatian 134–137, 139
cross–cultural communication (see: intercultural communication)
Crystal, D. 50, 53
cultural background and address 81, 83–87, 93
   Central European 83–84, 86
   English–speaking 83–84
   Northern European 83–84, 86
cultural conceptualisations 49, 54–57, 59
cultural standards (*Kulturstandards*) 64, 68, 75
Cummings, P.J. 56

Dahl, Ö. 24
Damari, R.R. 105
David, M.K. 40–41
Dawkins, J. 168, 197 fn
De Courcy, M. 229
de Weck, R. 66
deafness 149–161
   and multilingualism 149–161
   diagnosis 153–155, 157–158
deafness service providers 152–153, 156–160
DEECD (Department of Education and Early Childhood Development) 111, 176–177, 184–185, 189–190, 192–195, 200
Delsing, L. 18
Denmark (see: Scandinavia)
Department of Employment, Education and Training 177

Department of Immigration and Citizenship 135
Department of Statistics 34, 37, 39, 41
Deutsche Schule Melbourne 227, 229, 231–239
Di Biase, B. 187
Dickins, J. 119
Diebold, A.R. 175
diglossic situation
   as a consequence of domain loss 24
   in Aegean Macedonia 133, 139
   in German–speaking Switzerland 65
   in Singapore 36, 44
Dillon, L. 225 fn
Dinka 114, 116, 118, 121–123, 125–127
diversification of English (see: varieties of English)
Dixon, L.Q. 40
domain (see: family domain; friendship domain; neighbourhood domain; school domain; transactional domain; workplace domain)
domain loss 23–25, 29–30
domain–based analysis 131–132, 137
Döpke, S. 131
Doucet, J. 34
Douglas, E.L. 228, 231–232
Du Bois, J.W. 98, 104
Dubiner, D. 228, 238–239

early intervention services for deaf children (see: deafness service providers)
EC (European Commission) 4, 21–22
Ellis, E. 2–3
Elspaß, S. 71
Elter, I. 64, 67–68, 71, 75
Englebretson, R. 98
English 49–62
   glocalisation of 50, 54–57 (see also: varieties of English)
   in Australia 132–133, 139, 141, 145, 166, 170–173, 176, 228
   in Scandinavia 17–32
   in Singapore 33–39, 41–42, 44
   in Sudan 119
   in Sweden 17–32
English as a lingua franca 50, 58–60
   at international conferences 78, 81–85, 88–89, 91, 93
   in Scandinavia 18
   in Singapore 42–43

English as a pluricentric language (*see*: pluricentricity English)
English as an international language 49–62
English as language of instruction at Swedish universities 22–23, 25–26
English language proficiency 99–100, 108, 151, 153, 155, 157, 159
  in Scandinavia 18–22, 29
English language teaching 49, 57–60
English plus 1 (*see*: bilingualism with English)
English-knowing bilinguals (*see*: bilingualism with English)
enrolments in language programmes 190–195
Eritrea 113, 124
ESAV (Ethnic Schools Association of Victoria) 120, 122, 124, 200, 205
Ethiopia 113, 124
Ethnic Communities Council of Queensland 166–167
ethnic communities in Australia (*see*: immigrant communities)
ethnic communities in Singapore 34, 37–38
  Chinese 38–40, 44
  Indian 40–41
  Malay 41
ethnic schools (*see* community languages schools)
Ethnic Schools Association of Victoria (*see*: ESAV)
Ethnologue 115–119, 121, 123, 128 fn
Eurobarometer 21–22
European Charter for Regional and Minority Languages 133
European Commission (*see*: EC)
exogamy 135–136, 140

family domain 133, 139–142 (*see also*: home language)
Federation of Community Languages Schools 200
Federation of Ethnic Communitites' Councils of Australia 166–167, 170–171, 174
Fesl, E. 170
Finland (*see*: Scandinavia)
Fishman, J.A. 175
formality of address 65–72, 74, 84–91
  (*see also*: social distance)
Fox, B. 99

Freeman, D. 202–203, 210
French
  influence on address in Switzerland 69–70, 72, 74
  teaching of 183, 191–195, 221–222
Friedman, V. 133
friendship domain 142–143
Funch, C. 213–216
funding of bilingual programmes 227, 232–234, 238

Galtung, J. 83, 91
Gándara, P. 231, 238
Garcia, O. 172
Garcia, Y. 231
Garrick, A.J. (Toby) 213–214, 217–225
Geers, A.E. 150
Genesee, F. 230–231, 238
German 99–100, 102–103, 108
  address in 63–77, 91–92
  as a pluricentric language (*see*: pluricentricity German)
  as home language 235–236
  bilingual programme 227, 231–239
  teaching of 183, 191–195
German-speaking older migrants 100, 106, 108
Germany, address in 63–64, 66–69, 71, 74, 91–92
Gerner de Garcia, B. 151, 160
Giles, H. 131
Gilley, L. 121, 125
Gilmore, A. 215
globalisation 49–50, 57, 59
glocalisation of English 50, 54–57
  (*see also*: varieties of English)
Goffman, E. 79, 98
Gogolin, I. 2
Goh, I. 35
Gopinathan, S. 36
Gorter, D. 166
Graddol, D. 22, 50, 52–53, 60
Greek 132–137, 139, 142
  as a community language 185–188
  teaching of 194–195
Greek community in Australia 184–189, 194, 196
Greek Orthodox Church 186, 188
greetings (*see*: politeness formula)
Gregory, S. 150, 155
Grosjean, F. 171, 175
Grossman, M. 115

Group of Eight 213
Gunnarsson, B. 23
Gupta, A.F. 34, 36, 39, 41

Hafner, K. 68
Hajek, J. 1, 69, 115–118, 126, 185, 188
Hallo Schweiz 67, 72–74
Hämmerli, F. 74
Hatoss, A. 115
Hatton–Yeo, A. 110
Haugen, E. 18, 175
Haumann, S. 63
Hauser, A. 66, 69, 71
He, A.W. 142
hearing aid 150, 154
hearing loss (see: deafness)
heritage languages (see: community languages)
Herriman, M. 183
high school second language learners 97–112, 191–195
higher education 18, 22–23, 25–26, 29–30, 58
Hill, P. 138
Hlavac, J. 134, 143
Hodge, J. 178 fn
Hoffmann, C. 49
Hokkien 34, 36, 38 (see also: Chinese varieties)
Hollister, J. 52
home language(s) 36–37, 39, 41, 44, 135–136, 139 (see also: family domain)
Hong Kong English 56–57, 59
Hook, D.D. 81
Hornberger, N. 204, 210
Hotzenköcherle, R. 64, 66, 69, 71
House, J. 49, 51, 63, 74–75
Howard, E.R. 229–231
Hsieh, P.S.P. 102
Hu, X.Q. 54
Huang, H. 100, 110
Hui, L. 108
Huijser, H. 115
Hult, F.M. 27
Huss, L. 29
Hyltenstam, K. 132

identity 18, 20–22, 29–30, 39, 42–43, 51, 58, 98, 105, 138, 146, 188, 204–205
ideology of bilingualism 168, 171, 173–174, 176
Idris, H.F. 119

ihr 65–66, 69–70, 74 (see also: pronominal address)
Ikea 68–69
immersion 229–239 (see also: bilingual education)
immigrant communities in Australia
 from the Horn of Africa 113, 124–125
 Greek 184–189, 194, 196
 Italian 182, 184–188, 194, 196
 Macedonian 131–148
 recently arrived 113, 122
 refugee 124, 127
 Sudanese 113–130
immigrant languages (see: community languages)
Indian languages 35, 37, 40–41 (see also: Tamil)
Indigenous languages 166, 170, 172–173, 228
Indonesian, teaching of 183, 191–195, 221
Ingram, D. 166
intercultural communication 12, 64, 75, 78–79, 93, 104–106, 109–110, 225
intercultural competence 49, 57–60, 204, 211
intercultural pragmatics 64, 75, 78–79, 87, 93
intergenerational communication 40, 45, 97–112, 120, 139–142
intergenerational language transmission 38, 135–137, 141–142, 185–188, 195–196
international students
 in Australian secondary schools 193
 in Swedish universities 22–23, 29–30
internationalisation of higher education 22–23, 26, 29–30, 58
introductions 78–94 (see also: address)
Islam 119–121, 146 fn, 156
Italian 154–155, 182–198
 as a community language 184–188, 196
 teaching of 182–184, 189–196
Italian community in Australia 182, 184–188, 194, 196
Izon, M. 115, 121

Jaffe, A. 98–99, 101
Japanese, teaching of 183, 191–195, 214–216
Jernudd, B.H. 35, 39
Johnson, K. 202–203, 209–210
Johnson, M. 55

Johnstone, B. 99
Josephson, O. 24
Juba Arabic 119–121
Jupp, J. 166, 169

Kachru, B.B. 50, 54
Karan, M. 145
Kaspir, N. 119
Kevlihan, R. 119
Khartoum Arabic 119
King, M.G. 183
Kipp, S. 7, 115, 131, 134–135, 138, 142, 185–186
Kirkpatrick, A. 52, 55
Knoors, H. 150
Kracht, A. 151
Kramer, C. 133
Kramsch, C. 58–59, 204, 211
Kretzenbacher, H.L. 64, 67, 71, 91–92
Kritz, M. 97
Kühntopf, M. 72
Kuo, E. 34–35, 37, 39
Kwan–Terry, A. 39

Ladd, P. 150
Ladd, R.D. 125
Lakoff, G. 55
Lambert, B. 109
Lambert, W. 172
language attitudes 33, 39, 42–43 (*see also*: attitudes)
language background
  and address 81, 83–87, 89–91
  of students in bilingual programmes 234–239
language curriculum 166, 168, 175–176, 178 fn, 232, 237–238
language demography (*see*: census data)
language ecology 134–137, 145, 151, 158–159
language education 168–178 (*see also*: language teaching and learning; English language teaching)
  in Australia 9, 183, 185, 189–197
language education policies
  in Australia 184–185
  in Singapore 35, 39–40
language identity (*see*: identity)
language laboratory (*see*: language teaching technology)
language legislation 24–25

language maintenance 114, 120, 123, 126–127, 131–148, 170, 184–188, 196, 199
  with deaf children 149, 151, 160
language of instruction 35, 139–140, 229–230 (*see also*: English as language of instruction)
language policy
  in Australia 9, 165–181
  in Singapore 33, 35, 39, 42, 45
  in Sudan 119
  in Sweden 24, 29–30
  in Swedish universities 25–26, 30
language proficiency 99–100, 108, 160, 174, 231 (*see also*: English language proficiency)
language resources in the community 98, 172
language shift to English and Mandarin in Singapore 33, 35, 37–45
language teacher qualifications 121–122, 125, 190, 200, 203, 219–220
language teacher training 99–211
language teaching and learning 213–225
language teaching materials 122–123, 222, 238
language teaching methodology 122, 205–206, 210, 219, 224
language teaching strategies 103–104, 109, 209–210
language teaching technology 219, 223
language teaching to monolingual English speakers 165, 168–175, 183, 185
languages as school subjects in Australian schools 182–184, 189–196 (*see also*: language teaching to monolingual English speakers)
languages from the Horn of Africa 124–125
languages of international communication 51–53, 119
  (*see also*: English as a lingua franca; English as an international language)
Languages Other Than English (LOTE) (*see*: community languages)
Latin America 100, 104–106
Latuka (*see*: Otuho)
Lau, K.E. 37
Leane, S. 158
leave–taking formula (*see*: politeness formula)
Lee Kuan Yew 39

Lee, M.S. 97
Leoni, F. 184
Levinson, S. 79
Lewis, M.P. 115–118, 120–121, 123
Li Wei 39, 42, 142, 205
Li, Y. 150
Liddicoat, A. 97–98, 185, 204, 211, 213
Lindholm–Leary, K. 229–231
linguistic diversity 4, 34–35, 114–115, 118, 126, 182
  in Australia 2, 7, 170, 178 fn, 199
linguistic landscape 18, 26–29
linguistic politeness (see: politeness)
linguists, public engagement of (see: academics, public engagement of)
literacy 44, 123, 125, 139–140, 142, 144–145, 190, 197 fn, 228, 234, 236 (see also: biliteracy)
literacy testing (see: NAPLAN)
Litwin, H. 97
Liu, P. 205
Lo Bianco, J. 10, 165–166, 172–174, 182–184, 187, 213, 229, 231, 239
Long, M.H. 102–103, 109
Lopez, M. 166
LOTE (Languages Other Than English) (see: community languages)
Lowe, D. 216
Lundin–Åkesson, K. 18
Lynas, W. 150–151, 159
Lynch, T. 109

Macedonia (see: Republic of Macedonia; Aegean Macedonia)
Macedonian
  in Australia 133–148
  in Greece 132–133, 139–140
  in the Republic of Macedonia 133, 139–140
Macedonian community in Australia 131–148
Macedonian Welfare Workers' Network of Victoria (see: MWWNV)
Macklin, M. 178 fn
mainstreaming (of a community language as a subject in the education system) 182, 184, 187–189, 194–196
Maiworm, F. 22
Malay 34–38, 41
Malayalam (see: Indian languages)
Mandarin (see: Chinese Mandarin)

Manno, G. 6, 63, 67, 71, 74–75
manual communication with deaf children 149–161
marginalisation 172, 228
Martin, P.W. 205
McDougall, G. 132–133, 146 fn
McKay, P. 229
McKay, S.L. 51, 58
McMahon, A.M.S. 51
McPake, J. 201
Meadow–Orlans, K. 150
Meany, N. 216
Meehan, E. 167
Melander, B. 23, 29
Melbourne (Australia) 99–100, 114–118, 121, 123–124, 127, 132–134, 137, 143, 145, 201, 205, 231–239
metaphors (see: cultural conceptualisations)
migration experience 99, 104–106, 109, 184
migration vintage 135, 138
Miller, C. 119
Milne, F. 168, 170
Minister for Education 176
Ministerial Council on Education, Employment, Training and Youth Affairs 178 fn
Mirza, H.S. 205
mixed language abilities of students in bilingual programmes 234–239
Modern Language Aptitude Test 223
Möller, R. 71
Molyneux, P. 229
Monash University 202, 205
monolingual mindset 1–3, 10, 30, 158, 160, 171, 213, 224, 227–228
Moog, J.S. 150
Moore, M. 150
Morgan, M. 206
motivation 219, 222
Mphande, C. 115–118, 123, 126
multiculturalism 3, 166, 199–200, 228
multilingualism 2–3, 9, 12, 165, 168, 171, 175, 178, 183, 199, 228 (see also: bilingualism)
  and English as an International Language 49–62
  reduction in 33–48
Musgrave, S. 114–118, 126
MWWNV (Macedonian Welfare Workers' Network of Victoria) 146 fn

NAPLAN (National Assessment Program Literacy and Numeracy) 228, 237, 238
National Policy on Languages 165, 169, 172, 183, 197 fn
native speakers of English 50–52, 57–58, 60, 81, 83–83
Ndhlovu, F. 115
neighbourhood domain 144–145
Nettelbeck, C. 1
New South Wales Conference on National Language Policy 166–167
Newman, S. 97
Ng, B.C. 40, 42–43
Nicholas, N. 188
nominal address 63, 70–71, 73, 78–94
non–native speakers of English 4, 50–51, 81, 91 (*see also*: English as a lingua franca)
non–reciprocal address 66, 82–83
non–Tamil Indian languages (*see*: Indian languages)
Norrby, C. 24–25, 29, 64, 69
Northern Territory Government 228
Norway (*see*: Scandinavia)

Oakes, D. 113, 128 fn
Oakes, L. 20, 22
Ochs, E. 99
older Chinese–speaking Singaporeans 38, 40, 44
older migrants of non–English speaking background 97–112
    Chinese–speaking 100, 106–108
    German–speaking 100, 106, 108
    Spanish–speaking 100, 104–105, 108
oral communication with deaf children 149–161
orthography of Dinka 121–122, 125–126
Orton, J. 196 fn
Osborn, T.A. 2
Otuho 114, 116, 123–124, 126
Ozolins, U. 149, 166, 183

Pakir, A. 35
pan–Hellenist ideology 132–134
Papen, U. 27
parents
    from non–English speaking backgrounds raising deaf children 149–161
    involvement in bilingual school 227, 232–235, 238

Park, J.S.-Y. 3
Pauwels, A. 131
Peal, E. 172
Pennycook, A. 49
Phillipson, R. 49, 51
Pillai, A.D. 42
PLANLangPol Committee 166–167, 171
Platt, J. 35, 38
pluricentricity
    and address 63–65, 74–75, 91–92
    English 49, 54–55, 60 (*see also*: varieties of English)
    German 63–65, 91–92
politeness 63–65, 74–75, 78–79, 90–91
    (*see also*: address; introductions)
politeness formula (greeting, leave–taking) 63–64, 71–74
Polzenhagen, F. 56
positionality 98–100, 104
Poulton, H. 146 fn
Preisler, B. 18–20, 29
Price, S. 218
priority structure 167, 178
professional development of community languages teachers 199–211
pronominal address 63–72, 74
Pyke, J. 115

RAAF School of Languages 213–226
Radin, M. 138
Ramiah, K. 42
Rampton, B. 7
Rando, G. 184
Rash, F. 67, 70–71, 73–75
Rathje, S. 58
Reagan, T.G. 2
Reay, D. 205
recently arrived immigrant communities 113, 122
Reihl, B. 67
Republic of Macedonia 131–132, 135, 137–146 (*see also*: Aegean Macedonia)
Republic of South Sudan (*see*: South Sudan; Sudan)
Research Unit for Multilingualism and Cross–Cultural Communication (RUMACC) 127
retention rates 192–196
Review of Post Arrival Programs and Services to Migrants 166
Ricento, T. 35
Rindal, U. 20
Romaine, S. 175

Royal Australian Air Force School of Languages (see: RAAF School of Languages)
Rubino, A. 7
Rudd, K. 177
Russian, teaching of 216–218, 221

Salö, L. 22–23
Samimy, K.K. 58
Sarangi, S. 101
Saravanan, V. 41
Sasaki, M. 223
Saunders, G. 131
Saville–Troike, M. 103, 109
Scandinavia 17–32
Scarino, A. 204, 211
Schallert, D.L. 102
schemas (see: cultural conceptualisations)
Schiffman, H.F. 41
Schmidt, R. 103
Schmieger, R. 132–133
school domain 139–140
Schüpbach, D. 79
second language learners (secondary students) 97–112, 191–195
second language learning by monolingual English speakers 165, 168–175, 183, 185
second–generation speakers (see: intergenerational language transmission)
Seeman, T.E. 97
semicommunication 18
Senate Standing Committee on Education and the Arts 166, 170, 172
Serbian 132–137, 139
service encounters, address in 68, 74
Serwe, S. 39, 41–42
Sharifian, F. 1, 3–4, 49–50, 54–60
Sharkey, H.J. 119
Sharp, H. 18, 29
Sharples, J. 115
Sheeley, T. 115
Shohamy, E. 27, 167
Siegenthaler, M. 70
Siew, P.Y. 39, 41
sign language 149–150, 152, 155 (see also: Auslan)
signage in public spaces 26–29
Simon, H.J. 69–70
Singapore 33–48
Singapore Colloquial English 43–44

Singapore English 36, 43–44
Singlish (see: Singapore Colloquial English)
Sitzler, S. 68, 72–73
Skutnabb–Kangas, T. 51, 150
Slaughter, Y. 10, 182–185, 187, 190–191, 196 fn, 213, 229, 231, 239
Smith, L.E. 58
Smolicz, J. 186
social distance and address 79–82, 84–86, 88–90
social exclusion 40, 44
social inclusion 97, 109
social networks 142–143
sociocultural knowledge 99, 104–106
Söderlundh, H. 23, 26
Somalia 113, 124
South Eastern Region Migrant Resource Centre 120
South Sudan 114, 119–121, 128 fn (see also: Sudan)
Spanish 99–100, 102–105, 107, 194
Spanish–speaking older migrants 100, 104–105, 108
Speak Good English Campaign 35, 43
Speak Mandarin Campaign 35, 39
Spolsky, B. 159, 167
Språkrådet (see: Swedish Language Council)
spread of English 22, 49–62
stance 98–101, 105–106, 108
  ethical–moral adviser 101, 106–109
  language instructor 101–104, 109
  language learner 102, 104
  sociocultural guide 101, 104–106, 109
Standard Singapore English (see: Singapore English)
status and address 90–92
Steinberg, A. 150
Stockholm (Sweden) 18, 27–29
Stoessel, S. 142
Stroud, C. 132
Sudan 113–114, 118–121, 128 fn (see also: South Sudan)
Sudanese community in Australia 113–130
Sudanese languages 114–117, 123–125 (see also: Arabic, Dinka, Juba Arabic, Khartoum Arabic, Otuho)
Sudanese Luacjang Group of Australia 122
superdiversity 7–8, 34, 118, 152, 158, 160
Sussex, R. 1, 3–4

Svennevig, J. 79
Sweden 17–32
Swedish 17–18, 23–27, 29–30
Swedish Language Act 24–25, 29–30
Swedish Language Council (Språkrådet) 23–24
Swiss-German 63–77
Switzerland, address in 63–77

Tamil 35–41 (*see also*: Indian languages)
Tamis, A. 134
Tan, D.K.H. 43
Tan, J. 35
Tan, P.K.W. 43
Tan, S. 40
Tan, Y.Y. 35
Tannenbaum, M. 141
teachers in bilingual programmes 232, 238
teaching (*see*: language teaching)
Teague, B. 166, 173–174
terms of address (*see*: address)
Thelander, T. 23
third-generation speakers (*see*: intergenerational language transmission)
Thomas, E. 151
titles 64, 70–71, 74, 78–93 (*see also*: nominal address)
Torney-Parlicki, P. 214
transactional domain 68, 74, 144–145
Truckenbrodt, A. 188, 229
Trümpy, H. 66, 68, 70
Tucker, G. 228, 238–239
Turner, B. 213, 220, 224–225
Turner, S. 150–151, 159

universities (*see*: higher education)
University of Gothenburg 25–26
University of Melbourne 127, 214
University of Sydney 214–215

Van Boeschoten, R. 133
varieties of English 50, 54, 57–58 (*see also*: English; pluricenticity English)
  Hong Kong English 56–57, 59
  Singapore Colloquial English 43–44
  Singapore English 36, 43–44
VCAA (Victorian Curriculum Assessment Authority) 111 fn
VCE (Victorian Certificate of Education) 99, 111 fn, 183, 194–195

Vélez Rendón, G. 206–207, 210
VELS (Victorian Essential Learning Standards) 232, 237–238
Veltman, C. 38
Verhoeven, L. 230
Verschik, A. 143
Vertovec, S. 7, 34, 118, 152
Victoria (Australia) 97, 114–115, 118, 120–121, 152–153, 175–176, 183–185, 189–196, 200–202, 229, 231–233
Victorian Certificate of Education (*see*: VCE)
Victorian Curriculum Assessment Authority (*see*: VCAA)
Victorian Deaf Society 152
Victorian Education Act (1958) 229, 233
Victorian Essential Learning Standards (*see*: VELS)
Victorian Multicultural Commission (*see*: VMC)
Victorian Registration and Qualifications Authority (*see*: VRQA)
Victorian School of Languages (*see*: VSL)
Vidoeski, B. 133
VMC (Victorian Multicultural Commission) 123–124
Voss, C. 133
VRQA (Victorian Registration and Qualifications Authority) 201, 232–234, 236–237
VSL (Victorian School of Languages) 118, 120–122, 124–126, 128 fn, 189

Wächter, B. 22
Waltzman, S. 151, 155
Washburn, L. 17
Watson, R.L. 119
Wee, L. 34, 36
Weinreich, U. 175
Westoby, P. 115
White Australia Policy 169–170, 178 fn
White, P. 213
Wiadrowski, M. 214–215, 217
Wigglesworth, G. 228–229, 237
Willmeroth, S. 74
Willoughby, L. 150, 152, 160
Wingstedt, M. 20
Wolf, H.G. 56
workplace, address in 66–68, 74
workplace domain 144–145

World Englishes (*see*: varieties of English)
Wykes, O. 183

Xinhua News Agency 119
Xu, D. 39
Xu, Z. 50, 54

Yağmur, K. 131–132
Yeddi, A.R.M. 119

youth 18–21, 29, 38, 40–42 (*see also*: high school second language learners)
Yu, N. 55
Yu-lan Fung 108

Zentella, A. 145
Zhu Hua 142
Zollinger–Escher, A. 71–72
Zumoberhaus, D. 68

For Product Safety Concerns and Information please contact our EU Authorised Representative:

Easy Access System Europe

Mustamäe tee 50

10621 Tallinn

Estonia

gpsr.requests@easproject.com

www.ingramcontent.com/pod-product-compliance
Lightning Source LLC
Chambersburg PA
CBHW070558300426
44113CB00010B/1305